Better Homes and Gardens®

Carb
COUNTER'S
Diabetic Cookbook

Better Homes and Gardens® Books
Des Moines, Iowa

Better Homes and Gardens® Books
An imprint of Meredith® Books

Carb Counter's Diabetic Cookbook
Editor: Jan E. Miller, RD
Contributing Editors: Spectrum Communication Services, Inc., Mary Williams
Contributing Writer: Hope S. Warshaw, MMSc, RD, CDE
Copy Chief: Terri Fredrickson
Copy and Production Editor: Victoria Forlini
Editorial Operations Manager: Karen Schirm
Managers, Book Production: Pam Kvitne, Marjorie J. Schenkelberg
Contributing Copy Editor: Susie Fagan
Contributing Proofreaders: Maria Duryée, Gretchen Kauffman, Carolyn Petersen
Indexer: Elizabeth T. Parson
Electronic Production Coordinator: Paula Forest
Editorial and Design Assistants: Karen McFadden, Mary Lee Gavin
Test Kitchen Director: Lynn Blanchard
Test Kitchen Product Supervisor: Marilyn Cornelius

Meredith® Books
Editor in Chief: Linda Raglan Cunningham
Design Director: Matt Strelecki
Managing Editor: Gregory H. Kayko
Executive Editor, Food and Crafts: Jennifer Dorland Darling

Publisher: James D. Blume
Executive Director, Marketing: Jeffrey Myers
Executive Director, New Business Development: Todd M. Davis
Executive Director, Sales: Ken Zagor
Director, Operations: George A. Susral
Director, Production: Douglas M. Johnston
Business Director: Jim Leonard

Vice President and General Manager: Douglas J. Guendel

Better Homes and Gardens® Magazine
Editor in Chief: Karol DeWulf Nickell
Deputy Editor, Food and Entertaining: Nancy Hopkins

Meredith Publishing Group
President, Publishing Group: Stephen M. Lacy
Vice President-Publishing Director: Bob Mate

Meredith Corporation
Chairman and Chief Executive Officer: William T. Kerr

Chairman of the Executive Committee: E. T. Meredith III

Our seal assures you that every recipe in *Carb Counter's Diabetic Cookbook* has been tested in the Better Homes and Gardens® Test Kitchen. This means that each recipe is practical and reliable, and meets our high standards of taste appeal. We guarantee your satisfaction with this book for as long as you own it.

All of us at Better Homes and Gardens® Books are dedicated to providing you with the information and ideas you need to create delicious foods. We welcome your comments and suggestions. Write to us at: Better Homes and Gardens Books, Cookbook Editorial Department, 1716 Locust St., Des Moines, IA 50309-3023.

If you would like to purchase any of our cooking, crafts, gardening, home improvement, or home decorating and design books, check wherever quality books are sold. Or visit us at: bhgbooks.com

Pictured on front cover: Flank Steak with Corn Relish (see recipe, page 70)

The Basics

Managing diabetes has come a long way in a relatively short time! And more medicines and tools are on the way. With new combinations of diabetes pills, a wider variety of insulins, insulin pens and pumps, and more realistic approaches to meal planning such as carbohydrate counting, it's not necessary to turn your lifestyle upside down to control your blood sugar levels. The key to managing diabetes today is to find a plan that fits diabetes into your lifestyle. Not the converse.

Carbohydrate counting is a flexible and real-life approach to meal planning and fits this new philosophy perfectly. It's a practical, easier-to-understand guide for people of all ages with type 1 or type 2 diabetes. Within the pages of this book, you'll learn the basics of carb counting and find resources to advance your knowledge. In addition, you'll find many delicious healthful recipes to please your palate and help you count carbs.

Diabetes basics: The types of diabetes

Before you learn the basics of carb counting, here's a quick review of the major types of diabetes and the nutrition goals for each.

Type 1: The diagnosis of type 1 diabetes (previously called juvenile diabetes) most often occurs during childhood or the teenage years, although more people are developing it in adulthood. Type 1 diabetes is an autoimmune disease, which means the body, in a sense, turns on itself to attack the insulin-making cells in the pancreas. People with type 1 diabetes make essentially no insulin.

This is why they need a consistent source of insulin via shots, a pen, or a pump. People with type 1 need to balance their insulin doses with food intake and activity. There's no doubt that managing type 1 is a challenge, but it's easier to do today than ever before.
Type 1 nutrition goals: First, keep blood glucose in control. Second, follow a healthful eating plan that's similar to your usual food intake and flexible enough to fit your lifestyle. People with type 1 diabetes should learn and use Advanced Carbohydrate Counting, which is addressed on page 6.

Type 2: The diagnosis of type 2 diabetes (previously called adult onset diabetes) most often occurs after age 40, although people are being diagnosed with type 2 diabetes at younger ages than ever before. In fact, type 2 diabetes has reached epidemic numbers due in part to a rapidly growing overweight and underactive population. Type 2 typically takes 7 to 10 years to develop. At the early stage of type 2, people often make plenty of their own insulin, but their bodies aren't able to use it effectively. At this stage many people can control diabetes with a healthful eating and activity plan, while others may also need one or more oral diabetes medications. As the years progress, the pancreas makes less insulin. In the late stages of type 2, people make almost no insulin. At this point, it's necessary to take insulin to control blood sugars.
Type 2 nutrition goals: First, keep blood glucose, lipids (cholesterol, HDL, LDL, and triglycerides), and blood pressure in control. Second, follow a healthful eating plan to

achieve nutrition and diabetes goals. Many people with type 2 are overweight and underactive. Ten to 20 pounds of weight loss and an increase in activity can improve blood glucose as well as blood lipids and blood pressure. People with type 2 can use Basic Carbohydrate Counting to eat a consistent amount of carbohydrate and help keep glucose in check. If insulin is required they should learn Advanced Carbohydrate Counting.

A word about prediabetes
In early 2002, the term "prediabetes" was first used to describe the increasingly common condition that occurs when blood glucose levels are higher than normal but not high enough to be called diabetes. Why is this a concern? Research shows that some long-term damage to the heart and circulatory system may occur with prediabetes. More importantly, before people develop type 2 diabetes they almost always have prediabetes.

Are you at risk for prediabetes? The risk factors for prediabetes are the same as those for type 2 diabetes. Check your risk:
- a fasting and/or post-meal blood glucose level that is higher than normal (see table below)
- a sibling or parent who has or had diabetes

- a body mass index (BMI) above 25
- a triglyceride level higher than 250
- a high density lipoprotein level (HDL or good cholesterol) equal to or less than 35
- high blood pressure equal to or higher than 140/90
- lack of physical activity
- older than 45
- member of an ethnic group that has higher than average incidences of diabetes: African American, Hispanic American, American Indian, Asian American, and Pacific Islander
- gestational diabetes (diabetes during pregnancy) or having a baby or babies weighing more than 9 pounds

The good news? If you have prediabetes or are at risk for it, you can take steps to reduce your blood glucose to normal levels and possibly prevent type 2 diabetes. First, work toward shedding a few extra pounds (if you have them) and become more active. Even a small weight loss (7 percent of body weight) and an increase in activity level (30 minutes five times per week) may reduce blood glucose to a normal range, improve blood lipids, and lower blood pressure. Talk with your health care provider before you start an exercise program if you've been inactive.

How do you know if you have diabetes?

Diagnostic Numbers for Prediabetes and Diabetes	Normal Glucose Levels	Prediabetes* Glucose Levels	Diabetes** Glucose Levels
Fasting	< 110 mg/dl	≥ 110 and < 125 mg/dl	≥ 126
2 hours after eating a large amount of glucose	< 140 mg/dl	≥ 140 and < 199 mg/dl	≥ 200 mg/dl
Anytime			Symptoms of diabetes and casual plasma glucose ≥ 200 mg/dl

*It's more likely for a person with prediabetes and/or early onset type 2 diabetes to have a normal fasting glucose but a higher-than-normal level 2 hours after eating. **A diagnosis of diabetes has to be confirmed on a subsequent day by measuring a fasting glucose, 2 hours after eating or casual (any time of day) glucose.

What is carb counting?

Carb counting is a meal-planning method that helps you learn what and how to eat to achieve your diabetes and nutrition goals. To put carb counting into practice, you learn how to count the amount of carbohydrate in the foods you eat. The emphasis is on carbohydrate because it is the nutrient that has the greatest effect on your blood glucose levels. The goal of Basic Carb Counting is to eat about the same amount of carbohydrate at the same times each day to keep blood glucose levels in your target range. **It's a good meal-planning method if you have type 2 diabetes and don't take any or, at the most, one or two oral diabetes medications.**

Advanced Carb Counting is more complex to learn and use and is appropriate for individuals with type 1 diabetes who take multiple insulin injections daily or use an insulin pump. Its advantage is greater flexibility in meal planning. With Advanced Carb Counting you estimate the amount of carbohydrate you eat and adjust your mealtime insulin dose based on your carbohydrate-to-insulin ratio. If you take insulin before each meal or use an insulin pump, then you'll likely want to improve your carb counting skills to master Advanced Carb Counting. This book focuses on Basic Carb Counting. Seek the guidance of a registered dietitian or certified diabetes educator for Advanced Carb Counting information (see resources, page 16).

Why count carbs?

Foods have three calorie-containing nutrients—carbohydrate, protein, and fat. Why only count carbs? The thinking today is that the carbohydrate content of foods and beverages has the greatest effect on blood glucose levels. So, if you focus on carbohydrate content, you can eat a variety of foods and still control your blood glucose.

Since the mid-1990s carb counting has become a favored meal-planning approach by diabetes experts. In 1994 the American Diabetes Association (ADA) dramatically changed its recommendation about sugars and sweets—two sources of carbohydrate. Research studies led ADA in 1994 and again in 2002 to state: **It is the total amount of carbohydrate you eat that most affects your blood glucose levels, not the source or type.** This means whether you eat equal amounts of carbohydrate as the simple sugar in gumdrops or fruit juice or starch in bread or

---

Does the recommendation about carbohydrate from ADA mean that all sources of carbohydrate raise blood glucose levels exactly the same?

No, it means, in general, the source or type of carbohydrate doesn't matter much. Here are a few factors that affect how quickly blood glucose levels rise: how fast you eat, the fiber content of the food, what else you eat with the carbohydrate, and how the food is cooked. This recommendation doesn't mean that you shouldn't watch for those occasional foods that raise your blood glucose levels too quickly or too much. If you require insulin, these might be foods for which you adjust your insulin dose (if you can) or simply choose to eat occasionally.

noodles, your blood glucose rises to about the same level in a similar amount of time.

Which foods contain carbohydrate?
Many people think foods with carbohydrate are starches—end of story. The reality is many foods contain carbohydrate: cereals, crackers, starchy and nonstarchy vegetables, fruits and fruit juices, milk, yogurt, other dairy foods, and, of course, sugary foods and sweets.

How do carbohydrate, protein, and fat change blood glucose levels?
Carbohydrate: All the carbohydrate you eat breaks down into glucose (sugar) about 2 hours after you start to eat. Your body doesn't know whether the glucose came from a bowl of pasta or a piece of blueberry pie.

Protein: For many years people with diabetes were taught that about half of the protein eaten as beef, cheese, poultry, milk, or eggs turns into glucose, although more slowly than carbohydrate. Newer research refutes this. New evidence shows protein, when eaten in reasonable servings (3 to 4 ounces of cooked meat, poultry, or fish), doesn't raise blood glucose. However, large portions of protein can increase blood glucose levels. Because high-protein meals may be high in fat, they can also delay the rise of blood glucose levels.

Fat: Fat minimally raises blood glucose levels. If you eat a high-fat meal, the fat can actually delay the rise of blood glucose from the carbohydrate.

Advice about sugars and sweets
Can people with diabetes still enjoy sugars and sweets? Yes! But lifting the ban on sweets is hardly a license to eat unlimited desserts. Nutrition and calories still count! Continue to make whole grains, fruits,

Then why not avoid carbs?

Once you realize carbohydrates are the main nutrient that raises blood glucose, you might think it's logical to avoid them. Don't! Yes, you should be careful to eat the amount that is appropriate for you. But don't think skimping on carbs is a positive nutrition step. Foods that contain carbohydrates are among the healthiest foods—vegetables, fruits, whole grains, and low- or no-fat dairy foods.

vegetables, and low-fat dairy foods the centerpiece of your daily food choices. When you want a small serving of your favorite sweet or want to split a dessert at a restaurant, learn how to fit the carb from sweets into your healthy eating plan without feeling guilty or sending your blood sugar skyrocketing.

How can you fit the carbs from sweets into your healthy eating plan?
Fitting sweets into your eating plan depends on the type of diabetes you have, how you control your blood glucose and fat levels, and your nutrition goals. You have options. If you enjoy sweets, don't give them up. You'll be more successful controlling your diabetes if you learn to fit in desserts.

When you experiment with sweets, check your blood glucose level 2 hours after the start of a meal or snack with sweets. This may help you to see how much the sweet raises your glucose.

Try these tips:

Limit the sweets you eat to a few favorites. Think about this question: "How much do I really need to eat to satisfy my sweet tooth?" You may need just a few bites.

Learn the carb count of your favorite sweets. If you eat a packaged sweet, the carb count is on the Nutrition Facts label. Observe the Nutrition Facts panels of similar packaged sweets to estimate grams of carbs. If you eat a bakery or home-baked sweet, use a book with carb counts (see page 11) or purchase a cookbook with grams of carbs for each recipe.

Once in a while, feel free to substitute some carbs in your meal for the carbs in a sweet. For example, if you have 60 grams of carb for dinner and you want to celebrate a birthday with a piece of cake, eat more nonstarchy vegetables with fewer calories and omit a slice of bread and serving of fruit to leave enough carbs for a small slice of cake.

Balance extra calories from sweets by burning more calories with more activity. Eat a small peanut butter cookie, then walk a mile or two. But remember that you can rack up the calories from sweets more quickly than you can burn them.

Note: If you take insulin at meals according to your blood glucose results and carbohydrate counts, adjust your insulin dose to account for the carbohydrate in a dessert. Don't do this too often or you may begin to gain weight.

How much carbohydrate should you eat?

There is no set amount of carbohydrate that is right for everyone (see chart below). The amount of carbohydrate you should eat daily is based on several factors:

- **Height and weight**
- **Desire or need for weight loss**
- **Usual food habits**
- **Food preferences**
- **Activity level**
- **Blood lipids**
- **Diabetes medications and regimen**
- **Results of self blood glucose checks**

How much carbohydrate do you need?

This gives you a starting point. For good blood glucose control if you don't require insulin or if you aren't adjusting your dose of insulin at meals, divide the servings of carb foods evenly throughout the day. To learn more about carb counting and to develop a carb counting plan based on your individual needs and situation, work with a dietitian with expertise in diabetes. See resources, page 16, to learn how to find these health care providers.

Calories & Carbohydrates	Starches Servings/day (about 15 grams carb/serving)	Nonstarchy vegetables Servings/day (about 5 grams carb/serving)	Fruit Servings/day (about 15 grams carb/small serving)	Milk (fat-free or low fat) Servings/day (about 12 grams carb/serving)	Total grams carb/day (Carb should be about 45-50% of calories)
1,200 to 1,500 (for women who want to lose weight and older women who want to maintain weight)	6	4	3	2	180
1,600 to 1,900 (for larger build and/or active women and men who want to lose weight)	8	4	3	2	210
2,000 to 2,200 (for some children, teen girls, active larger women, and most men)	10	4	4	2	250

What to count: choices or grams?

If you read other carb counting books, you may discover some sources that teach how to count carb choices instead of carb grams. Using the choice method assumes there's an average amount of carbohydrate in the different groups of foods (see the average grams for the food groups in the chart on page 8). For example, a cup of potatoes or pasta contains 30 grams of carbohydrate while ½ cup canned peaches or applesauce contains 15 grams of carbohydrate. Your dietitian might encourage you to eat a certain number of servings of carbs or number of grams of carbohydrate that are derivative of 15 per meal, say 45 or 60 grams per meal. Counting carb grams instead of choices is a more precise method and most beneficial for anyone who uses insulin.

Meals and snacks: How many are right for you?

You may assume people with diabetes must eat three square meals and three snacks a day. That's old thinking. New oral diabetes medications, insulin, and other technologies help individuals and their health care providers develop more flexible diabetes management plans.

Bottom line: Your diabetes plan should include the number of meals and snacks that fit your lifestyle and desired eating habits. Don't settle for less! Let your health care providers know about your eating style and daily schedule. Let them know if you eat three meals and a snack before bed, two large meals and no snacks, or you do best with three small meals and two snacks. The more they know about how you eat, the better they can help you design a plan that fits your needs. If you don't control your diabetes by adjusting your insulin doses, you'll get the best glucose control if you eat about the same amount of carbs at similar times each day. See the 1,600 to 1,900 Calorie Sample Menu on pages 14 and 15.

Portion control tips:
When you shop, eat in, and eat out

Controlling portion sizes is an important part of counting carbs and is a tough challenge. That's because the messages to overeat are constant whether it's a buy-one-get-one-free offer, super-sizing a fast-food meal, chowing down at an all-you-can-eat buffet, or simply being tempted by the extras on the family dinner table. Concentrate on eating reasonable portions. Downsize or double-check the accuracy of your portions with these portion-control tools and tips.

Portion-control tools:

Measuring cups, spoons, and a food scale are must-have tools.

Nutrition Facts label: Check the serving size listed on the food labels of products you regularly purchase. These reasonable portions provide you with a reference point. The Total Carbohydrate count on the label helps you calculate the grams of carb for the portion you eat (see page 11).

Your eyes: Don't underestimate a well-trained and honest set of eyes. Train your eyes by using your measuring equipment at home.

Your hands are always with you and provide a a quick visual guide to portions:

Tip of the thumb (to first knuckle)=1 tsp.

Whole thumb=1 Tbsp.

Palm of your hand or the size of a deck of playing cards=3 ounces (This is the portion size of cooked meat [protein] most people need at a meal.)

Tight fist=½ cup

Loose fist or open handful=1 cup

Note: These guidelines hold true for most women's hands, but some men's hands are much larger. Check the size of your hand's measurements with measuring cups, spoons, and a scale.

Portion control tips: when you shop

Buy just enough food. If it's sandwich fixings, how many sandwiches do you want to make? If it's a steak, how many servings do you get from one steak?

When you buy fresh produce, become familiar with portions and the related carb content. If you regularly buy a certain type of apple, take three or four of them and individually weigh them on the food scale in the produce aisle or at home. What's the average weight? Match that to the correct carb count.

Review the Nutrition Facts label of foods similar to those you might eat out or make from scratch—pizza, macaroni and cheese, spaghetti with meatballs, or desserts. Learn the carb count.

Portion control tips: when you eat in

When you begin to carb count, weigh and measure all foods. This helps you learn about correct serving sizes. Don't be overwhelmed; you will quickly recognize common portion sizes without having to measure foods every time. Once you've mastered estimating portions, occasionally weigh or measure foods to keep your eyes in line. Always weigh or measure new foods.

Serve foods in the same size plates, bowls, and glasses. This helps you stay precise.

Don't prepare too much food. This usually promotes overeating.

Don't serve family-style (bowls of food on the table). This puts food an arm's distance away. That's too close if you don't have the willpower to say "no" to additional servings.

Put leftovers away quickly. Have someone else store the leftovers if it's too tempting to nibble while you put them away.

Purchase a cookbook with complete nutrition information such as this cookbook so you know the carb content of your favorite recipes. Visit bhgbooks.com to purchase additional *Better Homes and Gardens* diabetic cookbooks, including *Better Homes and Gardens® Diabetic Cookbook* and *Better Homes and Gardens® Easy Diabetic Meals for 2 or 4.*

Portion control tips: when you eat out

Watch for the words that give clues to portion size. Small portion terms: regular, junior, petite. Large portion terms: jumbo, supreme, grande, giant, extra-large. Try to order small portion size entrées when possible and avoid those dishes that fall in the large category.

Split items. Because restaurant portions are often too generous, order one dish for two people. Or divide the single portion in half and save one portion for lunch the next day.

Order smart. Order items that complement each other and help you eat more balanced meals. Choose from salads, appetizers, and/or soups and request one item as an appetizer and another as a main course.

Use the carb counts of restaurant foods when available. If there is no nutrition information for a particular restaurant you frequent, use the information available from similar restaurants (see resources, page 16).

Use the nutrition information from the Nutrition Facts of foods in the supermarket to estimate what you might eat in a restaurant.

If you regularly eat ethnic foods for which you find no nutrition information, buy a few cookbooks that contain recipes for the foods you enjoy. Then use a nutrient database or book with nutrition information to estimate the nutrient content for each ingredient.

Resources

How to determine carb counts

If you're going to count grams of carbohydrate, you need resources at your fingertips. You'll need resources for three categories of foods:

1. foods with a Nutrition Facts panel

2. foods you buy (outside of restaurant foods) that don't have a Nutrition Facts label, such as fresh produce and meats

3. restaurant foods

Foods with a Nutrition Facts label:

If you have a packaged food with a Nutrition Facts label, it's your best resource. It's accurate, up-to-date, and doesn't cost a penny. Pay attention to two lines:

1) Total Carbohydrate grams. There's no need to pay attention to or count grams of sugars or other information under Total Carbohydrate. These are already included in Total Carbohydrate.

2) The serving size. Make sure the serving size you'll eat is equal to the amount on the Nutrition Facts label. If it's more or less, adjust the amount of carb accordingly.

Foods without a Nutrition Facts label:

Most fresh produce, meat, poultry and fish do not include a Nutrition Facts label. Fresh meat, poultry, and fish don't contain significant amounts of carbohydrate unless they are breaded or stuffed. See pages 12 and 13 for carb values of fresh produce.

Books

Numerous books provide an extensive list of foods and their corresponding carb counts. You only need one. They all contain similar foods with similar information. Look for one that only provides grams of carb (unless you want other nutrition information) and lists foods in alphabetical order. Here are a few:

Calories and Carbohydrates by Barbara Kraus, Signet, 14th edition, 2001.

The Corinne T. Netzer Carbohydrate Counter by Corinne T. Netzer, Dell Publishing, 2nd edition, 1998.

The Diabetes Carbohydrate and Fat Gram Guide by LeaAnn Holzmeister, RD, CDE. American Diabetes Association, 2nd edition, 2000.

The Doctor's Pocket Calorie, Fat and Carbohydrate Counter by Allan Borushek, Family Health Publisher, 2000.

Bowes and Church Food Values of Portions Commonly Used by Janet Pennington, 17th edition, J.P Lippincott Company, 1998.

The Complete Guide to Carb Counting by Hope Warshaw, MMSc, RD, CDE and Karmeen Kulkarni, MS, RD, CDE, American Diabetes Association, 2001. A soup-to-nuts education about carb counting. An appendix with the carb counts for hundreds of everyday foods is included.

Nutrition Facts

Serving Size 1 cup (240ml)
Servings Per Container about 16

Amount Per Serving

Calories 90   Calories from Fat 0

	% Daily Value*
Total Fat 0g	**0%**
Saturated Fat 0g	**0%**
Cholesterol 5mg	**2%**
Sodium 130mg	**5%**
Total Carbohydrate 13g	**4%**
Dietary Fiber 0g	**0%**
Sugars 12g	**15%**
Protein 9g	
Vitamin A	10%
Vitamin C	4%
Calcium	30%
Iron	0%

* Percent Daily Values are based on a 2,000 calorie diet. Your Daily Values may be higher or lower depending on your calorie needs:

		Calories	2,000	2,500
Total Fat	Less than		65g	80g
Sat Fat	Less than		20g	25g
Cholesterol	Less than		300mg	300mg
Sodium	Less than		2,400mg	2,400mg
Total Carbohydrate			300g	375g
Dietary Fiber			25g	30g

Carb Counts of Fresh Fruits & Vegetables

Fresh Fruit	Serving	Calories	Carb (g)
Apple, with skin	1 medium (5 oz.)	81	21
Apricots	4 (1 oz. each)	68	16
Banana	1 small (6 inch)	93	24
Blackberries	¾ cup	56	14
Blueberries	¾ cup	61	15
Cantaloupe	1 cup, cubes	56	13
Cherries, sweet	13	62	15
Cranberries	1 cup	47	12
Figs, large	1 (2½ inch)	48	12
Grapefruit	½ large	51	13
Grapes, seedless	17	60	15
Honeydew melon	1 cup, cubes	59	16
Kiwifruit	1 large (4 oz.)	56	14
Mango	½ cup, sliced	54	14
Nectarine	1 (2½ inch)	67	16
Orange	1 (5 oz.)	62	15
Papaya	1 cup, cubes	55	14
Peach	1 large (6 oz.)	67	17
Pear	½ of a large	62	16
Pineapple	¾ cup	57	14
Plums	2 (2 inch)	73	17
Raspberries	1 cup	60	14
Strawberries, whole	1½ cups	65	15
Tangerines, medium	2 (3 inch)	74	19
Watermelon	1¼ cups, cubes	62	14

Fresh Vegetables (nonstarchy)	Serving	Calories	Carb (g)
Asparagus, cooked	½ cup	22	4
Asparagus, cooked	8 spears	29	5
Beans, snap green, cooked	½ cup	22	5
Bean sprouts, raw	1 cup	31	6
Beets, cooked	½ cup	37	8
Broccoli, raw	1 cup	25	5
Broccoli, cooked	½ cup	22	4
Brussels sprouts, cooked	½ cup	30	7

Fresh Vegetables (nonstarchy)	Serving	Calories	Carb (g)
Cabbage, cooked	½ cup	17	3
Cabbage, raw	1 cup	18	4
Carrot, raw,	1 medium (2 oz.)	26	6
Carrot, cooked	½ cup	35	8
Cauliflower, raw	1 cup	25	5
Cauliflower, cooked	½ cup	14	3
Celery, raw	1 cup	19	4
Cucumber, raw	1 cup	14	3
Eggplant, cooked	½ cup	13	3
Greens, cooked			
Collard	½ cup	17	4
Kale	½ cup	21	4
Mustard	½ cup	10	2
Turnip	½ cup	14	3
Lettuce, iceberg	1 cup	7	1
Mushrooms, raw, whole	1 cup	24	4
Mushrooms, cooked	¾ cup	32	6
Okra, cooked	½ cup	25	6
Pea pods, raw	1 cup	61	11
Pea pods, cooked	½ cup	34	6
Romaine	1 cup	8	2
Spinach, raw	1 cup	7	1
Spinach, cooked	½ cup	20	4
Squash, summer, raw	1 cup	25	5
Squash, summer, cooked	½ cup	18	4
Tomato, raw, chopped	1 cup	38	8
Tomato, raw, whole, sliced	1 (2½ inch)	26	6
Turnips, cooked	1 cup cubes	33	8
Zucchini, raw	1 cup	17	4
Zucchini, cooked	1 cup	29	7

Fresh vegetables (starchy)	Serving	Calories	Carb (g)
Corn, sweet, yellow, cooked	½ cup	88	21
Peas, green cooked	½ cup	67	13
Potato, white, baked	3 oz.	93	22
Potato, white, boiled	½ cup	68	16
Squash, winter	1 cup	82	22
Potato, sweet, baked	½ of a medium (4 oz.)	59	14

Source: USDA Nutrient database for Standard Reference

Sample Menu

1,600—1,900 Calories • 210 grams of carbohydrate

All underlined menu items are recipes in this book.

Monday

Breakfast 58 g

Fresh Fruit with
   Minted Yogurt 27 g
½ of a small (3 inch)
   oat bran bagel 19 g
2 teaspoons margarine 0 g
8 ounces fat-free milk 12 g
Hot tea/coffee

Lunch 51 g

Tomato Basil Bisque 10 g
Turkey sandwich:
   3 ounces turkey 0 g
   2 slices whole wheat
   bread 26 g
   Mustard, lettuce
½ of a large pear 15 g
Sparkling water

Snack 25 g

Energy Bar 25 g

Dinner 55 g

Red Snapper and
   Vegetable Packets 25 g
1 whole wheat roll
   (2½ inch diameter) 18 g
1 tablespoon margarine 0 g
8 ounces fat-free milk 12 g

Snack 25 g

Nectarine-Orange Smoothie 25 g

Tuesday

Breakfast 57 g

Five Grain Cereal
   with Honey Fruit 50 g
1 scrambled egg 1 g
4 ounces fat-free milk 6 g
Hot tea/coffee

Lunch 52 g

Curried Chicken Salad 13 g
½ cup papaya 8 g
3 crisp rye crackers 20 g
1 cup baby carrots 11 g
Diet soda

Snack 23 g

White Bean and Pine Nut Dip
   (with pita chips) 18 g
1 cup raw broccoli 5 g

Dinner 56 g

Tomato Polenta Pizza 39 g
1½ cups torn spinach
   with 1 tablespoon
   salad dressing 5 g
Espresso Granita 12 g

Snack 25 g

1¼ cups strawberries 12 g
¾ cup fat-free yogurt 13 g

Wednesday

Breakfast 52 g

Cream Cheese and
   Raspberry Coffee Cake 20 g
1½ cups cantaloupe 20 g
8 ounces fat-free milk 12 g
Hot tea/coffee

Lunch 56 g

Pesto Bean Wraps 44 g
1 plum 8 g
1 cup celery 4 g
Sparkling water

Snack 27 g

¾ cup plain
   fat-free yogurt 13 g
¾ cup blueberries 14 g

Dinner 55 g

Beef-Broccoli Stir-Fry
   with cooked rice 30 g
Cheese Batter Rolls 18 g
1 tablespoon margarine 0 g
Basil Beets and Onions 7 g
Hot jasmine tea

Snack 24 g

Devil's Food Cookie 12 g
8 ounces fat-free milk 12 g

Thursday

Breakfast 56 g

Fruit-Topped
   Grapefruit Halves 26 g
Whole grain English muffin,
   2 halves 30 g
1 tablespoon margarine 0 g
Hot tea/coffee

Lunch 50 g

Dilled Tuna and
   Potato Salad 19 g
17 seedless green grapes 15 g
2 slices wheat crispbread 16 g
Diet soda

Snack 27 g

Tropical Fruit Pop 15 g
8 ounces fat-free milk 12g

Dinner 57 g

Skillet-Style Lasagna 20 g
1 cup steamed green beans 4 g
Shortcut Olive Flatbread 21 g
8 ounces fat-free milk 12 g

Snack 21 g

2 tablespoons
  peanut butter 6 g
5 whole wheat crackers 15 g

Friday

Breakfast 54 g

Baked French Toast
  with Orange Syrup 38 g
2 ounces lean ham 0 g
¾ cup mixed berries 16 g
Hot tea/coffee

Lunch 58 g

Gazpacho Sandwich 36 g
1 sliced kiwifruit 14 g
1 Date Bar 8g
Iced tea

Snack 20 g

Savory Corn-Cracker Mix 15 g
1 cup mixed raw vegetables 5 g
Diet soda

Dinner 53 g

Jamaican Pork Chops
  with Melon Salsa 10 g
Ginger-Lime Peas and Carrots 11 g
1½ cups mixed greens
  with 1 tablespoon salad
  dressing 3 g

Crème Caramel 17 g
8 ounces fat-free milk 12 g

Snack 18 g

2 Vanilla Bean Biscotti 18 g
Iced coffee

Saturday

Breakfast 55 g

Potato, Apple,
  and Ham Skillet 22 g
1 slice whole grain toast 13 g
1 tablespoon margarine 0 g
6 ounces orange juice 20 g

Lunch 49 grams

Grilled Chicken Salad with
  Strawberry Dressing 33 g
1 slice toasted French
  bread, 16 g
1 tablespoon margarine 0 g
Iced tea

Snack 25 g

3 cups light popcorn 11 g
2 tablespoons raisins 14 g
Diet soda

Dinner 58 g

Pan-Seared Scallops
  in Lemon Vinaigrette 7 g
⅓ cup cooked brown
  rice 15 g
1 cup steamed yellow
  summer squash 8 g
8 ounces fat-free milk 12 g
Strawberry Bavarian Pie 16 g

Snack 23 g

Honey-Peach Frozen Yogurt 23 g

Sunday

Breakfast 54 g

Southwest Breakfast
  Strata 20 g
1 fresh orange,
  sectioned 15 g
½ cup raspberries 7 g
8 ounces fat-free milk 12 g

Lunch 52 g

Greek Pizza 38 g
Fruit Verde 14 g
Diet soda

Snack 26 g

Cranberry-Raspberry
  Freeze 16 g
2 gingersnap cookies 10 g

Dinner 56 g

Chicken with
  Cherry Tomatoes 4 g
Skinny Mashed Potatoes 26 g
1 cup steamed
  broccoli spears 12 g
1 dinner roll 14 g
1 tablespoon margarine 0 g
Sparkling water

Snack 23 g

1 ounce reduced-fat
  cheddar cheese 1 g
5 saltine crackers 10 g
8 ounces fat-free milk 12 g

Additional Resources
Internet

www.nal.usda.gov This is the federal government's nutrient database. Download this database of 6,000 basic foods for free. Go to Publications/Databases. Click on Databases. Go down to USDA Nutrient Database for Standard Reference. Go to for more information; Download.

www.calorieking.com This site contains nutrient databases for supermarket and restaurant foods. A downloadable database for hand-held computers is also available.

www.animascorp.com EZManager from Animas is a downloadable database of 9,000 foods including supermarket and restaurant items. This software also allows people who do Advanced Carbohydrate Counting to adjust insulin doses based on data they enter. There is a fee for this software.

www.healthetech.com Several products for nutrition information and blood glucose management are available for a cost.

For more diabetic recipes check out this *Better Homes and Gardens* website: www.bhg.com/diabeticrecipes
Visit *Better Homes and Gardens* Recipe Center at www.bhg.com/bkrecipe

Restaurant Foods

Nutrition information is generally available from national chains that fit into the "walk up and order" category. It's easiest to find this information on their websites. Look under the menu and then click your way to nutrition. Limited nutrition information is available for the "sit down and order" category of restaurants. This is where using your portion control tools comes in handy. You always have your eyes and hands with you to estimate.

Books and Booklets for Restaurant Foods:
Guide to Healthy Restaurant Eating by Hope Warshaw, MMSc, RD, CDE, American Diabetes Association, 2002. This guide provides strategies for healthful restaurant eating plus nutrition information for more than 3,500 menu items from nearly 55 major restaurant chains.

Nutrition in the Fast Lane—The Fast Food Dining Guide, Franklin Publishing, Inc. Indianapolis, 800/634-1993 or www.fastfoodfacts.com. This booklet, updated annually, provides nutrition information for 54 popular chain restaurants.

Education and Support

To learn more about how to count carbs and how carb counting can help you control your diabetes, get to know a diabetes educator who can provide you with both the knowledge and support you need to manage this challenging disease. The following resources are excellent when it comes to locating quality diabetes care:

To find a recognized diabetes education program (a teaching program approved by the American Diabetes Association near you) call 800/DIABETES (800/342-2383) or look at the American Diabetes Association's home page www.diabetes.org or go to www.diabetes.org/education/eduprogram.asp.
To find diabetes educators (who may be dietitians, nurses, pharmacists, counselors, or other health professionals) near you, call the American Association of Diabetes Educators (AADE) toll-free at 800/TEAM-UP (800/832-6874) or click on AADE's Internet site at http://www.aadenet.org and go to "Find an Educator."

Appetizers & Snacks

34 g carb

Fresh Fruit Float

Mix and match fresh fruit, a carbonated beverage, and sherbet to create your favorite combination. You can also substitute any flavor of sorbet for the sherbet.

1 Divide fruit evenly among 4 tall glasses. Slowly pour 1 cup carbonated beverage over fruit in each glass. Top each serving with ½ cup sherbet.

Nutrition Facts per serving: 155 cal., 2 g total fat (1 g sat. fat), 5 mg chol., 80 mg sodium, 34 g carbo., 29 g sugar, 2 g fiber, 2 g pro.
Daily Values: 2% vit. A, 75% vit. C, 6% calcium, 2% iron
Exchanges: 2 Fruit, ½ Fat

Start to Finish: 10 minutes
Makes: 4 servings

2 cups cut-up fruit (such as strawberries, seedless grapes, peeled oranges or bananas, and/or apples)

4 cups low-calorie lemon-lime carbonated beverage or low-calorie ginger ale

2 cups fruit-flavored sherbet

Sangria-Style Cooler

For the most eye-appealing cooler, don't use red grape juice in this recipe. When combined with orange juice, it discolors slightly. White grape juice lends the same flavor without a color change.

1 In a large bowl or pitcher stir together the orange juice and grape juice. Slowly pour in ginger ale; stir gently. Add the fruit and ice cubes.

2 Ladle the juice mixture with the fruit into tall glasses. If desired, garnish with fresh mint sprigs.

Nutrition Facts per serving: 121 cal., 0 g total fat (0 g sat. fat), 0 mg chol., 12 mg sodium, 29 g carbo., 28 g sugar, 1 g fiber, 1 g pro.
Daily Values: 6% vit. A, 114% vit. C, 2% calcium, 2% iron
Exchanges: 2 Fruit

Start to Finish: 15 minutes
Makes: 10 (8-ounce) servings

- 1 quart (4 cups) orange juice, chilled
- 1½ cups white or red unsweetened grape juice, chilled
- 1 1-liter bottle ginger ale, chilled
- 2 cups cut-up fruit (such as oranges, lemons, limes, pineapple, seedless grapes, peaches, and/or strawberries)
- 2 cups ice cubes
  Fresh mint sprigs (optional)

Nectarine-Orange Smoothie

Protein-rich soy milk provides the base for this vitamin-packed drink. Make sure you purchase calcium-fortified soy milk to get the benefit of this important nutrient.

1 In a blender container or food processor bowl combine nectarines, soy milk, orange juice, and sugar. Cover and blend or process until mixture is thick and smooth.

2 Serve the fruit mixture over ice cubes. If desired, garnish with fresh mint sprigs.

Nutrition Facts per serving: 132 cal., 3 g total fat (0 g sat. fat), 0 mg chol., 15 mg sodium, 25 g carbo., 19 g sugar, 3 g fiber, 5 g pro.
Daily Values: 18% vit. A, 43% vit. C, 1% calcium, 5% iron
Exchanges: 1½ Fruit, ½ Medium-Fat Meat

Start to Finish: 15 minutes
Makes: 2 (1¼-cup) servings

8 ounces nectarines or peaches, peeled
　　and cut up (1½ cups)
1 cup soy milk, chilled
⅓ cup orange juice
1 tablespoon sugar
　Ice cubes
　Fresh mint sprigs (optional)

Cranberry-Raspberry Freeze

As beautifully colored as it is tasty, this freeze is just the thing to quench your thirst (and stave off hunger) in the afternoon.

1 Place the 2 cups raspberries in a fine-mesh sieve set over a large glass measure or pitcher. Pour boiling water over raspberries. Using the back of a spoon, press berries to release juice. Discard berry pulp; reserve juice (you should have about 1 cup). Cover and chill.

2 In a blender container combine the reserved raspberry juice and the cranberry juice. With blender running, add the ice cubes through opening in lid. Blend until slushy.

3 Transfer cranberry mixture to a pitcher. Slowly pour in carbonated beverage; stir gently. Serve over additional ice cubes. If desired, garnish with lemon slices and additional fresh raspberries.

Nutrition Facts per serving: 67 cal., 0 g total fat (0 g sat. fat), 0 mg chol., 13 mg sodium, 16 g carbo., 15 g sugar, 3 g fiber, 0 g pro.
Daily Values: 1% vit. A, 65% vit. C, 1% calcium, 2% iron
Exchanges: 1 Fruit

Start to Finish: 15 minutes
Makes: 5 or 6 servings

- 2 cups raspberries or one 12-ounce package frozen lightly sweetened red raspberries, thawed
- ½ cup boiling water
- 1½ cups cranberry juice, chilled
- 1 cup ice cubes
- 1 12-ounce can reduced-calorie lemon-lime carbonated beverage, chilled
- Lemon slices (optional)

15 g
carb

Tropical Fruit Pops

You may think you're making this treat for kids, but as soon as the adults taste them—all bets are off! Experiment with gelatin flavors to determine which you like best or keep an assortment on hand for easy healthful snacking.

1 In a 1- or 2-cup glass measure stir together boiling water and gelatin until gelatin dissolves. Pour into a blender container. Add undrained pineapple and banana chunks. Cover and blend until smooth.

2 Pour a scant ½ cup of the fruit mixture into each of eight 5- to 6-ounce paper or plastic drink cups. (Or pour a scant ⅓ cup into each of twelve 3-ounce cups.) Cover each cup with foil. Using the tip of a knife, make a small hole in the foil over each cup. Insert a wooden stick into the cup through the hole. Freeze about 6 hours or until firm.

3 To serve, quickly dip the cups in warm water to slightly soften the fruit mixture. Remove foil and loosen sides of pops from drink cups. Tear off the paper.

Prep: 15 minutes
Freeze: 6 hours
Makes: 8 or 12 pops

½ cup boiling water
1 4-serving-size package sugar-free lemon-, mixed fruit-, or strawberry-flavored gelatin
1 15¼-ounce can crushed pineapple (juice pack)
2 medium bananas, cut into chunks

Nutrition Facts per pop: 65 cal., 0 g total fat (0 g sat. fat), 0 mg chol., 29 mg sodium, 15 g carbo., 12 g sugar, 1 g fiber, 1 g pro.
Daily Values: 1% vit. A, 13% vit. C, 1% calcium, 1% iron
Exchanges: 1 Fruit

Berry Good Fruit Dip

Make a gorgeous party platter with attractively cut fresh fruit fanned around a bowl of this light and flavorful dip. Estimate the amount of fruit you use as dippers. Add 15 grams of carb for a small apple, half of a large pear, or 1½ cups strawberries.

1 Place the 1 cup strawberries in a blender container or food processor bowl. Cover and blend or process until smooth.

2 In a medium bowl stir together the pureed strawberries, yogurt, cinnamon, and ginger. Fold in the dessert topping. Cover and chill for up to 24 hours.

3 Transfer the yogurt mixture to a serving dish. Serve with fresh fruit dippers.

Nutrition Facts per serving (dip only): 32 cal., 1 g total fat (1 g sat. fat), 0 mg chol., 7 mg sodium, 4 g carbo., 2 g sugar, 0 g fiber, 1 g pro.
Daily Values: 11% vit. C, 2% calcium
Exchanges: ½ Other Carbo.

Chill: up to 24 hours
Start to Finish: 15 minutes
Makes: 12 servings

- 1 cup strawberries
- ¾ cup fat-free vanilla yogurt
- ½ teaspoon ground cinnamon
- ¼ teaspoon ground ginger
- ½ of an 8-ounce container frozen light whipped dessert topping, thawed
  Apple wedges, pear wedges, whole strawberries, or other fruit dippers

Curried Apple Spread

Fresh apple gives this bread spread a refreshing juiciness. Curry powder tints the mixture gold. For entertaining, mix the spread ahead so it's ready for munching as soon as your guests arrive.

1 In a small bowl combine cream cheese, orange peel, orange juice, and curry powder. Gently stir in apple.

2 Serve the spread with mini bagels or Melba toast rounds.

Nutrition Facts per serving (1 tablespoon spread + 1 mini bagel half): 75 cal., 2 g total fat (1 g sat. fat), 7 mg chol., 132 mg sodium, 10 g carbo., 1 g sugar, 1 g fiber, 3 g pro.
Daily Values: 2% vit. A, 2% vit. C, 2% calcium, 4% iron
Exchanges: ½ Starch, ½ Fat

Start to Finish: 10 minutes
Makes: 12 (1-tablespoon) servings

½ of an 8-ounce package reduced-fat cream cheese (Neufchâtel), softened
1 teaspoon finely shredded orange peel
1 tablespoon orange juice
½ teaspoon curry powder
¼ of a medium apple (such as Delicious, Gala, or Braeburn), finely chopped
 Mini bagels, halved, or Melba toast rounds

White Bean and Pine Nut Dip

Similar in consistency to hummus, this easy blender dip has a nutty, herb flavor all its own. For a twist, use a different seasoning blend or toasted nut each time you make it.

1 In a small bowl combine the bread crumbs and milk. Cover and let stand for 5 minutes.

2 Meanwhile, in a blender container or food processor bowl combine beans, sour cream, pine nuts, seasoning blend, and ground red pepper. Cover and blend or process until nearly smooth. Add bread crumb mixture. Cover and blend or process until smooth. Stir in oregano. Cover and chill for 2 to 24 hours to blend flavors.

3 If desired, sprinkle chives over dip. Serve the dip with Toasted Pita Chips.

Toasted Pita Chips: Split 4 large pita bread rounds in half horizontally. Using a sharp knife, cut each pita half into 6 wedges. Arrange wedges in a single layer on ungreased baking sheets. Coat pita wedges with nonstick cooking spray. Sprinkle lightly with paprika. Bake in a 350° oven for 12 to 15 minutes or until wedges are crisp and golden brown. Makes 48 chips.

Nutrition Facts per serving (2 tablespoons dip + 4 chips): 94 cal., 1 g total fat (0 g sat. fat), 1 mg chol., 175 mg sodium, 18 g carbo., 1 g sugar, 2 g fiber, 5 g pro.
Daily Values: 1% vit. A, 4% calcium, 6% iron
Exchanges: 1 Starch, ½ Very Lean Meat

Prep: 15 minutes
Bake: 12 minutes
Chill: 2 to 24 hours
Oven: 350°F
Makes: 12 (2-tablespoon) servings

¼ cup soft bread crumbs
2 tablespoons fat-free milk
1 15-ounce can white kidney (cannellini) beans or Great Northern beans, rinsed and drained
¼ cup fat-free dairy sour cream
3 tablespoons pine nuts, toasted
¼ teaspoon salt-free garlic and herb or other salt-free seasoning blend
⅛ teaspoon ground red pepper
2 teaspoons snipped fresh oregano or basil or ½ teaspoon dried oregano or basil, crushed
   Snipped fresh chives (optional)
1 recipe Toasted Pita Chips

15 g
carb

Layered Southwestern Dip

If you want a crowd pleaser, seven layers of fresh, colorful Southwestern flavors will do the trick. Be sure to make the tortilla chips—they take little time to prepare and will save you lots of calories compared with their fried counterparts.

1 Line a 12-inch platter with shredded lettuce. In a medium bowl stir together black beans, sweet pepper, and jalapeño peppers. Spoon over lettuce, leaving a border of lettuce. Spoon sour cream over bean mixture; gently spread in a smooth layer, leaving a border of bean mixture.

2 Drain excess liquid from salsa. Spoon salsa over sour cream layer, leaving a border of sour cream. Sprinkle cheese over salsa. If desired, top with olives. Serve immediately or cover and chill for up to 6 hours. Serve the dip with Homemade Tortilla Chips.

Homemade Tortilla Chips: Cut each of eight 7- to 8-inch flour tortillas into 6 wedges. Arrange wedges in a single layer on ungreased baking sheets. Bake in a 350° oven for 5 to 8 minutes or until dry and crisp, rotating baking sheets once. Makes 48 chips.

Nutrition Facts per serving (1 tablespoon of dip + 3 chips): 92 cal., 2 g total fat (1 g sat. fat), 3 mg chol., 229 mg sodium, 15 g carbo., 0 g sugar, 2 g fiber, 5 g pro.
Daily Values: 3% vit. A, 10% vit. C, 8% calcium, 5% iron
Exchanges: 1 Starch, ½ Very Lean Meat

Prep: 30 minutes
Bake: 5 minutes
Oven: 350°F
Makes: 16 (1-tablespoon) servings

- 2 cups shredded lettuce
- 1 15-ounce can black beans, rinsed and drained
- ½ cup chopped green sweet pepper
- 2 tablespoons bottled chopped red jalapeño peppers or canned diced green chile peppers
- 1 8-ounce carton fat-free dairy sour cream
- 1 8-ounce jar chunky salsa
- ½ cup shredded reduced-fat cheddar cheese (2 ounces)
- 2 tablespoons chopped pitted ripe olives (optional)
- 1 recipe Homemade Tortilla Chips

Double Tomato Spread

Two kinds of tomatoes—fresh and dried—are cooked with shallots, garlic, and fresh ginger in this colorful spread. It's perfect served as an appetizer with toasted baguette slices or as an accompaniment to grilled chicken or beef.

1 Place the Roma tomatoes on the unheated rack of a broiler pan. Broil 3 to 4 inches from the heat about 4 minutes or until skin is blistered, turning once. Cool slightly and coarsely chop.

2 In a small bowl pour the boiling water over dried tomatoes. Cover and let stand for 5 minutes. Meanwhile, in a large skillet heat oil over medium-high heat. Add shallots; cook and stir about 2 minutes or until golden brown. Add ginger and garlic; cook and stir for 30 seconds.

3 Carefully add the Roma tomatoes and undrained dried tomatoes. Cook for 20 to 25 minutes or until mixture thickens and most of liquid evaporates, stirring occasionally. Stir in vinegar, brown sugar, salt, and pepper. Cook for 1 minute more.

4 Transfer to a serving dish; cool. Serve the spread with toasted baguette slices or assorted crackers.

Make-Ahead Tip: Prepare spread as directed. Cover and chill for up to 3 days.

Prep: 20 minutes
Cook: 20 minutes
Makes: 48 (1-tablespoon) servings

12	Roma tomatoes (about 2 pounds)
½	cup boiling water
¼	cup dried tomatoes (not oil-packed)
2	tablespoons olive oil
1	cup thinly sliced shallots
2	teaspoons grated fresh ginger
3	cloves garlic, minced
2	tablespoons balsamic vinegar
1	tablespoon brown sugar
½	teaspoon salt
¼	teaspoon freshly ground black pepper
	Baguette slices, toasted, or assorted crackers

Nutrition Facts per serving (1 tablespoon spread + 1 baguette slice): 52 cal., 1 g total fat (0 g sat. fat), 0 mg chol., 119 mg sodium, 9 g carbo., 2 g sugar, 1 g fiber, 2 g pro.
Daily Values: 3% vit. A, 6% vit. C, 1% calcium, 3% iron
Exchanges: ½ Starch

15 g

carb

Savory Corn-Cracker Mix

Air-popped popcorn is the best choice for this snack mix. One cup contributes only 30 calories. If you choose to purchase microwave popcorn, read the package labels carefully. Many varieties contain extra fat and calories.

1 Pop the popcorn in a hot-air popper or microwave oven according to package directions (you should have 6 cups of popped corn). In a large bowl combine popcorn and cheese crackers.

2 In a small saucepan melt margarine over medium heat. Cook chili powder and garlic in hot margarine for 1 to 2 minutes or until garlic is tender. Stir in salt. Drizzle over popcorn mixture; toss gently to coat.

Nutrition Facts per serving: 106 cal., 4 g total fat (1 g sat. fat), 0 mg chol., 216 mg sodium, 15 g carbo., 0 g sugar, 2 g fiber, 2 g pro.
Daily Values: 4% vit. A, 1% vit. C, 2% calcium, 4% iron
Exchanges: 1 Starch, ½ Fat

Start to Finish: 15 minutes
Makes: 6 servings

- ¼ cup unpopped popcorn
- 2 cups bite-size reduced-fat cheese crackers
- 1 tablespoon margarine or butter
- ¾ teaspoon chili powder
- 1 clove garlic, minced
- ¼ teaspoon salt

Mini Spinach Pockets

A savory spinach-and-onion mixture packs these miniature stuffed pizzas. They're sure to please the palate and the cook. The refrigerated pizza dough makes them incredibly easy.

1 Line a baking sheet with foil; lightly grease the foil. Set baking sheet aside. For filling, in a medium bowl stir together spinach, cream cheese, green onion, Parmesan cheese, and pepper. Set aside.

2 Unroll pizza dough on a lightly floured surface; roll dough into a 15-inch square. Cut into twenty-five 3-inch squares. Spoon 1 rounded teaspoon filling onto each square. Brush edges of dough with water. Lift a corner of each square and stretch dough over filling to opposite corner, making a triangle. Press edges with fingers or a fork to seal.

3 Arrange the pockets on prepared baking sheet. Prick tops of pockets with a fork. Brush with milk. Bake in a 425° oven for 8 to 10 minutes or until golden brown. Let stand for 5 minutes before serving. If desired, serve with spaghetti sauce.

Nutrition Facts per pocket: 38 cal., 2 g total fat (1 g sat. fat), 4 mg chol., 62 mg sodium, 5 g carbo., 0 g sugar, 0 g fiber, 1 g pro.
Daily Values: 9% vit. A, 1% vit. C, 1% calcium, 2% iron
Exchanges: ½ Starch

Prep: 40 minutes
Bake: 8 minutes
Stand: 5 minutes
Oven: 425°F
Makes: 25 pockets

- ½ of a 10-ounce package frozen chopped spinach, thawed and well drained
- ½ of an 8-ounce package reduced-fat cream cheese (Neufchâtel), softened
- 2 tablespoons finely chopped green onion
- 1 tablespoon grated Parmesan cheese
  Dash black pepper
- 1 10-ounce package refrigerated pizza dough
- 1 tablespoon milk
  Bottled light spaghetti sauce, warmed (optional)

13 g
carb

Siesta Rolls

Two kinds of peppers—sweet red peppers and spicy poblano peppers—combine for just the right "warmth" in the filling, but you may adjust the ratio to your taste. For another twist, try vegetable-flavored tortillas in place of the plain variety.

1 To roast poblano and sweet peppers, halve peppers and remove stems, seeds, and membranes. Place peppers, cut sides down, on a foil-lined baking sheet. Roast in a 425°F oven about 20 minutes or until skin is bubbly and browned. Wrap peppers in the foil; let stand for 20 to 25 minutes or until cool enough to handle. Using a paring knife, pull the skin off gently and slowly. Cut peppers into thin strips.

2 Meanwhile, in a small bowl stir together cream cheese, cilantro, lime juice, ground red pepper, and garlic. Spread tortillas with cream cheese mixture. Arrange the pepper strips on top of cream cheese mixture; roll up tortillas.

3 If desired, wrap tortilla rolls in plastic wrap and chill for up to 6 hours. To serve, slice tortilla rolls into 1¼-inch pieces.

Start to Finish: 40 minutes
Oven: 425°F
Makes: 8 to 10 servings

2 large fresh poblano peppers
2 medium red sweet peppers
½ of an 8-ounce tub fat-free cream cheese
1 tablespoon snipped fresh cilantro
2 teaspoons lime juice
⅛ teaspoon ground red pepper
2 cloves garlic, minced
4 7- to 8-inch flour tortillas

Nutrition Facts per 3-piece serving: 75 cal., 1 g total fat (0 g sat. fat), 2 mg chol., 62 mg sodium, 13 g carbo., 0 g sugar, 1 g fiber, 4 g pro.
Daily Values: 37% vit. A, 174% vit. C, 7% calcium, 7% iron
Exchanges: 1 Vegetable, ½ Starch

Crab and Vegetable Roll-Ups

This pseudo sushi, without the rice and seaweed, uses zucchini ribbons to wrap up a crab-filled package of flavor. Create an assembly line with the ingredients, then wrap and roll with ease.

1 Trim ends of zucchini. Using a sharp vegetable peeler, slice zucchini lengthwise into wide, flat "ribbons." Discard first and last slices, and the seedy portions in the middle. (You will need 32 ribbons.) Set ribbons aside.

2 Carefully clean crabmeat, removing any shell or cartilage pieces. Drain crabmeat well in a colander, pressing with the back of a spoon to remove most of the liquid. Pat dry with paper towels. In a small bowl combine crabmeat, mayonnaise, wasabi paste, and salt. Seed and peel the avocado; cut into thin strips.

3 On a clean work surface, place one zucchini ribbon on top of another. For each roll-up, place 1 slightly rounded teaspoon of crab mixture at one end of two layers of zucchini ribbon. Top with avocado strips, a few shreds of carrot, and a basil leaf. Roll up; secure with toothpicks. If desired, cover and chill up to 30 minutes.

Start to Finish: 40 minutes
Makes: 16 appetizers

- 2 medium zucchini or yellow summer squash
- ½ cup cooked lump crabmeat
- 1 tablespoon mayonnaise or salad dressing
- 1 teaspoon wasabi paste
- ⅛ teaspoon salt
- ½ of a medium avocado
- 2 tablespoons coarsely shredded carrot
- 16 small fresh basil leaves

Nutrition Facts per appetizer: 23 cal., 2 g total fat (0 g sat. fat), 4 mg chol., 37 mg sodium, 1 g carbo., 1 g sugar, 1 g fiber, 1 g pro.
Daily Values: 8% vit. A, 5% vit. C, 1% calcium, 1% iron
Exchanges: ½ Fat

9 g
carb

Baked Vegetable Dippers

Folks of all ages will love these oven-fried vegetables. Be sure to make more than enough because these crowd-pleasers disappear fast.

1 Coat a large baking sheet with cooking spray; set aside.

2 In a small bowl combine the cornflake crumbs, cheese, garlic powder, and ground red pepper. In another small bowl beat together egg whites and water.

3 Dip squash, cauliflower, and mushrooms in egg white mixture and coat with crumb mixture. Place in a single layer on the prepared baking sheet. Bake in a 400° oven for 8 to 10 minutes or until vegetables are crisp-tender and coating is golden brown.

4 Meanwhile, in a small saucepan cook and stir pizza sauce over low heat until heated through. Serve the baked vegetables with pizza sauce for dipping.

Nutrition Facts per serving: 51 cal., 1 g total fat (0 g sat. fat), 1 mg chol., 232 mg sodium, 9 g carbo., 2 g sugar, 1 g fiber, 3 g pro.
Daily Values: 3% vit. A, 18% vit. C, 3% calcium, 3% iron
Exchanges: 2 Vegetable

Prep: 20 minutes
Bake: 8 minutes
Oven: 400°F
Makes: 8 servings

Nonstick cooking spray
¾ cup cornflake crumbs
2 tablespoons grated Romano or Parmesan cheese
⅛ teaspoon garlic powder
⅛ teaspoon ground red pepper
2 egg whites
2 tablespoons water
2 small zucchini or yellow summer squash, cut into ¼-inch slices
1 cup cauliflower florets
1 cup halved small fresh mushrooms or broccoli florets
1 8-ounce can pizza sauce

Eggplant with Herbed Goat Cheese

These broiled eggplant slices—topped with a basil-goat cheese mixture, chopped tomato, and additional fresh basil—make an elegant appetizer for any gathering.

1 Cut eggplant crosswise into sixteen ½-inch slices. Lightly sprinkle both sides of eggplant slices with salt. Place on paper towels; let stand for 20 minutes. Pat dry with paper towels.

2 Meanwhile, in a small bowl combine goat cheese, basil, onion powder, and pepper. If mixture seems dry, stir in enough of the milk to moisten.

3 Brush the eggplant slices with oil. Place eggplant in a single layer on the unheated rack of a broiler pan. Broil 4 to 5 inches from the heat for 8 to 9 minutes or until tender and lightly browned, turning once.

4 Remove eggplant from broiler and spread with the goat cheese mixture. Sprinkle with additional pepper. Broil about 1 minute more or until cheese mixture is heated through.

5 To serve, sprinkle eggplant slices with chopped tomato and, if desired, additional snipped fresh basil.

Make-Ahead Tip: Prepare cheese mixture as directed. Cover and chill for up to 24 hours.

Nutrition Facts per appetizer: 49 cal., 4 g total fat (2 g sat. fat), 4 mg chol., 37 mg sodium, 2 g carbo., 1 g sugar, 1 g fiber, 2 g pro.
Daily Values: 1% vit. A, 3% vit. C, 2% calcium, 2% iron
Exchanges: ½ Vegetable, 1 Fat

Prep: 30 minutes
Broil: 9 minutes
Makes: 16 appetizers

- 1 medium eggplant (about 1 pound)
  Salt
- 1 5½- to 6-ounce package soft goat cheese (chèvre)
- 1 tablespoon snipped fresh basil or thyme or 1 teaspoon dried basil or thyme, crushed
- 1 teaspoon onion powder
  Dash black pepper
- 1 tablespoon milk (optional)
- 2 tablespoons olive oil
- 1 small tomato, seeded and chopped
  Snipped fresh basil or thyme (optional)

7 g
carb

Broiled Portobello Mushrooms

This hearty, meaty appetizer will thrill carnivores and vegetarians alike, and it couldn't be easier to make. Broil a few extra mushrooms to have on hand for fast and easy open-face sandwiches.

1 Remove stems from mushrooms. Wipe mushrooms with a clean, damp cloth or paper towel. Place mushrooms, stemmed sides up, in a small shallow baking pan. Drizzle with oil.

2 In a small bowl combine the garlic and seasoned salt; set aside.

3 Broil mushrooms 3 to 4 inches from the heat for 8 to 10 minutes or until tender, sprinkling with garlic mixture halfway through broiling.

4 Sprinkle the mushrooms with basil and Parmesan cheese. Serve immediately.

Prep: 15 minutes
Broil: 8 minutes
Makes: 4 servings

- 4 extra-large fresh portobello mushrooms (about 4½ inches in diameter)
- 4 teaspoons olive oil
- 4 cloves garlic, minced
- ½ teaspoon seasoned salt
- 2 tablespoons snipped fresh basil
- 2 tablespoons freshly grated Parmesan cheese

Nutrition Facts per serving: 97 cal., 5 g total fat (1 g sat. fat), 2 mg chol., 262 mg sodium, 7 g carbo., 1 g sugar, 4 g fiber, 5 g pro.
Daily Values: 1% vit. A, 2% vit. C, 10% calcium, 3% iron
Exchanges: 1½ Vegetable, 1 Fat

Potato Skins with Roasted Peppers

These Italian-flavored stuffed potato skins are as packed with nutrients as they are with flavor. Use the reserved "flesh" of the potato to make mashed potatoes within a day or two.

1 Scrub potatoes; prick with a fork. Bake in a 425° oven for 40 to 45 minutes or until tender; cool.

2 Halve each potato lengthwise. Scoop out the insides of potato halves, leaving ¼-inch shells. Cover and chill scooped-out potato for another use.

3 Line a 15×10×1-inch baking pan with foil. Arrange potato shells, cut sides up, on the prepared baking sheet. Lightly sprinkle with the salt and black pepper. Sprinkle with roasted sweet peppers and green onions. Top with mozzarella cheese.

4 Bake in a 450° oven for 8 to 10 minutes or until cheese is melted and potato shells are heated through.

5 Meanwhile, in a small bowl stir together sour cream, Italian seasoning, and garlic. If desired, sprinkle potato skins with additional green onions. Serve warm with sour cream mixture.

Make-Ahead Tip: Assemble potato shells as directed. Cover and chill for up to 24 hours before baking.

Prep: 50 minutes
Bake: 8 minutes
Oven: 425°F/450°F
Makes: 12 appetizers

- 6   medium baking potatoes (about 2 pounds)
- ¼   teaspoon salt
- ⅛   teaspoon black pepper
- 1   7-ounce jar roasted red sweet peppers, drained and chopped
- 3   tablespoons thinly sliced green onions
- 1   cup shredded reduced-fat mozzarella cheese (4 ounces)
- ½   cup light dairy sour cream
- ¼   teaspoon dried Italian seasoning, crushed
- 1   clove garlic, minced
  Sliced green onion tops (optional)

Nutrition Facts per appetizer: 79 cal., 3 g total fat (2 g sat. fat), 8 mg chol., 110 mg sodium, 11 g carbo., 0 g sugar, 1 g fiber, 4 g pro.
Daily Values: 3% vit. A, 63% vit. C, 8% calcium, 5% iron
Exchanges: ½ Starch, ½ Medium-Fat Meat

1 g
carb

Asian Barbecued Meatballs

Sure to be the hit of any party, these savory meatballs can be dressed up by adding chunks of pineapple to the skewers. Be sure to add 15 grams of carb per ¾ cup of pineapple.

1 In a medium bowl combine ground beef, green onions, the ¼ cup chopped onion, the soy sauce, sesame seeds, and sugar. Shape into 36 meatballs, about 1 inch in size.

2 Thread 2 meatballs onto each of eighteen 6-inch skewers, leaving ¼ inch between meatballs. (If using wooden skewers, soak in water for 30 minutes before broiling.) Place skewers on the unheated rack of a broiler pan. Broil 4 to 5 inches from the heat for 8 to 10 minutes or until meat is done (160°F), turning skewers once. If desired, serve the meatball skewers with mustard.

Grill Method: Place skewers on the rack of an uncovered grill directly over medium coals. Grill for 8 to 10 minutes or until meat is done (160°F), turning once.

Nutrition Facts per appetizer: 59 cal., 4 g total fat (1 g sat. fat), 16 mg chol., 168 mg sodium, 1 g carbo., 1 g sugar, 0 g fiber, 5 g pro.
Daily Values: 1% vit. C, 3% iron
Exchanges: 1 Medium-Fat Meat

Prep: 25 minutes
Broil: 8 minutes
Makes: 18 appetizers

1   **pound lean ground beef**
⅓   **cup finely chopped green onions**
¼   **cup chopped onion**
3   **tablespoons soy sauce**
2   **tablespoons sesame seeds, toasted**
1   **tablespoon sugar**
     Prepared Chinese-style hot mustard
        (optional)

Potted Shrimp

There's a generous amount of butter in classic potted shrimp, but not in this version. A jalapeño pepper, cumin, and oregano pump up the flavor. You'll never miss the extra fat.

1 Thaw shrimp, if frozen. Peel and devein shrimp. Rinse shrimp; pat dry with paper towels. Set aside. In a large nonstick skillet melt butter over medium heat. Cook jalapeño pepper and garlic in hot butter for 30 to 40 seconds or until pepper is tender. Add shrimp and cook for 2 minutes, stirring occasionally. Stir in salt, cumin seeds, and oregano; cook and stir about 1 minute more or until shrimp are opaque.

2 Transfer the shrimp mixture to a food processor bowl. Cover and process with on/off pulses until shrimp is finely chopped. Transfer to a medium bowl; stir in mayonnaise.

3 Pack the shrimp mixture into a serving bowl. Using a rubber spatula, smooth the surface. Cover and chill for up to 24 hours. Let stand at room temperature about 30 minutes before serving. Serve the spread with assorted crackers.

Test-Kitchen Tip: Hot peppers contain volatile oils that can burn eyes, lips, and sensitive skin. When working with chile peppers, wear plastic or rubber gloves to protect your skin. If your bare hands touch the peppers, wash your hands well with soap and water.

Prep: 25 minutes
Chill: up to 24 hours
Stand: 30 minutes
Makes: 16 (2-tablespoon) servings

1 pound fresh or frozen large shrimp in shells (about 24 shrimp)
1 tablespoon butter or margarine
1 large fresh jalapeño pepper, seeded and finely chopped
2 teaspoons bottled minced garlic
¾ teaspoon salt
¼ teaspoon cumin seeds
¼ teaspoon dried oregano, crushed
3 tablespoons mayonnaise or salad dressing
   Assorted crackers

Nutrition Facts per serving (2 tablespoons spread + 3 crackers): 92 cal., 5 g total fat (1 g sat. fat), 35 mg chol., 234 mg sodium, 6 g carbo., 0 g sugar, 0 g fiber, 5 g pro.
Daily Values: 1% vit. A, 2% vit. C, 2% calcium, 5% iron
Exchanges: ½ Starch, ½ Lean Meat, ½ Fat

5 g
carb

Fiesta Shrimp Skewers

Light up your palate with spicy shrimp, tempered by a flame-taming dip. Cilantro adds a unique fresh flavor to the dip. If it's not your favorite herb, substitute fresh parsley.

1 Prepare Cool Cilantro Dip. Cover and chill until ready to serve. Thaw shrimp, if frozen. Peel and devein shrimp. Rinse shrimp; pat dry with paper towels. Place shrimp in a plastic bag set in a shallow dish.

2 For marinade, in a small bowl combine ale, lime peel, lime juice, cilantro, jalapeño pepper, cumin, ground red pepper, and garlic. Pour over shrimp; seal bag. Marinate in the refrigerator for 30 to 60 minutes, turning bag occasionally. Drain shrimp, reserving the marinade.

3 Alternately thread shrimp, poblano pieces, and lime pieces onto ten to twelve 6-inch skewers, leaving ¼ inch between pieces. (If using wooden skewers, soak in water for 30 minutes before grilling.) Brush with reserved marinade; discard any remaining marinade.

4 Place skewers on rack of an uncovered grill directly over medium coals. Grill for 8 to 10 minutes or until shrimp are opaque, turning once. Serve shrimp skewers with Cool Cilantro Dip.

Cool Cilantro Dip: In a small bowl stir together one 8-ounce carton light dairy sour cream, 2 tablespoons snipped fresh cilantro, 1 tablespoon bottled salsa, ½ teaspoon finely shredded lime peel, and 1 garlic clove, minced. Makes 1 cup.

Prep: 25 minutes
Marinate: 30 minutes
Grill: 8 minutes
Makes: 10 to 12 servings

1 recipe Cool Cilantro Dip
1 pound fresh or frozen large shrimp in shells (about 24 shrimp)
½ cup amber ale or other ale
½ teaspoon finely shredded lime peel
¼ cup lime juice
2 tablespoons snipped fresh cilantro
1 small fresh jalapeño pepper, seeded and finely chopped (see tip, page 37)
¼ teaspoon ground cumin
⅛ teaspoon ground red pepper
1 clove garlic, minced
2 fresh poblano peppers, seeded and cut into 1-inch pieces
2 limes, cut into 1-inch pieces

Nutrition Facts per serving: 81 cal., 3 g total fat (1 g sat. fat), 59 mg chol., 71 mg sodium, 5 g carbo., 2 g sugar, 1 g fiber, 9 g pro.
Daily Values: 8% vit. A, 50% vit. C, 7% calcium, 7% iron
Exchanges: ½ Vegetable, 1 Very Lean Meat, ½ Fat

Breakfast & Brunch

Baked Breakfast Apples

Fill your home with an irresistible aroma when you make this treat for breakfast. Rely on the microwave for hurried mornings.

1 Combine apples and dates. Add half of the apple mixture to each of two 10- or 12-ounce casseroles. Sprinkle each with half of the cinnamon. Pour half of apple juice over apple mixture in each casserole.

2 Bake, covered, in a 350° oven for 20 to 25 minutes or just until apples are tender. Stir spreadable fruit; spoon over apple mixture. Sprinkle with granola. Serve warm.

Microwave Directions: In two 10- or 12-ounce microwave-safe casseroles combine apples and dates. Sprinkle with cinnamon. Reduce the apple juice to ¼ cup; pour over apple mixture. Cover and microwave on 100 percent power (high) for 3 to 4 minutes or just until apples are tender. Continue as directed.

Nutrition Facts per serving: 210 cal., 1 g total fat (0 g sat. fat), 0 mg chol., 32 mg sodium, 52 g carbo., 40 g sugar, 6 g fiber, 2 g pro.
Daily Values: 5% vit. A, 15% vit. C, 3% calcium, 6% iron
Exchanges: 3 Fruit, ½ Starch

Prep: 10 minutes
Bake: 20 minutes
Oven: 350°F
Makes: 2 servings

2 medium apples, cored and cut into bite-size pieces
2 tablespoons snipped pitted whole dates
¼ teaspoon ground cinnamon
½ cup apple juice or apple cider
1 tablespoon raspberry spreadable fruit
¼ cup low-fat granola

Fruit-Topped Grapefruit Halves

Grapefruit never had it so good! Even people who are not grapefruit enthusiasts may change their minds when they taste this sweet and flavorful dish. An ideal, healthful way to start the day, it has plenty of vitamin C (90% of your recommended daily intake) and fiber.

1 Halve each grapefruit; cut a very thin slice from bottom of each half so grapefruit will sit flat. Using a grapefruit knife or other small knife, cut around the outer edge to loosen fruit from shell. Cut between each segment to loosen fruit from membrane.

2 In a small bowl combine orange sections, banana slices, dried plums, and, if desired, orange liqueur. Mound the orange mixture on top of grapefruit halves. Dot with margarine. Combine brown sugar and cinnamon; sprinkle over orange mixture. Place grapefruit halves in a 3-quart rectangular baking dish.

3 Bake in a 450° oven about 12 minutes or until grapefruit is warm and topping is heated through.

Prep: 15 minutes
Bake: 12 minutes
Oven: 450°F
Makes: 6 servings

3   red grapefruit
1   large orange, peeled and sectioned
1   medium banana, sliced
⅓   cup orange- or lemon-flavored or regular pitted dried plums (prunes), coarsely snipped
2   tablespoons orange liqueur or orange juice (optional)
1   tablespoon margarine or butter, cut into small pieces
2   tablespoons brown sugar
½   teaspoon ground cinnamon

Nutrition Facts per serving: 118 cal., 2 g total fat (0 g sat. fat), 0 mg chol., 25 mg sodium, 26 g carbo., 18 g sugar, 3 g fiber, 1 g pro.
Daily Values: 12% vit. A, 90% vit. C, 3% calcium, 3% iron
Exchanges: 1½ Fruit, ½ Fat

Fresh Fruit with Minted Yogurt

When summer produce is at its peak, you'll have no trouble finding your favorite fruits to mix and match in this "plum good" yogurt topper. You don't have to wait for summer, however; it's just as refreshing spooned over a bowl of fall fruit.

1 In a small bowl stir together yogurt, honey, and mint. Cover and chill until ready to serve.

2 In a medium bowl combine plums and berries. Spoon fruit mixture into serving bowls. Top with the yogurt mixture. If desired, garnish with additional fresh mint.

Nutrition Facts per serving: 135 cal., 2 g total fat (1 g sat. fat), 5 mg chol., 55 mg sodium, 27 g carbo., 21 g sugar, 3 g fiber, 5 g pro.
Daily Values: 5% vit. A, 46% vit. C, 15% calcium, 4% iron
Exchanges: ½ Milk, 1½ Fruit

Start to Finish: 15 minutes
Makes: 6 servings

1   16-ounce carton plain low-fat yogurt
3   tablespoons honey
2   tablespoons snipped fresh mint
4   medium plums, pitted and thinly sliced
       (about 3 cups)
3   cups assorted berries (such as sliced
       strawberries, whole raspberries,
       and/or blueberries)
    Snipped fresh mint (optional)

Lemon Breakfast Parfaits

Serve these lively, layered parfaits of fruit and couscous for a smart start in the morning. Although the combination may sound unusual, the couscous mixture is a new twist on an old classic—rice pudding.

1 In a medium saucepan combine milk and salt. Bring to boiling. Stir in couscous; reduce heat. Simmer, covered, for 1 minute. Remove from heat; let stand for 5 minutes. Fluff with a fork. Cool.

2 In a small bowl combine yogurt, sour cream, honey, and lemon peel; stir into couscous mixture.

3 Spoon half of the fruit into 6 parfait glasses. Spoon the couscous mixture over the fruit; top with remaining fruit.

Nutrition Facts per serving: 127 cal., 2 g total fat (1 g sat. fat), 9 mg chol., 70 mg sodium, 22 g carbo., 13 g sugar, 2 g fiber, 5 g pro.
Daily Values: 5% vit. A, 69% vit. C, 13% calcium, 2% iron
Exchanges: ½ Fruit, 1 Starch, ½ Fat

Start to Finish: 25 minutes
Makes: 6 servings

- ¾ cup fat-free milk
  Dash salt
- ⅓ cup quick-cooking couscous
- ½ cup lemon low-fat yogurt
- ½ cup light dairy sour cream
- 1 tablespoon honey
- ¼ teaspoon finely shredded lemon peel
- 3 cups assorted fruit (such as sliced strawberries, nectarines, or star fruit; sliced peeled kiwifruit; blueberries; and/or raspberries)

Apple Butter-Oat Bran Muffins

Oat bran is loaded with soluble fiber, the type associated with lowering blood cholesterol and controlling blood sugar. Here's a great way to get your oat bran—in a moist, delicious muffin.

1 Lightly coat twelve 2½-inch muffin cups with cooking spray; set aside.

2 In a large bowl stir together oat bran, flour, baking powder, baking soda, and salt. Make a well in the center of flour mixture.

3 In a medium bowl combine apple butter, buttermilk, egg product, honey, and oil. Add all at once to flour mixture. Stir just until moistened (batter should be lumpy). Fold in the dates.

4 Spoon batter into prepared muffin cups, filling each about three-fourths full. Bake in a 400° oven for 18 to 20 minutes or until golden brown. Cool muffins in pan on a wire rack for 5 minutes. Remove from muffin cups. Serve muffins warm.

*Note: Choose 100-percent oat bran with no added ingredients. If you can't find oat bran, place 1 cup rolled oats in a food processor bowl or blender container. Cover and process or blend until oats are the consistency of a coarse flour (you should have about ¾ cup). Substitute the ¾ cup oat flour for the 1¼ cups oat bran.

Prep: 15 minutes
Bake: 18 minutes
Oven: 400°F
Makes: 12 muffins

Nonstick cooking spray
1¼ cups oat bran*
1 cup all-purpose flour
1¼ teaspoons baking powder
½ teaspoon baking soda
¼ teaspoon salt
¾ cup apple butter, spiced apple butter, or peach butter
½ cup buttermilk
¼ cup refrigerated or frozen egg product, thawed
2 tablespoons honey
1 tablespoon cooking oil
⅓ cup finely snipped pitted whole dates

Nutrition Facts per muffin: 193 cal., 2 g total fat (0 g sat. fat), 0 mg chol., 165 mg sodium, 44 g carbo., 26 g sugar, 3 g fiber, 4 g pro.
Daily Values: 2% vit. A, 1% vit. C, 6% calcium, 7% iron
Exchanges: 2 Fruit, 1 Starch

Blueberry Gems

**Plump blueberries make these bite-size orange-accented muffins scrumptious.
They are so tender, you won't even need to top them with butter.**

1 Lightly coat thirty-six 1¾-inch muffin pans with cooking spray; set aside.

2 In a medium bowl stir together flour, sugar, baking powder, and salt. Make a well in the center of flour mixture.

3 In a small bowl combine egg whites, juice, oil, and vanilla. Add all at once to flour mixture. Stir just until moistened (batter should be lumpy). Fold in the blueberries.

4 Spoon batter into prepared muffin cups, filling each about two-thirds full. Bake in a 400° oven for 15 to 18 minutes or until muffins are golden brown and a wooden toothpick inserted in centers comes out clean. Cool in pans on wire racks for 5 minutes. Remove from muffin cups. Serve warm.

Prep: 15 minutes
Bake: 15 minutes
Oven: 400°F
Makes: 36 muffins

Nonstick cooking spray
1½ cups all-purpose flour
¼ cup sugar
1½ teaspoons baking powder
¼ teaspoon salt
2 egg whites
⅔ cup orange juice
2 tablespoons cooking oil
1 teaspoon vanilla
1 cup fresh or frozen blueberries

Nutrition Facts per muffin: 35 cal., 1 g total fat (0 g sat. fat), 0 mg chol., 36 mg sodium, 6 g carbo., 2 g sugar, 0 g fiber, 1 g pro.
Daily Values: 5% vit. C, 1% calcium, 1% iron
Exchanges: ½ Starch

18 g
carb

Whole Wheat Pumpkin Muffins

Canned pumpkin keeps these low-fat muffins moist and tender and lends lots of great flavor. The pumpkin also contributes a hefty dose of health-promoting carotene.

1 Lightly coat twelve 2½-inch muffin cups with cooking spray; set aside.

2 In a large bowl stir together all-purpose flour, whole wheat flour, sugar, baking powder, pumpkin pie spice, baking soda, and salt. Make a well in the center of flour mixture.

3 In a small bowl combine egg, milk, and margarine; stir in pumpkin. Add all at once to flour mixture. Stir just until moistened (batter should be lumpy).

4 Spoon the batter into the prepared muffin cups, filling each about two-thirds full. Bake in a 375° oven for 15 to 18 minutes or until a wooden toothpick inserted in centers comes out clean. Cool in pan on a wire rack for 5 minutes. Remove from muffin cups. Serve warm.

Nutrition Facts per muffin: 104 cal., 3 g total fat (1 g sat. fat), 18 mg chol., 154 mg sodium, 18 g carbo., 4 g sugar, 1 g fiber, 3 g pro.
Daily Values: 48% vit. A, 1% vit. C, 7% calcium, 5% iron
Exchanges: 1 Starch, ½ Fat

Prep: 15 minutes
Bake: 15 minutes
Oven: 375°F
Makes: 12 muffins

Nonstick cooking spray
1 cup all-purpose flour
¾ cup whole wheat flour
3 tablespoons sugar
2 teaspoons baking powder
1 teaspoon pumpkin pie spice
¼ teaspoon baking soda
⅛ teaspoon salt
1 beaten egg
¾ cup fat-free milk
2 tablespoons margarine or butter, melted
½ cup canned pumpkin

Up-and-Down Biscuits

An unusual configuration makes these light-as-air biscuits an attractive opener for your breakfast brunch. Dust the dough with cinnamon for a little more flavor; it also makes the layers easier to see.

1 Grease twelve 2½-inch muffin cups; set aside. In a large bowl stir together flour, baking powder, cream of tartar, and salt. Using a pastry blender, cut in shortening until the mixture resembles coarse crumbs. Make a well in the center of flour mixture. Add milk all at once to flour mixture. Stir just until dough clings together.

2 Turn dough out onto a lightly floured surface. Quickly knead dough by gently folding and pressing for 10 to 12 strokes or until nearly smooth. Divide dough in half.

3 Roll one portion into a 12×10-inch rectangle. If desired, sprinkle dough lightly with cinnamon. Cut dough into five 12×2-inch strips. Stack the strips; cut stack into six 2-inch squares. Place each stack of squares, cut sides down, in the prepared muffin cups. Repeat with the remaining dough.

4 Bake in a 450° oven for 10 to 12 minutes or until golden brown. Serve warm.

Prep: 20 minutes
Bake: 10 minutes
Oven: 450°F
Makes: 12 biscuits

- 2 cups all-purpose flour
- 4 teaspoons baking powder
- ½ teaspoon cream of tartar
- ¼ teaspoon salt
- ¼ cup shortening
- ¾ cup fat-free milk
  Ground cinnamon (optional)

Nutrition Facts per biscuit: 115 cal., 4 g total fat (1 g sat. fat), 0 mg chol., 188 mg sodium, 16 g carbo., 1 g sugar, 1 g fiber, 3 g pro.
Daily Values: 1% vit. A, 8% vit. C, 5% calcium, 5% iron
Exchanges: 1 Starch, 1 Fat

15 g
carb

Berry-Lemon Cornmeal Biscuits

Cornmeal adds a crunchy bite to these citrusy berry-studded biscuits. Use fresh berries—frozen berries may make the batter too wet and discolor the biscuits.

1 Coat a large baking sheet with cooking spray; set aside. In a large bowl stir together flour, cornmeal, sugar, lemon peel, baking powder, baking soda, and salt. Using a pastry blender, cut in butter until mixture resembles coarse crumbs. Make a well in the center of the flour mixture.

2 In a small bowl combine milk and sour cream. Add all at once to flour mixture. Stir just until moistened. Gently fold in the raspberries.

3 Drop dough by rounded tablespoons 1 inch apart on the prepared baking sheet, forming 16 biscuits. Bake in a 400° oven for 14 to 16 minutes or until golden brown. Cool slightly on a wire rack. Serve warm.

Nutrition Facts per biscuit: 99 cal., 3 g total fat (2 g sat. fat), 9 mg chol., 142 mg sodium, 15 g carbo., 4 g sugar, 1 g fiber, 3 g pro.
Daily Values: 4% vit. A, 4% vit. C, 7% calcium, 4% iron
Exchanges: 1 Starch, ½ Fat

Prep: 15 minutes
Bake: 14 minutes
Oven: 400°F
Makes: 16 biscuits

Nonstick cooking spray
1½ cups all-purpose flour
½ cup cornmeal
2 tablespoons sugar
1 tablespoon finely shredded lemon peel
2 teaspoons baking powder
¼ teaspoon baking soda
¼ teaspoon salt
3 tablespoons butter
¾ cup fat-free milk
½ cup light dairy sour cream
1 cup fresh raspberries and/or blueberries
  (do not use frozen berries)

Apricot Hot Cross Buns

There's nothing like the smell of these buns baking to get sleepyheads out of bed. To streamline your morning, mix the dry ingredients the night before and put them in a sealed plastic bag. Mix the wet ingredients and store them, covered, in the refrigerator.

1 In a large mixing bowl combine 2 cups of the flour, the yeast, and cinnamon; set aside. In a medium saucepan heat and stir milk, butter, sugar, and salt until warm (120°F to 130°F) and butter is almost melted.

2 Add milk mixture to flour mixture. Add the 3 eggs. Beat with an electric mixer on low to medium speed for 30 seconds, scraping sides of bowl constantly. Beat on high speed for 3 minutes. Using a wooden spoon, stir in apricots and as much of the remaining flour as you can.

3 Turn dough out onto a lightly floured surface. Knead in enough remaining flour to make a moderately soft dough that is smooth and elastic (3 to 5 minutes total). Shape into a ball. Place in a lightly greased bowl, turning once to grease surface. Cover; let rise in a warm place until double in size (about 1½ hours).

4 Punch dough down. Turn out onto a lightly floured surface. Cover and let rest for 10 minutes. Lightly grease 2 baking sheets; set aside.

5 Divide dough into 20 portions. Shape each into a smooth ball. Place 1½ inches apart on the prepared baking sheets. Cover and let rise in a warm place until nearly double in size (45 to 60 minutes).

Prep: 45 minutes
Rise: 2¼ hours
Bake: 12 minutes
Oven: 375°F
Makes: 20 buns

4	to 4½ cups all-purpose flour
1	package active dry yeast
¾	teaspoon ground cinnamon
¾	cup reduced-fat milk
½	cup butter
⅓	cup sugar
½	teaspoon salt
3	eggs
1	cup snipped dried apricots
1	slightly beaten egg white
1	tablespoon water

6 Using a sharp knife, make a criss-cross slash across top of each bun. In a small bowl combine egg white and water; brush over buns.

7 Bake in a 375° oven for 12 to 15 minutes or until golden brown. Cool slightly on wire racks.

Nutrition Facts per bun: 180 cal., 6 g total fat (3 g sat. fat), 46 mg chol., 126 mg sodium, 27 g carbo., 6 g sugar, 1 g fiber, 4 g pro.
Daily Values: 15% vit. A, 2% calcium, 9% iron
Exchanges: 2 Starch, ½ Fat

21 g
carb

Orange-Glazed Cinnamon Rolls

To slice the dough for these easy orange-scented rolls, put a piece of heavy-duty thread under the dough. Crisscross the thread over the dough and pull quickly.

1 Lightly coat a 9×1½-inch round baking pan with cooking spray; set aside. On a lightly floured surface, roll dough into a 12×8-inch rectangle. (If the dough is difficult to roll out, let it rest for a short time and roll out again. Repeat as necessary.)

2 Brush dough with melted margarine; sprinkle evenly with granulated sugar and cinnamon.

3 Roll up dough, starting from a long side; seal seam. Cut into twelve 1-inch slices. Place rolls, cut sides down, in the prepared baking pan. Cover and let rise in a warm place until nearly double in size (about 30 minutes).

4 Bake in a 375° oven for 20 to 25 minutes or until light brown. Cool slightly in pan on a wire rack. Remove from pan. Drizzle rolls with Orange Glaze. Serve warm.

Orange Glaze: In a bowl combine ½ cup sifted powdered sugar and ¼ teaspoon finely shredded orange peel. Stir in enough orange juice (2 to 3 teaspoons) to make of drizzling consistency.

Make-Ahead Tip: Prepare and bake rolls as directed. Cool completely; do not drizzle with glaze. Wrap in foil or freezer wrap and freeze for up to 3 months. To serve, heat wrapped rolls in a 300° oven for 20 to 30 minutes or until warm. Drizzle with Orange Glaze.

Prep: 15 minutes
Rise: 30 minutes
Bake: 20 minutes
Oven: 375°F
Makes: 12 rolls

Nonstick cooking spray
1   1-pound loaf frozen bread dough, thawed
1   tablespoon margarine or butter, melted
1   tablespoon granulated sugar
1   teaspoon ground cinnamon
1   recipe Orange Glaze

Nutrition Facts per roll: 119 cal., 1 g total fat (0 g sat. fat), 0 mg chol., 11 mg sodium, 21 g carbo., 8 g sugar, 0 g fiber, 3 g pro.
Daily Values: 1% vit. A, 1% vit. C, 4% calcium, 1% iron
Exchanges: 1½ Starch

Coffee Cake Show-Off

Although this gorgeous cake looks like it must have come from a professional bakery, no one will know how simple it is to make. Spreadable fruit comes in a variety of flavors—choose your family's favorite.

1 In a medium mixing bowl stir together 1 cup of the flour and the yeast; set aside. In a small saucepan heat and stir evaporated milk, water, granulated sugar, butter, and salt just until warm (120°F to 130°F) and butter is almost melted. Add milk mixture to flour mixture; add egg. Beat with an electric mixer on low speed for 30 seconds, scraping sides of bowl. Beat on high speed for 3 minutes. Using a wooden spoon, stir in as much remaining flour as you can.

2 Turn dough out onto a lightly floured surface. Knead in enough remaining flour to make a moderately stiff dough that is smooth and elastic (6 to 8 minutes total). Shape into a ball; place in a lightly greased bowl, turning once. Cover; let rise in a warm place until double in size (about 1 hour). Punch dough down. Turn out onto a lightly floured surface. Divide into 2 portions, with three-fourths of the dough in larger portion. Cover; let rest for 10 minutes.

3 Grease a 10-inch springform pan with a removable bottom; set aside. Beat together cream cheese, powdered sugar, and vanilla until smooth. Roll larger portion of dough into an 11-inch circle. Fit into the prepared pan, covering bottom and ½ inch up sides. Spread cream cheese mixture over bottom; top with spreadable fruit.

4 Roll remaining dough into a 9×5-inch rectangle; cut into five 9×1-inch strips. Twist each strip; place 3 strips on spreadable fruit at 2-inch intervals, stretching strips to fit.

Prep: 45 minutes
Rise: 1½ hours
Bake: 35 minutes
Oven: 350°F
Makes: 10 servings

- 2 to 2¼ cups all-purpose flour
- 1 package active dry yeast
- ⅓ cup evaporated fat-free milk
- 3 tablespoons water
- 1 tablespoon granulated sugar
- 1 tablespoon butter
- ¼ teaspoon salt
- 1 egg
- 6 ounces reduced-fat cream cheese (Neufchâtel), softened
- 2 tablespoons powdered sugar
- 1 teaspoon vanilla
- ½ cup spreadable fruit, any flavor

Place remaining strips across strips already in place. Press ends into sides of crust; trim, if necessary. Cover; let rise in a warm place until nearly double in size (about 30 minutes).

5 Bake in a 350° oven for 35 minutes or until crust is golden brown. Cover with foil, the last 10 minutes, if necessary. Cool on a wire rack about 45 minutes.

Nutrition Facts per serving: 201 cal., 6 g total fat (3 g sat. fat), 38 mg chol., 155 mg sodium, 32 g carbo., 10 g sugar, 1 g fiber, 6 g pro. **Daily Values:** 6% vit. A, 4% calcium, 7% iron **Exchanges:** 1 Starch, 1 Other Carbo., 1 Fat

20 g carb

Cream Cheese and Raspberry Coffee Cake

You can easily change the flavor of this time-honored recipe by substituting different fruit preserves—such as strawberry or blackberry—for the raspberry.

1 Grease and flour a 13×9×2-inch baking pan; set aside. In a large mixing bowl beat cream cheese, granulated sugar, and butter with an electric mixer on medium speed until fluffy. Add half of the flour, the eggs, milk, baking powder, baking soda, vanilla, and salt. Beat about 2 minutes or until combined. Beat in the remaining flour on low speed until combined.

2 Spread batter in the prepared baking pan. Spoon preserves in 8 to 10 portions on top of batter. Using a knife, swirl the preserves into batter to marble.

3 Bake in a 350° oven for 30 to 35 minutes or until a wooden toothpick inserted near center comes out clean. Cool slightly on a wire rack. Sift powdered sugar over top. Cut into squares; serve warm.

Nutrition Facts per serving: 157 cal., 8 g total fat (5 g sat. fat), 39 mg chol., 145 mg sodium, 20 g carbo., 12 g sugar, 0 g fiber, 2 g pro.
Daily Values: 6% vit. A, 1% vit. C, 3% calcium, 3% iron
Exchanges: ½ Starch, 1 Other Carbo., 1½ Fat

Prep: 20 minutes
Bake: 30 minutes
Oven: 350°F
Makes: 24 servings

1   8-ounce package cream cheese or reduced-fat cream cheese (Neufchâtel), softened (do not use fat-free cream cheese)
1   cup granulated sugar
½   cup butter, softened
1¾   cups all-purpose flour
2   eggs
¼   cup milk
1   teaspoon baking powder
½   teaspoon baking soda
½   teaspoon vanilla
¼   teaspoon salt
½   cup seedless raspberry preserves
2   teaspoons sifted powdered sugar

Stuffed French Toast

It seems decadent, but one slice of French toast oozing with cream cheese and drizzled with melted fruit spread offers about the same number of calories and grams of fat as a bowl of most breakfast cereals.

1. In a small bowl combine cream cheese and the 2 tablespoons spreadable fruit. Using a serrated knife, form a pocket in each bread slice by making a horizontal cut halfway between the top and bottom crust, slicing almost all the way through to the opposite side. Fill pockets with cream cheese mixture.

2. In another small bowl beat together egg whites, whole egg, milk, vanilla, and apple pie spice. Lightly coat a nonstick griddle with cooking spray. Heat griddle over medium heat.

3. Dip stuffed bread slices in egg mixture, coating both sides. Place bread slices on hot griddle. Cook about 3 minutes or until golden brown, turning once.

4. Meanwhile, in a small saucepan heat the ½ cup spreadable fruit until melted, stirring frequently. Drizzle the melted spreadable fruit over French toast.

Make-Ahead Tip: Stuff each bread slice as directed; place in an airtight container. Cover and chill overnight. In the morning, prepare egg mixture and cook French toast as directed.

Start to Finish: 25 minutes
Makes: 8 servings

- 6 ounces fat-free cream cheese
- 2 tablespoons strawberry or apricot spreadable fruit
- 8 1-inch slices French bread
- 2 egg whites
- 1 egg
- ¾ cup fat-free milk
- ½ teaspoon vanilla
- ⅛ teaspoon apple pie spice
  Nonstick cooking spray
- ½ cup strawberry or apricot spreadable fruit

Nutrition Facts per serving: 159 cal., 1 g total fat (0 g sat. fat), 30 mg chol., 186 mg sodium, 31 g carbo., 12 g sugar, 1 g fiber, 7 g pro.
Daily Values: 2% vit. A, 11% calcium, 4% iron
Exchanges: 2 Starch

Baked French Toast with Orange Syrup

Start the day with two slices of golden French toast dripping with an orange-flavored syrup. It's a generous serving that will keep you satisfied all morning. Give each slice of bread just a quick dip in the egg mixture so you have enough for all eight slices.

1 Coat a large baking sheet with cooking spray; set aside. In a shallow dish combine the whole egg, egg white, milk, and vanilla. Dip bread slices in egg mixture, coating both sides. Place slices on the prepared baking sheet.

2 Bake in a 450° oven about 6 minutes or until bread is lightly browned. Turn bread over and bake 5 to 8 minutes more or until golden brown. Serve French toast with warm Orange Syrup.

Orange Syrup: In a small saucepan combine ⅔ cup orange juice, 1 tablespoon honey, 1½ teaspoons cornstarch, and ⅛ teaspoon ground cinnamon. Cook and stir over medium heat until thickened and bubbly. Cook and stir for 2 minutes more.

Start to Finish: 20 minutes
Oven: 450°F
Makes: 4 servings

Nonstick cooking spray
1   slightly beaten egg
1   slightly beaten egg white
¾   cup fat-free milk
1   teaspoon vanilla
8   ½-inch slices French bread
1   recipe Orange Syrup

Nutrition Facts per serving: 218 cal., 3 g total fat (1 g sat. fat), 54 mg chol., 358 mg sodium, 38 g carbo., 13 g sugar, 2 g fiber, 9 g pro.
Daily Values: 5% vit. A, 35% vit. C, 11% calcium, 9% iron
Exchanges: ½ Fruit, 2 Starch, ½ Lean Meat

Lemon-Poppy Seed Pancakes

A honey-sweetened raspberry sauce makes these crepelike pancakes special. When fresh berries aren't in season, use loose-pack frozen raspberries, thawed.

1 In a medium bowl stir together flour, sugar, baking powder, baking soda, and salt. In another medium bowl combine yogurt, milk, egg product, and poppy seeds. Add all at once to flour mixture. Stir just until moistened (batter should be lumpy).

2 For each pancake, pour about ¼ cup batter onto a hot, lightly greased or nonstick griddle or heavy skillet and spread to a 4-inch circle. Cook over medium heat about 2 minutes on each side or until pancakes are golden brown, turning to second sides when pancakes have bubbly surfaces and edges are slightly dry.

3 Serve pancakes with Raspberry Sauce. If desired, garnish with a few additional fresh raspberries.

Raspberry Sauce: In a small saucepan stir together ⅓ cup orange juice, 2 tablespoons honey, and 2 teaspoons cornstarch. Add 1¼ cups fresh or frozen raspberries, thawed. Cook and stir over medium heat until thickened and bubbly. Cook and stir for 2 minutes more. Pour berry mixture through a sieve to remove seeds.

Nutrition Facts per 2 pancakes + 1½ tablespoons sauce: 176 cal., 1 g total fat (0 g sat. fat), 3 mg chol., 304 mg sodium, 35 g carbo., 19 g sugar, 2 g fiber, 6 g pro.
Daily Values: 3% vit. A, 23% vit. C, 19% calcium, 8% iron
Exchanges: 1 Fruit, 1½ Starch

Start to Finish: 30 minutes
Makes: 6 servings (12 pancakes)

- 1 cup all-purpose flour
- 1 tablespoon sugar
- 1½ teaspoons baking powder
- ¼ teaspoon baking soda
- ¼ teaspoon salt
- 1 8-ounce carton lemon low-fat yogurt
- ½ cup fat-free milk
- ¼ cup refrigerated or frozen egg product, thawed, or 1 egg
- 1 tablespoon poppy seeds
- 1 recipe Raspberry Sauce
  Raspberries (optional)

Fruit-Filled Puff Pancakes

These puff pancakes deflate after baking to form a bowl—just right for filling with fresh fruit. They're a unique, colorful addition to any breakfast menu and easily double as a light dessert.

1 Coat four 5-inch individual pie pans or 4½-inch tart pans with cooking spray; set aside.

2 In a medium mixing bowl beat thawed egg product, flour, milk, oil, and salt with a rotary beater or wire whisk until smooth. Divide batter among prepared pans. Bake in a 400° oven about 25 minutes or until pancakes are puffed and golden brown. Turn off oven; let stand in oven for 5 minutes.

3 To serve, immediately transfer pancakes to serving plates. Spoon the fruit into centers of pancakes. Drizzle the warm orange marmalade over fruit.

Prep: 15 minutes
Bake: 25 minutes
Stand: 5 minutes
Oven: 400°F
Makes: 4 servings

Nonstick cooking spray
½ cup refrigerated or frozen egg product, thawed, or 1 whole egg plus 1 egg white
¼ cup all-purpose flour
¼ cup fat-free milk
1 tablespoon cooking oil
¼ teaspoon salt
2 cups assorted fruit (such as sliced strawberries, nectarines, or apricots; sliced peeled kiwifruit or peaches; halved seedless grapes or pitted sweet cherries; blackberries; and/or blueberries)
2 tablespoons orange marmalade, warmed

Nutrition Facts per serving: 123 cal., 4 g total fat (1 g sat. fat), 0 mg chol., 204 mg sodium, 18 g carbo., 11 g sugar, 2 g fiber, 5 g pro.
Daily Values: 3% vit. A, 68% vit. C, 4% calcium, 6% iron
Exchanges: 1 Fruit, ½ Very Lean Meat, 1 Fat

Five-Grain Cereal with Honey Fruit

This recipe makes eight servings, but you can prepare it ahead, chill it, and reheat it in the microwave oven when you want a speedy breakfast for one.

1 In a large saucepan bring water to boiling. Stir in brown rice, barley, wheat berries, rye berries, millet, and salt. Return to boiling; reduce heat. Simmer, covered, for 45 to 60 minutes or until grains are tender, stirring occasionally. (If mixture becomes too dry during cooking, stir in a small amount of additional water.)

2 To serve, stir together the orange juice and honey. Spoon hot cereal into serving bowls. Drizzle with the juice mixture. Top with strawberries and banana.

Make-Ahead Tip: Cover and chill cooked cereal for up to 3 days. To reheat 1 serving, measure ¾ to 1 cup cereal into a microwave-safe bowl. Cover with waxed paper. Microwave on 100 percent power (high) for 1 to 1½ minutes or until heated through. To serve, stir together 1 tablespoon of the orange juice and 1 teaspoon of the honey; drizzle over hot cereal. Top with ¼ cup of the strawberries and a few slices of banana.

Nutrition Facts per serving: 226 cal., 2 g total fat (0 g sat. fat), 0 mg chol., 45 mg sodium, 50 g carbo., 15 g sugar, 5 g fiber, 5 g pro.
Daily Values: 1% vit. A, 49% vit. C, 2% calcium, 8% iron
Exchanges: 1 Fruit, 2 Starch

Prep: 15 minutes
Cook: 45 minutes
Makes: 8 servings

- **6** cups water
- **½** cup uncooked regular brown rice
- **½** cup regular pearl barley
- **⅓** cup wheat berries
- **⅓** cup rye berries
- **⅓** cup millet
- **⅛** teaspoon salt
- **½** cup orange juice or unsweetened pineapple juice
- **¼** cup honey
- **2** cups sliced strawberries
- **1** medium banana, sliced

Warm and Fruity Breakfast Bowl

This hearty warm breakfast provides the energy you need to make it through any kind of day. Try a mixture of dried fruits to create a powerful "nutrient cocktail."

1 In a self-sealing plastic bag combine cracked wheat, rice, dried fruit, cinnamon, and salt. Mix thoroughly to ensure dried fruit and seasonings are evenly distributed. (You may have to use your hands to separate pieces of dried fruit.) Seal bag and store in the refrigerator up to 1 month.

2 To cook 1 serving, in a small saucepan combine ⅔ cup water and ½ cup fat-free milk. Bring to boiling; reduce heat. Stir in ½ cup wheat mixture. Simmer, uncovered, for 15 to 20 minutes or just until wheat is tender, mixture is creamy, and most of the liquid is absorbed, stirring occasionally. (If mixture becomes too dry during cooking, stir in a small amount of additional water.) Serve warm.

Prep: 10 minutes
Cook: 15 minutes
Makes: 5 servings

1½ cups cracked wheat
¾ cup instant brown rice
½ cup dried cherries, cranberries, blueberries, or raisins
½ teaspoon ground cinnamon
¼ teaspoon salt
⅔ cup water (per serving)
½ cup fat-free milk (per serving)

Nutrition Facts per serving: 274 cal., 1 g total fat (0 g sat. fat), 9 mg chol., 189 mg sodium, 58 g carbo., 16 g sugar, 9 g fiber, 11 g pro.
Daily Values: 5% vit. A, 2% vit. C, 17% calcium, 7% iron
Exchanges: ½ Milk, 3 Starch

Energy Bars

**These moist and chewy treats are a great grab-and-go breakfast bite.
What's their good-for-you secret ingredient? Don't tell the kids. It's the beans!**

1 Line a 13×9×2-inch baking pan with foil. Lightly coat foil with cooking spray; set pan aside.

2 In a large bowl stir together granola, dates, coconut, brown sugar, flour, and cinnamon. Stir in beans, raisins, and nuts. In a small bowl combine honey, margarine, oil, vanilla, and salt. Add to granola mixture; stir until combined. Spread in prepared baking pan.

3 Bake in a 350° oven for 40 to 45 minutes or until edges of bars are light brown and center is firm to touch. Cool in pan on a wire rack. Using foil, lift out of pan; cut into bars.

Make-Ahead Tip: Wrap bars in foil or freezer wrap and freeze for up to 3 months.

Nutrition Facts per bar: 141 cal., 5 g total fat (1 g sat. fat), 0 mg chol., 85 mg sodium, 25 g carbo., 17 g sugar, 2 g fiber, 2 g pro.
Daily Values: 3% vit. A, 1% vit. C, 2% calcium, 4% iron
Exchanges: ½ Fruit, 1 Starch, ½ Fat

Prep: 20 minutes
Bake: 40 minutes
Oven: 350°F
Makes: about 30 bars

Nonstick cooking spray
1⅔ cups low-fat granola
1 cup chopped pitted dates
1 cup flaked coconut
⅔ cup packed light brown sugar
½ cup whole wheat pastry flour
1 teaspoon ground cinnamon
1 15-ounce can pinto or Great Northern beans, rinsed, well drained, and coarsely chopped
½ cup dark raisins
½ cup chopped walnuts or almonds
½ cup honey
3 tablespoons margarine or butter, melted
2 tablespoons cooking oil
1 teaspoon vanilla
⅛ teaspoon salt

11 g
carb

Fluffy Omelet Squares

Topped with a savory zucchini and tomato sauce, these fluffy squares provide a delicious, quick choice for breakfast or brunch. They're also just right for a light lunch or supper.

1 Lightly coat a 2-quart square baking dish with cooking spray; set aside.

2 For omelet, in a medium mixing bowl beat egg yolks, onion powder, salt, and ⅛ teaspoon pepper with an electric mixer on medium speed about 4 minutes or until thick and lemon colored; set aside.

3 Wash and dry beaters thoroughly. In a large mixing bowl beat egg whites until soft peaks form (tips curl). Gently fold yolk mixture into beaten egg whites. Spread egg mixture evenly in the prepared baking dish.

4 Bake in a 350° oven for 22 to 25 minutes or until a knife inserted near the center comes out clean.

5 Meanwhile, for sauce, in a medium saucepan combine undrained tomatoes, zucchini, and the remaining ⅛ teaspoon pepper. Bring to boiling; reduce heat. Simmer, covered, about 5 minutes or until the zucchini is tender. Simmer, uncovered, for 10 to 12 minutes more or until desired consistency. To serve, cut the omelet into quarters. Top with sauce.

Nutrition Facts per serving: 157 cal., 8 g total fat (2 g sat. fat), 319 mg chol., 689 mg sodium, 11 g carbo., 7 g sugar, 2 g fiber, 11 g pro.
Daily Values: 20% vit. A, 17% vit. C, 6% calcium, 8% iron
Exchanges: 2 Vegetable, 1½ Medium-Fat Meat

Start to Finish: 40 minutes
Oven: 350°F
Makes: 4 servings

Nonstick cooking spray
6 egg yolks
½ teaspoon onion powder
¼ teaspoon salt
⅛ teaspoon black pepper
6 egg whites
1 14½-ounce can chunky pasta-style tomatoes
1 medium zucchini, quartered lengthwise and sliced (about 1 cup)
⅛ teaspoon black pepper

Mexican-Style Scrambled Eggs

Extra-sharp cheddar cheese is more flavorful than its milder cousins, so you don't have to use as much, which means fewer calories and less fat.

1 In a small saucepan combine water, green onions, and sweet pepper. Bring to boiling; reduce heat. Simmer, uncovered, for 5 to 7 minutes or until vegetables are tender. Drain well. In a medium bowl stir together egg product, milk, and black pepper. Stir in cooked vegetables.

2 Stack tortillas; wrap in foil. Bake in a 350° oven about 10 minutes or until warm. [Or just before serving, cover and microwave tortillas on 100 percent power (high) about 1 minute.]

3 Meanwhile, in a large skillet melt margarine over medium heat. Pour in egg mixture. Cook, without stirring, until mixture begins to set on bottom and around edges. Using a spatula or large spoon, lift and fold partially cooked eggs so uncooked portion flows underneath. Sprinkle with cheese. Continue cooking for 2 to 3 minutes or until eggs are cooked through but still glossy and moist.

4 To serve, immediately spoon the egg mixture down the center of each warm tortilla. Fold tortilla in half or roll up. Top with salsa.

Start to Finish: 30 minutes
Oven: 350°F
Makes: 4 servings

- 1 cup water
- ¼ cup thinly sliced green onions
- ¼ cup chopped red or green sweet pepper
- 1 8-ounce carton refrigerated or frozen egg product, thawed
- ¼ cup fat-free milk
- ⅛ teaspoon black pepper
- 4 7-inch flour tortillas
- 1 teaspoon margarine or butter
- ½ cup shredded reduced-fat sharp cheddar cheese (2 ounces)
- ⅓ cup bottled salsa

Nutrition Facts per serving: 183 cal., 6 g total fat (2 g sat. fat), 10 mg chol., 381 mg sodium, 19 g carbo., 2 g sugar, 1 g fiber, 12 g pro.
Daily Values: 17% vit. A, 30% vit. C, 18% calcium, 12% iron
Exchanges: 1 Vegetable, 1 Starch, 1½ Lean Meat

Double-Egg Skillet

Bake a puff pancake in one ovenproof skillet, scramble eggs in another skillet, and combine them for an extraordinary breakfast entrée.

1 For puff pancake, in a 10-inch ovenproof nonstick skillet heat margarine in a 400° oven for 3 to 5 minutes or until melted. Meanwhile, in a medium mixing bowl beat ¾ cup of the egg product, ½ cup of the milk, the flour, and Parmesan cheese with a rotary beater or wire whisk until smooth. Tilt skillet to coat with melted margarine. Immediately pour egg mixture into hot skillet. Bake egg mixture in the 400° oven about 25 minutes or until puffed and browned.

2 Meanwhile, for eggs, in a medium bowl combine the remaining egg product, remaining milk, basil, thyme, salt, and pepper. Lightly coat a large skillet with cooking spray. Heat skillet over medium heat. Pour in egg mixture. Cook, without stirring, until mixture begins to set on bottom and around edges.

3 Using a spatula or large spoon, lift and fold partially cooked eggs so uncooked portion flows underneath. Continue cooking for 3 to 4 minutes or until eggs are cooked through but still glossy and moist. To serve, immediately spoon egg mixture into puff pancake. Cut into wedges.

Prep: 15 minutes
Bake: 25 minutes
Oven: 400°F
Makes: 4 servings

1   tablespoon margarine or butter
3   8-ounce cartons refrigerated or frozen
      egg product, thawed
1   cup fat-free milk
½   cup all-purpose flour
2   tablespoons grated Parmesan cheese
2   tablespoons snipped fresh basil or
      parsley or 2 teaspoons dried basil
      or parsley, crushed
¾   teaspoon snipped fresh thyme or
      ¼ teaspoon dried thyme, crushed
⅛   teaspoon salt
      Dash black pepper
      Nonstick cooking spray

Nutrition Facts per serving: 195 cal., 4 g total fat (1 g sat. fat), 3 mg chol., 463 mg sodium, 17 g carbo., 4 g sugar, 0 g fiber, 21 g pro.
Daily Values: 18% vit. A, 2% vit. C, 17% calcium, 21% iron
Exchanges: 1 Starch, 2½ Very Lean Meat, ½ Fat

Potato, Apple, and Ham Skillet

Frozen hash brown potatoes make short work of this hearty breakfast (or lunch or dinner) skillet dish. Read the package labels when buying the potatoes and be sure to purchase potatoes without added fat.

1 Press thawed potatoes between paper towels to remove moisture; set aside. In a 10-inch ovenproof skillet combine apple, onion, water, and sage. Bring to boiling; reduce heat to medium. Cook, uncovered, until onion is tender. Remove from heat. Stir in potatoes and ham.

2 In a medium bowl combine milk, egg product, cheese, and salt. Pour into skillet over potato mixture. Do not stir. Bake in a 350° oven for 30 to 35 minutes or just until center appears set.

Nutrition Facts per serving: 194 cal., 4 g total fat (2 g sat. fat), 22 mg chol., 614 mg sodium, 22 g carbo., 7 g sugar, 1 g fiber, 15 g pro.
Daily Values: 6% vit. A, 15% vit. C, 16% calcium, 8% iron
Exchanges: 1½ Starch, ½ Lean Meat

Prep: 20 minutes
Bake: 30 minutes
Oven: 350°F
Makes: 6 servings

3	cups loose-pack frozen diced hash brown potatoes with onion and peppers, thawed
1	large red apple, cored and chopped
1	small onion, chopped
2	tablespoons water
1	teaspoon dried sage, crushed
1	cup diced cooked ham
1½	cups fat-free milk
1	cup refrigerated or frozen egg product, thawed, or 4 eggs
½	cup shredded reduced-fat cheddar cheese (2 ounces)
¼	teaspoon salt

15 g
carb

Sausage-Egg Puffs

A golden puff of heavenly flavor is a tasty and appealing way to start your day. Make this dish the focus of a brunch with friends.

1 Coat four 4½-inch tart pans with cooking spray; set aside. In a small bowl combine sour cream, lemon-pepper seasoning, and cumin. Cover and chill until ready to serve.

2 In a medium skillet cook turkey sausage over medium heat until brown. Drain fat.

3 In a medium mixing bowl beat flour, egg product, milk, oregano, salt, and pepper with a rotary beater or wire whisk until smooth. Divide batter among prepared tart pans. Top with cooked sausage and green onion.

4 Bake in a 425° oven for 10 to 13 minutes or until pancakes are puffed and lightly browned. Sprinkle with cheese. Bake, uncovered, 1 minute more or until the cheese is melted. Serve pancakes immediately with the sour cream mixture.

Prep: 20 minutes
Bake: 11 minutes
Oven: 425°F
Makes: 4 servings

Nonstick cooking spray
¼ cup light dairy sour cream
¼ teaspoon lemon-pepper seasoning
⅛ teaspoon ground cumin
4 ounces uncooked bulk turkey sausage
½ cup all-purpose flour
½ cup refrigerated or frozen egg product, thawed, or 2 eggs
½ cup fat-free milk
¼ teaspoon dried oregano, crushed
⅛ teaspoon salt
Dash black pepper
2 tablespoons thinly sliced green onion
¼ cup shredded reduced-fat cheddar cheese (1 ounce)

Nutrition Facts per serving: 180 cal., 6 g total fat (3 g sat. fat), 21 mg chol., 485 mg sodium, 15 g carbo., 3 g sugar, 1 g fiber, 15 g pro.
Daily Values: 6% vit. A, 1% vit. C, 14% calcium, 10% iron
Exchanges: 1 Starch, 2 Lean Meat

Hash Brown Strata

A strata (Italian for "layered") is an egg and bread casserole. In this extra-easy version, frozen hash browns make a time-saving substitute for the bread.

1 Coat a 2-quart square baking dish with cooking spray. Arrange hash brown potatoes and broccoli in bottom of prepared baking dish; top with turkey bacon. Set aside.

2 In a medium bowl gradually stir milk into flour. Stir in egg product, half of the cheese, the basil, pepper, and salt. Pour egg mixture over potato mixture.

3 Bake in a 350° oven for 40 to 45 minutes or until a knife inserted near the center comes out clean. Sprinkle with the remaining cheese. Let stand for 5 minutes. If desired, garnish with additional fresh basil.

Make-Ahead Tip: Assemble strata as directed, except do not bake. Cover and chill for 4 to 24 hours. To serve, uncover and bake as directed.

Nutrition Facts per serving: 152 cal., 4 g total fat (0 g sat. fat), 14 mg chol., 407 mg sodium, 14 g carbo., 1 g sugar, 0 g fiber, 13 g pro.
Daily Values: 13% vit. A, 17% vit. C, 14% calcium, 10% iron
Exchanges: 1 Starch, 1½ Lean Meat

Prep: 15 minutes
Bake: 40 minutes
Stand: 5 minutes
Oven: 350°F
Makes: 6 servings

Nonstick cooking spray
2   cups loose-pack frozen diced hash brown
      potatoes with onion and peppers
1   cup broccoli florets
⅓   cup finely chopped turkey bacon or
      turkey ham (about 2 ounces)
⅓   cup evaporated fat-free milk
2   tablespoons all-purpose flour
2   8-ounce cartons refrigerated or frozen
      egg product, thawed
½   cup shredded reduced-fat cheddar
      cheese (2 ounces)
1   tablespoon snipped fresh basil or
      ½ teaspoon dried basil, crushed
¼   teaspoon black pepper
⅛   teaspoon salt
      Snipped fresh basil (optional)

20 g
carb

Southwest Breakfast Strata

The next time you have overnight guests, serve this colorful south-of-the-border strata. Make it easy on the cook and assemble it the night before, then pop it in the oven in the morning.

1 Lightly coat a 2-quart rectangular baking dish with cooking spray. Cover the bottom of the prepared baking dish with French bread slices, cutting to fit.

2 In a medium bowl combine egg product, chile peppers, and black pepper. Pour egg mixture evenly over bread. Sprinkle with Canadian bacon; top with tomato slices and cheese. Cover and chill for at least 4 hours or overnight.

3 Bake in a 350° oven about 25 minutes or until a knife inserted near the center comes out clean. Before serving, sprinkle with fresh cilantro.

Nutrition Facts per serving: 170 cal., 4 g total fat (1 g sat. fat), 11 mg chol., 511 mg sodium, 20 g carbo., 3 g sugar, 1 g fiber, 14 g pro.
Daily Values: 8% vit. A, 13% vit. C, 13% calcium, 12% iron
Exchanges: ½ Vegetable, 1 Starch, 1½ Lean Meat

Prep: 15 minutes
Bake: 25 minutes
Chill: 4 to 24 hours
Oven: 350°F
Makes: 6 servings

Nonstick cooking spray
8   ½-inch slices French bread or other firm-textured bread
1½ cups refrigerated or frozen egg product, thawed
2   tablespoons canned diced green chile peppers
⅛   teaspoon black pepper
2   slices Canadian-style bacon, cut into thin strips, or ½ cup diced cooked ham
2   Roma tomatoes, thinly sliced
½   cup shredded reduced-fat Monterey Jack cheese (2 ounces)
1   tablespoon snipped fresh cilantro

Beef, Pork & Lamb

10 g
carb

Beef Steak and Onions

Just three ounces of lean beef, such as the top loin steak in this dish, provides more than half of your day's supply of iron and more than a third of your requirement for zinc.

1 For glaze, in a small bowl stir together mustard, honey, thyme, black pepper, and garlic. Set aside. Trim fat from steak.

2 Place steak and onion slices on the rack of an uncovered grill directly over medium coals. Grill for 11 to 15 minutes for medium rare (145°F) or 14 to 18 minutes for medium (160°F), turning once. Brush steak and onions with glaze just before turning; generously brush with remaining glaze during the last half of grilling.

3 To serve, thinly slice steak across the grain. Serve the steak slices with glazed onion slices.

Broiler Method: Place steak and onion slices on the unheated rack of a broiler pan. Broil 3 to 4 inches from the heat for 12 to 14 minutes for medium rare (145°F) or 15 to 18 minutes for medium (160°F), turning once. Brush steak and onions with glaze just before turning and generously brush with remaining glaze the last half of broiling.

Nutrition Facts per serving: 164 cal., 6 g total fat (2 g sat. fat), 43 mg chol., 125 mg sodium, 10 g carbo., 5 g sugar, 1 g fiber, 18 g pro.
Daily Values: 5% vit. C, 4% calcium, 11% iron
Exchanges: ½ Other Carbo., 2½ Lean Meat

Prep: 15 minutes
Grill: 11 minutes
Makes: 4 servings

¼   cup Dijon-style, brown, or prepared mustard
1   tablespoon honey
1½   teaspoons snipped fresh thyme or ½ teaspoon dried thyme, crushed
⅛   teaspoon black pepper
1   clove garlic, minced
12   ounces boneless beef top loin steak, cut 1 inch thick
2   medium onions, cut into ½-inch slices

Beef Steak in Thai Marinade

Thai red curry paste, unsweetened coconut milk, and fish sauce are available in the Asian foods section of most grocery stores. The curry paste and fish sauce keep for months in the refrigerator. Once opened, keep the coconut milk in the refrigerator for no more than two days.

1 Trim fat from steak. Place steak in a plastic bag set in a shallow dish.

2 For marinade, in a blender container or food processor bowl combine coconut milk, lime juice, red curry paste, fish sauce, sugar, and lemongrass. Cover and blend or process until smooth. Pour over meat; seal bag. Marinate in the refrigerator for 4 to 24 hours, turning bag occasionally. Drain steak, reserving the marinade.

3 Place the steak on the rack of an uncovered grill directly over medium coals. Grill for 14 to 18 minutes for medium rare (145°F) or 18 to 22 minutes for medium doneness (160°F), turning and brushing once with the reserved marinade. Discard any remaining marinade. To serve, thinly slice steak across the grain.

Prep: 15 minutes
Marinate: 4 to 24 hours
Grill: 14 minutes
Makes: 10 servings

2½   **pounds boneless beef top sirloin steak, cut 1 inch thick**
½   **cup unsweetened coconut milk**
3   **tablespoons lime juice**
2   **to 4 tablespoons red curry paste**
2   **tablespoons fish sauce or soy sauce**
2   **teaspoons sugar**
½   **stalk lemongrass, trimmed and coarsely chopped, or ⅛ teaspoon finely shredded lemon peel**

Nutrition Facts per serving: 190 cal., 8 g total fat (4 g sat. fat), 69 mg chol., 462 mg sodium, 3 g carbo., 1 g sugar, 0 g fiber, 24 g pro.
Daily Values: 12% vit. C, 2% calcium, 18% iron
Exchanges: 3½ Lean Meat

21 g
carb

Flank Steak with Corn Relish

Sizzling steak on the grill is irresistible. Top it with a vibrant bean and corn relish and you'll have diners dashing to dinner. If you have relish left over, store it in an air-tight container in the refrigerator for up to 3 days.

1 For relish, in a small bowl combine black beans, corn relish, radishes, jalapeño pepper, lime juice, and cumin. Cover and chill for at least 30 minutes or for up to 4 hours.

2 Trim fat from steak. Score steak on both sides by making shallow diagonal cuts at 1-inch intervals in a diamond pattern. Lightly sprinkle with the salt and black pepper.

3 Place steak on the rack of an uncovered grill directly over medium coals. Grill for 17 to 21 minutes for medium (160°F), turning once.

4 To serve, thinly slice steak diagonally across the grain. Serve the steak slices with relish.

Broiler Method: Place the steak on the unheated rack of a broiler pan. Broil 3 to 4 inches from the heat for 15 to 18 minutes for medium (160°F), turning once.

Prep: 15 minutes
Chill: 30 minutes
Broil: 15 minutes
Makes: 4 servings

½ of a 15-ounce can black beans, rinsed and drained
⅔ cup corn relish
¼ cup halved and thinly sliced radishes
1 small fresh jalapeño pepper, seeded and finely chopped (see tip, page 37)
2 teaspoons lime juice
¼ teaspoon ground cumin
12 ounces beef flank steak
⅛ teaspoon salt
   Dash black pepper

Nutrition Facts per serving: 223 cal., 6 g total fat (2 g sat. fat), 34 mg chol., 358 mg sodium, 21 g carbo., 6 g sugar, 3 g fiber, 22 g pro.
Daily Values: 7% vit. C, 3% calcium, 11% iron
Exchanges: 1½ Starch, 2½ Very Lean Meat, ½ Fat

Fajita Steaks with Honey-Pickle Salsa

Part Southern, part Mexican, and part Asian—this dish is a global melting pot! You'll see just how great fusion cooking can be when you taste this irresistible combination of flavors in a new family favorite.

1 If using, prepare Honey-Pickle Salsa. Cover and chill for up to 8 hours. For glaze, in a small saucepan combine vinegar, brown sugar, lime peel, lime juice, mustard, soy sauce, and ginger. Bring to boiling over medium heat. Boil gently, uncovered, about 10 minutes or until reduced by half (about ⅓ cup).

2 Trim fat from steak. Place steak on the rack of an uncovered grill directly over medium coals. Grill for 17 to 21 minutes for medium (160°F), turning once and generously brushing with the glaze up to the last 5 minutes of grilling.

3 To serve, thinly slice steak across the grain. Serve the steak slices with salsa and, if desired, sour cream.

Honey-Pickle Salsa: In a small bowl stir together one 4-ounce can diced green chile peppers, drained, or 3 fresh Anaheim or New Mexico peppers, roasted, peeled, and chopped; ½ cup chopped dill pickle; 3 tablespoons finely chopped red onion; 2 tablespoons snipped fresh cilantro; 4 teaspoons lime juice; and 2 teaspoons honey. Makes about 1 cup.

Prep: 30 minutes
Grill: 17 minutes
Makes: 6 servings

1 recipe Honey-Pickle Salsa or 1 cup bottled salsa
¼ cup rice vinegar or white wine vinegar
2 tablespoons brown sugar
½ teaspoon finely shredded lime peel
2 tablespoons lime juice
1 tablespoon Dijon-style mustard
1 tablespoon soy sauce
1 teaspoon grated fresh ginger
1¼ pounds beef flank steak or beef skirt steak
Fat-free dairy sour cream (optional)

Nutrition Facts per serving: 186 cal., 7 g total fat (3 g sat. fat), 38 mg chol., 439 mg sodium, 8 g carbo., 5 g sugar, 0 g fiber, 22 g pro.
Daily Values: 3% vit. A, 17% vit. C, 4% calcium, 11% iron
Exchanges: ½ Other Carbo., 3 Lean Meat

Skinny Swiss Steak with Oven-Roasted Potatoes

A Swiss steak is always pounded with the notched side of a meat tenderizer and cooked "smothered." Even though the meat and potatoes are cooked in separate baking dishes, they conveniently take the same amount of time to cook.

1 Trim fat from meat. Cut meat into 4 serving-size pieces. Combine the flour and pepper. Using the notched side of a meat mallet, pound flour mixture into both sides of meat.

2 Coat a large skillet with cooking spray. Heat skillet over medium heat. Brown meat on both sides in hot skillet. Transfer to a 2-quart square baking dish. In a medium bowl combine undrained stewed tomatoes, carrots, and wine; pour over meat. Bake, covered, in a 350° oven for 1¼ to 1½ hours or until tender.

3 Meanwhile, cut potatoes into 1-inch pieces. Coat another 2-quart baking dish with cooking spray. Add potatoes, olive oil, salt, and garlic; toss to coat. Bake, covered, in the 350° oven for 45 minutes, stirring after 20 minutes. Uncover, stir gently, and bake about 25 minutes more or until potatoes are lightly browned on the edges. Serve meat and tomato mixture with the potatoes.

Nutrition Facts per serving: 341 cal., 9 g total fat (2 g sat. fat), 50 mg chol., 427 mg sodium, 40 g carbo., 8 g sugar, 4 g fiber, 23 g pro.
Daily Values: 154% vit. A, 53% vit. C, 5% calcium, 23% iron
Exchanges: 2 Vegetable, 2 Starch, 2 Lean Meat, ½ Fat

Prep: 20 minutes
Bake: 1¼ hours
Oven: 350°F
Makes: 4 servings

- 1   12-ounce boneless beef round steak, cut ¾ inch thick
- 2   tablespoons all-purpose flour
- ¼   teaspoon black pepper
-     Nonstick cooking spray
- 1   14½-ounce can Italian-style stewed tomatoes
- 2   medium carrots, sliced (1 cup)
- 2   tablespoons dry red wine or water
- 4   medium potatoes (about 1⅓ pounds), peeled
- 1   tablespoon olive oil
- ¼   teaspoon salt
- 1   clove garlic, minced

Roasted Tenderloin with Tricolor Potatoes

This beautiful dish is worthy of a formal dinner party. Don't worry if you can't get all three kinds of potatoes—it is also attractive when made with two. It is well worth buying fresh herbs to garnish the plates; they add an elegant look, and the aroma enhances your dining pleasure.

1 Trim any fat from meat. In a small bowl stir together dried marjoram, lemon peel, pepper, ½ teaspoon salt, and garlic. Brush meat with 1 tablespoon of the olive oil. Sprinkle with half of the garlic mixture; press to coat.

2 Place meat on a rack in a shallow roasting pan. Insert a meat thermometer into center of meat. Roast in a 425° oven for 35 to 40 minutes for medium rare (140°F) or 45 to 50 minutes for medium (155°F), spooning off any fat in roasting pan.

3 Meanwhile, in a large bowl combine potatoes, ½ teaspoon salt, the remaining 2 tablespoons olive oil, and the remaining garlic mixture. Add potato mixture to roasting pan the last 30 minutes of roasting.

4 Transfer meat and potatoes to a serving platter. Cover loosely with foil; let stand for 15 minutes (the meat's temperature will rise 5°F during standing). Cut meat into ½-inch slices. If desired, garnish with fresh marjoram, rosemary, and lemon wedges.

Prep: 15 minutes
Roast: 35 minutes
Stand: 15 minutes
Oven: 425°F
Makes: 8 servings

1	2- to 3-pound center-cut beef tenderloin
4	teaspoons dried marjoram, crushed
1	tablespoon finely shredded lemon peel
2	teaspoons cracked black pepper
½	teaspoon salt
3	tablespoons bottled minced garlic
3	tablespoons olive oil
1½	pounds small white, purple, and/or red potatoes, quartered
½	teaspoon salt
	Fresh marjoram sprigs (optional)
	Fresh rosemary sprigs (optional)
	Lemon wedges (optional)

Nutrition Facts per serving: 293 cal., 13 g total fat (4 g sat. fat), 69 mg chol., 350 mg sodium, 17 g carbo., 0 g sugar, 2 g fiber, 26 g pro.
Daily Values: 1% vit. A, 25% vit. C, 4% calcium, 27% iron
Exchanges: 1 Starch, 3 Lean Meat, 1 Fat

Italian-Style Steak Sandwiches

Save time by preparing the steak and pepper spread up to four days ahead. Refrigerate the cooked steak in a plastic bag and the spread in a tightly sealed container.

1 If desired, sprinkle eggplant slices with salt. Set aside. For pepper spread, in a medium skillet heat olive oil over medium heat. Add onion and garlic; cook and stir for 5 minutes. Add peppers, vinegar, and the ¼ teaspoon salt. Cook and stir for 2 minutes. Reduce heat to medium low. Cook, covered, for 5 minutes, stirring occasionally. Cool slightly.

2 Transfer pepper mixture to a food processor bowl or blender container. Cover and process or blend until smooth. Set aside.

3 Trim fat from steak. If using flank steak, score steak on both sides by making shallow diagonal cuts at 1-inch intervals in a diamond pattern. Rub Italian seasoning onto both sides of steak. If salted, rinse eggplant; pat dry with paper towels. Brush both sides of eggplant slices with cooking oil.

4 Place steak and eggplant on the rack of an uncovered grill directly over medium coals. Grill for 6 to 8 minutes or until eggplant is tender, turning eggplant once. Remove eggplant from grill. Continue grilling the steak for 11 to 14 minutes for medium (160°F), turning once. Slice steak diagonally across the grain into thick slices.

5 To assemble sandwiches, spread about 1 tablespoon of the pepper spread on the bottom half of each roll. Layer with salad greens, eggplant slices, and steak slices. If

Prep: 35 minutes
Grill: 17 minutes
Makes: 4 sandwiches

- 1 small eggplant (about 12 ounces), cut lengthwise into ¼- to ½-inch slices
- 2 teaspoons olive oil
- 1 medium onion, chopped (½ cup)
- 4 cloves garlic, minced
- 8 ounces fresh mild red cherry or banana peppers, halved and seeded
- 2 tablespoons balsamic vinegar
- ¼ teaspoon salt
- 12 ounces beef flank steak or boneless beef top sirloin steak, cut 1 inch thick
- 2 teaspoons dried Italian seasoning, crushed
- 1 teaspoon cooking oil
- 4 6-inch Italian rolls, split and toasted
  Mixed salad greens
- 2 ounces shaved Parmesan cheese (optional)

desired, sprinkle with Parmesan cheese. Replace roll tops.

Nutrition Facts per sandwich: 459 cal., 13 g total fat (4 g sat. fat), 34 mg chol., 724 mg sodium, 56 g carbo., 9 g sugar, 7 g fiber, 28 g pro.
Daily Values: 8% vit. A, 73% vit. C, 12% calcium, 27% iron
Exchanges: 2 Vegetable, 3 Starch, 2 Lean Meat, 1 Fat

Sloppy Josés

Here's a fun Tex-Mex twist on the family classic that makes it as healthy as it is delicious. Control the amount of heat to suit your group by cutting back or adding more green chile peppers.

1 In a medium skillet cook ground beef and onion until meat is brown and onion is tender. Drain fat.

2 Stir in refried beans, salsa, undrained chile peppers, beer, chili powder, and garlic. Bring to boiling; reduce heat. Simmer, uncovered, for 10 to 15 minutes or until desired consistency. Serve the meat mixture in toasted buns.

Nutrition Facts per serving: 264 cal., 8 g total fat (3 g sat. fat), 39 mg chol., 469 mg sodium, 30 g carbo., 3 g sugar, 3 g fiber, 16 g pro.
Daily Values: 3% vit. A, 17% vit. C, 11% calcium, 18% iron
Exchanges: 2 Starch, 1½ Medium-Fat Meat

Prep: 15 minutes
Cook: 10 minutes
Makes: 6 servings

- 12 ounces lean ground beef
- 1 small onion, chopped (⅓ cup)
- ½ of a 16-ounce can refried beans
- ½ cup bottled salsa
- 1 4-ounce can diced green chile peppers
- ¼ cup beer
- ½ teaspoon chili powder
- 1 clove garlic, minced
- 6 hamburger buns, split and toasted

Greek Pizza

A loaf of frozen wheat bread dough makes an easy pizza crust when rolled thin for this Greek-inspired pizza. It's topped with ground beef, garlic, spinach, tomato, and feta cheese.

1 Lightly coat a 12-inch pizza pan or a 13×9×2-inch baking pan with cooking spray. Press bread dough into the prepared pan, forming a 1-inch edge. Prick dough several times with a fork. Bake in a 375° oven for 10 minutes. Remove from oven.

2 Meanwhile, in a large skillet cook ground beef, onion, and garlic about 5 minutes or until meat is brown. Drain fat. Stir in spaghetti sauce; set aside. Squeeze all of the liquid from thawed spinach. Sprinkle the spinach over hot baked crust. Spoon the meat mixture over spinach. Sprinkle with tomato, Monterey Jack cheese, and feta cheese.

3 Bake for 30 to 35 minutes or until cheese is golden brown. Remove from oven. Let stand for 5 minutes. To serve, cut into wedges or squares.

Nutrition Facts per serving: 346 cal., 12 g total fat (5 g sat. fat), 52 mg chol., 566 mg sodium, 38 g carbo., 2 g sugar, 6 g fiber, 25 g pro.
Daily Values: 111% vit. A, 37% vit. C, 23% calcium, 16% iron
Exchanges: 1½ Vegetable, 2 Starch, 2 Medium-Fat Meat

Prep: 15 minutes
Bake: 40 minutes
Stand: 5 minutes
Oven: 375°F
Makes: 8 servings

Nonstick cooking spray
1 16-ounce loaf frozen honey wheat bread dough or whole wheat bread dough, thawed
1 pound lean ground beef
1 cup chopped onion
2 cloves garlic, minced
1 cup bottled light spaghetti sauce
2 10-ounce packages frozen chopped spinach, thawed and well drained
2 cups chopped tomato
1 cup shredded reduced-fat Monterey Jack or mozzarella cheese (4 ounces)
½ cup crumbled feta cheese (2 ounces)

Beef and Barley-Stuffed Peppers

This classic family meal gets a fun flavor twist with salsa, cumin, and Monterey Jack cheese. You'll love how fast and easy these peppers are to prepare.

1 Halve sweet peppers lengthwise; remove stems, seeds, and membranes. In a large Dutch oven cook pepper halves in a large amount of boiling salted water for 3 to 5 minutes or just until tender. Invert pepper halves over paper towels to drain.

2 In a large skillet cook ground beef and green onions about 5 minutes or until meat is brown. Drain fat. Stir in barley, salsa, carrot, and cumin. Stir in ½ cup of the cheese. Spoon the meat mixture into pepper halves. Place in a 3-quart rectangular baking dish.

3 Bake peppers, covered, in a 350° oven for 25 minutes. Sprinkle with the remaining cheese. Bake, uncovered, about 5 minutes more or until meat mixture is heated through and cheese is melted.

Make-Ahead Tip: Cook peppers in boiling water as directed. Drain and cool. Cover and chill for up to 24 hours.

Prep: 25 minutes
Bake: 30 minutes
Oven: 350°F
Makes: 6 servings

- **3** large yellow, orange, red, and/or green sweet peppers
- **1** pound lean ground beef
- **⅓** cup sliced green onions
- **1** cup cooked, regular or quick-cooking barley
- **1** cup bottled chunky salsa
- **⅓** cup shredded carrot
- **¼** teaspoon ground cumin
- **¾** cup shredded Monterey Jack cheese (3 ounces)

Nutrition Facts per serving: 243 cal., 12 g total fat (6 g sat. fat), 60 mg chol., 201 mg sodium, 16 g carbo., 3 g sugar, 3 g fiber, 19 g pro.
Daily Values: 44% vit. A, 249% vit. C, 13% calcium, 14% iron
Exchanges: 2 Vegetable, ½ Starch, 2 Medium-Fat Meat

30 g
carb

Beef-Broccoli Stir-Fry

In less than 30 minutes after you walk in the door, this family-pleasing, well-balanced meal can be on the table. Start the water boiling for the rice or spaghetti first thing, and the entire meal will be ready at the same time.

1 For marinade, in a medium bowl combine soy sauce, cornstarch, vinegar, ginger, crushed red pepper, and garlic. Trim fat from meat. Cut meat across the grain into ⅛-inch slices. Add meat to marinade; toss to coat. Cover and marinate at room temperature for 10 minutes. Drain meat, discarding marinade.

2 Meanwhile, cut broccoli florets from stems. If desired, peel stems. Cut stems into ¼-inch slices.

3 In a wok or large skillet heat 1 teaspoon of the oil over medium-high heat. Add meat; cook and stir in hot oil for 2 to 3 minutes or until slightly pink in center. Remove meat from wok.

4 Add the remaining 1 teaspoon oil to hot wok. Add broccoli, carrots, and green onions; cook and stir for 1 minute. Add beef broth; cook and stir for 5 to 7 minutes or until vegetables are crisp-tender, scraping up any brown bits on bottom of wok. Return cooked meat to wok; heat through. Serve immediately over hot cooked spaghetti or rice.

Start to Finish: 30 minutes
Makes: 4 servings

- 2 tablespoons reduced-sodium soy sauce
- 1 tablespoon cornstarch
- 1 tablespoon white vinegar
- 1 tablespoon grated fresh ginger
- ¼ teaspoon crushed red pepper
- 2 cloves garlic, minced
- 12 ounces boneless beef top sirloin steak
- 1 small bunch broccoli (about 1 pound)
- 2 teaspoons cooking oil
- 2 medium carrots, cut into ⅛-inch slices
- 4 green onions, sliced
- ¾ cup reduced-sodium beef broth
- 2 cups hot cooked spaghetti or rice

Nutrition Facts per serving: 279 cal., 7 g total fat (2 g sat. fat), 52 mg chol., 445 mg sodium, 30 g carbo., 5 g sugar, 5 g fiber, 25 g pro.
Daily Values: 176% vit. A, 101% vit. C, 7% calcium, 24% iron
Exchanges: 1½ Vegetable, 1½ Starch, 2½ Very Lean Meat, ½ Fat

Curried Beef and Rice

Brown rice gives this dish an extra boost of fiber (as well as other healthful nutrients), and you can keep it very low in fat by using lean meat. Pass hot sauce for diners who like their curry hot. Serve a cooling crisp salad for a complete meal.

1 In a 2-quart saucepan stir together the water, onion, carrot, bouillon granules, curry powder, and garlic. Bring to boiling. Stir in uncooked brown rice. Return to boiling; reduce heat. Simmer, covered, for 40 minutes.

2 Stir the cooked beef, peas, and tomato into rice mixture. Simmer, covered, about 5 minutes more or until rice and peas are tender.

Nutrition Facts per serving: 316 cal., 8 g total fat (3 g sat. fat), 45 mg chol., 743 mg sodium, 39 g carbo., 5 g sugar, 5 g fiber, 21 g pro.
Daily Values: 85% vit. A, 21% vit. C, 4% calcium, 17% iron
Exchanges: 1 Vegetable, 2 Starch, 2 Lean Meat, ½ Fat

Prep: 15 minutes
Cook: 45 minutes
Makes: 4 servings

1½   cups water
1   large onion, chopped (1 cup)
1   medium carrot, chopped
1   tablespoon instant beef bouillon granules
2   teaspoons curry powder
1   clove garlic, minced
¾   cup uncooked regular brown rice
1½   cups cubed cooked beef (8 ounces)
1   cup frozen peas
1   medium tomato, chopped

Pineapple-Teriyaki Beef

This sweet and salty flavor combination has universal appeal. Here the classic combination of pineapple and teriyaki makes an ideal marinade-turned-sauce. Be sure to simmer this and any marinade that has been exposed to raw meat or poultry for 5 minutes.

1 Trim fat from steak. Place steak in a plastic bag set in a shallow dish. Drain pineapple, reserving juice. Cover and chill pineapple for sauce.

2 For marinade, in a small bowl stir together the reserved pineapple juice, green onion, teriyaki sauce, ginger, and garlic. Pour over steak; seal bag. Marinate in the refrigerator for 6 to 24 hours, turning the bag occasionally. Drain steak, reserving marinade.

3 Place steak on the unheated rack of a broiler pan. Broil 4 to 5 inches from the heat for 18 to 20 minutes for medium rare (145°F), turning once.

4 For sauce, in a small saucepan combine the reserved marinade and pineapple. Bring to boiling; reduce heat. Simmer, uncovered, for 5 minutes. Remove from heat. To serve, cut steak into serving-size pieces. Spoon the sauce over steak.

Prep: 20 minutes
Marinate: 6 to 24 hours
Broil: 18 minutes
Makes: 6 to 8 servings

1 **2-pound boneless beef top round steak, cut 1½ inches thick**
1 **8-ounce can crushed pineapple (juice pack)**
2 **tablespoons finely chopped green onion**
2 **tablespoons reduced-sodium teriyaki sauce**
1 **teaspoon grated fresh ginger**
1 **teaspoon bottled minced garlic**

Nutrition Facts per serving: 204 cal., 3 g total fat (1 g sat. fat), 65 mg chol., 155 mg sodium, 7 g carbo., 5 g sugar, 0 g fiber, 35 g pro.
Daily Values: 7% vit. C, 2% calcium, 17% iron
Exchanges: ½ Fruit, 5 Very Lean Meat

Hearty Beef Stew

Make this dish on a cold afternoon and fill your home with a tantalizing aroma that beckons your family to the table. Make a double batch and freeze some to serve on a more hectic night when you're longing for the comfort of this warming stew.

1 Trim fat from meat. Cut meat into 1-inch pieces. In a 4-quart Dutch oven combine the meat, onion, beef broth, water, salt, thyme, pepper, and garlic. Bring to boiling; reduce heat. Simmer, covered, for 1 hour.

2 Stir in the potatoes, carrots, and mushrooms. Return to boiling; reduce heat. Simmer, covered, about 30 minutes more or until meat and vegetables are tender.

3 Stir in the undrained tomatoes and tomato paste. Stir in peas; heat through.

Nutrition Facts per serving: 277 cal., 6 g total fat (2 g sat. fat), 45 mg chol., 517 mg sodium, 34 g carbo., 9 g sugar, 7 g fiber, 24 g pro.
Daily Values: 395% vit. A, 55% vit. C, 7% calcium, 23% iron
Exchanges: 2 Vegetable, 1½ Starch, 2 Lean Meat

Prep: 15 minutes
Cook: 1½ hours
Makes: 6 servings

- 1 pound boneless beef round steak
- 2 cups chopped onion
- 1 14-ounce can reduced-sodium beef broth
- 1 cup water
- ½ teaspoon salt
- ½ teaspoon dried thyme, crushed
- ¼ teaspoon freshly ground black pepper
- 2 cloves garlic, minced
- 1 pound tiny new potatoes, quartered (3 cups)
- 1 pound carrots, sliced (3 cups)
- 8 ounces fresh mushrooms, quartered (3 cups)
- 1 14½-ounce can diced tomatoes
- 3 tablespoons tomato paste
- 1 cup frozen peas, thawed

Mediterranean Beef Kabobs

Broil or grill these flavorful meat kabobs, and serve them with other Mediterranean-inspired fare. Try a salad made with romaine, feta cheese, and kalamata olives; orzo tossed with lemon, parsley, and olive oil; and a dessert of fresh fruit.

1 Trim fat from meat. Cut meat into 1½-inch pieces. Place meat in a plastic bag set in a shallow dish.

2 For marinade, in a small bowl combine green onions, oil, lemon juice, tarragon, oregano, pepper, and garlic. Pour over meat; seal bag. Marinate in the refrigerator for 4 to 24 hours, turning bag occasionally. Drain meat, discarding marinade.

3 Thread meat onto six 12-inch skewers, leaving ¼ inch between pieces. (If using wooden skewers, soak in water for 30 minutes before broiling.) Place skewers on the unheated rack of a broiler pan. Broil 4 to 5 inches from the heat for 10 to 12 minutes or until meat is slightly pink in center, turning occasionally to brown evenly.

Prep: 15 minutes
Marinate: 4 to 24 hours
Broil: 10 minutes
Makes: 6 servings

1½   pounds boneless beef top sirloin steak
 3   green onions, sliced
 ¼   cup olive oil
 3   tablespoons lemon juice
 2   teaspoons dried tarragon, crushed
 ½   teaspoon dried oregano, crushed
 ¼   teaspoon freshly ground black pepper
1½   teaspoons bottled minced garlic

Nutrition Facts per serving: 160 cal., 8 g total fat (2 g sat. fat), 55 mg chol., 46 mg sodium, 1 g carbo., 0 g sugar, 0 g fiber, 19 g pro.
Daily Values: 1% vit. A, 6% vit. C, 2% calcium, 14% iron
Exchanges: 3 Lean Meat

Blueberry Pork

Blueberries and pork? Although it seems an unlikely combination, the pairing is divine. Choose berries that are deep indigo blue with a frosty sheen. To keep your berries fresh, wash them just before using them.

1 Trim fat from meat. Place meat on the unheated rack of a broiler pan. Broil 4 to 5 inches from the heat about 20 minutes or until juices run clear (160°F), turning occasionally. Transfer the meat to a serving platter; cover and keep warm.

2 Meanwhile, for sauce, in a large skillet melt margarine over medium-low heat. Add onions, salt, and pepper. Cook about 10 minutes or until onions are golden brown, stirring frequently.

3 Stir in sugar and cook for 3 minutes more, stirring frequently. Stir in port wine and vinegar. Bring to boiling. Boil gently, uncovered, for 3 minutes. Stir in the blueberries and cherry tomatoes. Cook, stirring gently, until heated through. To serve, thinly slice meat. Serve the meat slices with sauce.

Grill Method: In a grill with a cover arrange hot coals around a drip pan. Test for medium-hot heat above the pan. (You should be able to hold your hand above the drip pan for 3 to 4 seconds.) Place meat on grill rack over drip pan. Cover; grill for 40 to 50 minutes or until juices run clear (160°F).

Prep: 15 minutes
Broil: 20 minutes
Makes: 4 servings

1   ¾- to 1-pound pork tenderloin
2   tablespoons margarine or butter
2   medium onions, sliced
½   teaspoon salt
¼   teaspoon black pepper
2   tablespoons sugar
¼   cup port wine, sweet sherry, or
      chicken broth
2   tablespoons balsamic vinegar or vinegar
1   cup fresh or frozen blueberries
1   cup halved cherry tomatoes

Nutrition Facts per serving: 253 cal., 9 g total fat (2 g sat. fat), 55 mg chol., 405 mg sodium, 21 g carbo., 13 g sugar, 2 g fiber, 19 g pro.
Daily Values: 11% vit. A, 27% vit. C, 2% calcium, 8% iron
Exchanges: ½ Vegetable, 1 Fruit, 2½ Very Lean Meat, 1½ Fat

Pork Tenderloin with Nutty Pear Stuffing

This elegant-looking dish is far easier to prepare than it looks. Let the roast stand for a couple of minutes before slicing it. The stuffing makes a swirl of color in each slice and provides a sweet, nutty counterpoint to the tender pork.

1 For stuffing, in a small bowl combine pear, nuts, carrot, bread crumbs, onion, ginger, salt, and pepper; set aside.

2 Trim any fat from meat. Butterfly meat by making a lengthwise slit down the center to within ½ inch of the underside. Open flat; pound with the flat side of a meat mallet to about ¼-inch thickness.

3 Spread stuffing over meat. Fold in ends. Starting from a long side, roll up meat. Secure with 100-percent-cotton string or wooden toothpicks. Place meat roll on a rack in a shallow roasting pan. Brush lightly with oil. Insert a meat thermometer into center of meat.

4 Roast in a 425° oven for 30 to 40 minutes or until meat thermometer registers 155°F. Brush orange marmalade over top of meat. Roast about 5 minutes more or until meat thermometer registers 160°F.

Prep: 20 minutes
Roast: 30 minutes
Oven: 425°F
Makes: 4 servings

½ cup chopped pear
¼ cup chopped hazelnuts (filberts) or almonds, toasted
¼ cup finely shredded carrot
¼ cup soft bread crumbs
2 tablespoons chopped onion
1 teaspoon grated fresh ginger
¼ teaspoon salt
¼ teaspoon black pepper
1 12-ounce pork tenderloin
1 teaspoon cooking oil
2 tablespoons orange marmalade

Nutrition Facts per serving: 198 cal., 9 g total fat (1 g sat. fat), 55 mg chol., 193 mg sodium, 10 g carbo., 6 g sugar, 2 g fiber, 20 g pro.
Daily Values: 43% vit. A, 9% vit. C, 2% calcium, 9% iron
Exchanges: ½ Fruit, 3 Very Lean Meat, 1½ Fat

Sassy Mojo Pork

Mojo (pronounced mo-hoe) is short, in Spanish, for mojado, which means "wet." Mojo sauces and marinades are fundamental to many Spanish and Cuban cuisines and are found premade in many grocery stores.

1 Trim any fat from meat. Place meat in a plastic bag set in a shallow dish. For marinade, in a food processor bowl or blender container combine chipotle peppers, orange juice, onion, oregano, lime juice, honey, oil, salt, and garlic. Cover and process or blend until nearly smooth.

2 Pour marinade over meat; seal bag. Marinate in the refrigerator for 2 hours, turning bag occasionally. Drain meat, discarding marinade.

3 In a grill with a cover arrange hot coals around a drip pan. Test for medium-hot heat above the pan. (You should be able to hold your hand over the drip pan for 3 seconds.) Place meat on the grill rack over drip pan. Cover and grill for 40 to 50 minutes or until juices run clear (160°F). If desired, garnish the meat with additional fresh oregano.

Nutrition Facts per serving: 191 cal., 6 g total fat (2 g sat. fat), 73 mg chol., 344 mg sodium, 9 g carbo., 5 g sugar, 0 g fiber, 24 g pro.
Daily Values: 1% vit. A, 24% vit. C, 2% calcium, 9% iron
Exchanges: ½ Fruit, 3½ Very Lean Meat, 1 Fat

Prep: 15 minutes
Grill: 40 minutes
Marinate: 2 hours
Makes: 6 servings

2 ¾- to 1-pound pork tenderloins
4 canned chipotle peppers in adobo sauce, rinsed
½ cup orange juice
¼ cup coarsely chopped onion
2 tablespoons snipped fresh oregano or 2 teaspoons dried oregano, crushed
2 tablespoons lime juice
1 tablespoon honey
1 tablespoon cooking oil
½ teaspoon salt
3 cloves garlic, minced
Fresh oregano (optional)

10 g
carb

Saucy Apple Pork Roast

Chunky apple wedges sweetened with apple juice roast alongside an herb-crusted pork loin. For best results, choose firm red cooking apples such as Braeburn or Winesap.

1 Trim fat from meat. Cut small slits (about ½ inch wide and 1 inch deep) in meat; insert a slice of garlic in each slit. In a small bowl combine salt, rosemary, and black pepper. Rub rosemary mixture evenly over meat. Place meat on a rack in a shallow roasting pan. Insert a meat thermometer into center of meat. Roast in a 325° oven about 2 hours or until meat thermometer registers 155°F.

2 Meanwhile, in a large bowl combine apples, apple juice, brown sugar, lemon juice, and dry mustard. Add apple mixture to roasting pan the last 30 minutes of roasting.

3 Transfer meat to a serving platter. Cover meat loosely with foil; let stand for 10 minutes (the meat's temperature will rise 5°F during standing).

4 Remove the rack from roasting pan. Stir the apple wedges into pan juices. Cut the meat into slices. Serve the meat with apple mixture.

Nutrition Facts per serving: 262 cal., 8 g total fat (3 g sat. fat), 87 mg chol., 252 mg sodium, 10 g carbo., 9 g sugar, 1 g fiber, 35 g pro.
Daily Values: 1% vit. A, 8% vit. C, 4% calcium, 8% iron
Exchanges: ½ Fruit, 5 Very Lean Meat, 1½ Fat

Prep: 15 minutes
Roast: 2 hours
Stand: 10 minutes
Oven: 325°F
Makes: 10 to 12 servings

- 1 3½- to 4-pound boneless pork top loin roast (double loin, tied)
- 3 cloves garlic, cut into thin slices
- 1 teaspoon coarse salt or salt
- 1 teaspoon dried rosemary, crushed
- ½ teaspoon coarsely ground black pepper
- 3 medium apples, cored and cut into wedges
- ¼ cup apple juice or apple cider
- 2 tablespoons brown sugar
- 2 tablespoons lemon juice
- 2 teaspoons dry mustard

Jamaican Pork Chops with Melon Salsa

The beguiling contrast of the sweet fruit topping and the spicy rub on the chops makes this tropical-tasting dish seem exotic. You'll especially love the flavors for summer alfresco dining.

1 For salsa, in a small bowl stir together honeydew melon, cantaloupe, mint, and honey. Cover and chill until ready to serve.

2 Trim fat from chops. Rub jerk seasoning onto both sides of chops. Place chops on the rack of an uncovered grill directly over medium coals. Grill for 12 to 15 minutes or until juices run clear (160°F), turning once. Serve the chops with salsa. If desired, garnish with additional mint.

Nutrition Facts per serving: 201 cal., 5 g total fat (2 g sat. fat), 62 mg chol., 354 mg sodium, 12 g carbo., 11 g sugar, 1 g fiber, 25 g pro.
Daily Values: 26% vit. A, 48% vit. C, 3% calcium, 6% iron
Exchanges: 1 Fruit, 3½ Very Lean Meat, ½ Fat

Prep: 15 minutes
Grill: 12 minutes
Makes: 4 servings

1   cup chopped honeydew melon
1   cup chopped cantaloupe
1   tablespoon snipped fresh mint
1   tablespoon honey
4   boneless pork top loin chops, cut ¾ to 1 inch thick (about 1 pound total)
4   teaspoons Jamaican jerk seasoning
    Snipped fresh mint (optional)

Grilled Mustard Pork Chops

The pork chops get infused with flavor while they marinate in the refrigerator. Best of all, the marinade is a snap to put together, so these make a completely hassle-free main course.

1 Trim fat from chops. Place chops in a plastic bag set in a shallow dish. For marinade, in a small bowl stir together mustard, wine, green onion, curry powder, oil, crushed red pepper, and garlic.

2 Pour marinade over chops; seal bag. Marinate in the refrigerator for 6 to 24 hours, turning the bag occasionally. Drain chops, reserving marinade.

3 In a grill with a cover arrange medium-hot coals around a drip pan. Test for medium heat above the pan. (You should be able to hold your hand over the drip pan for 3 seconds.) Place chops on the grill rack over drip pan. Cover and grill for 22 to 24 minutes or until juices run clear (160°F), turning and brushing once with reserved marinade. Discard any remaining marinade.

Nutrition Facts per serving: 231 cal., 11 g total fat (2 g sat. fat), 62 mg chol., 457 mg sodium, 3 g carbo., 0 g sugar, 1 g fiber, 27 g pro.
Daily Values: 1% vit. A, 3% vit. C, 7% calcium, 10% iron
Exchanges: 4 Lean Meat

Prep: 15 minutes
Marinate: 6 to 24 hours
Grill: 22 minutes
Makes: 4 servings

4 boneless pork top loin chops, cut 1 inch thick (about 1 pound total)
½ cup spicy brown mustard
¼ cup dry white wine
1 green onion, sliced
1 tablespoon curry powder
1 tablespoon olive oil
¼ to ½ teaspoon crushed red pepper
1 clove garlic, minced

Barbecued Pork Sandwiches

Making your own barbecue sauce, rather than using a commercial sauce, reduces the sodium content in this recipe. If you're short on time, make the sauce ahead and store it in the refrigerator for up to 3 days.

1 For sauce, lightly coat a small saucepan with cooking spray. Heat saucepan over medium heat. Add onion and garlic; cook and stir about 5 minutes or until onion is tender. Stir in water, tomato paste, vinegar, brown sugar, chili powder, oregano, and Worcestershire sauce. Bring to boiling; reduce heat. Simmer, uncovered, about 10 minutes or until sauce is the desired consistency, stirring occasionally.

2 Meanwhile, trim any fat from meat. Cut meat into bite-size strips. Lightly coat a large skillet with cooking spray. Heat skillet over medium-high heat. Add meat and sprinkle with salt. Cook and stir for 2 to 3 minutes or until meat is slightly pink in center. Stir in the sauce and sweet pepper; heat through. Serve the meat mixture in toasted buns.

Nutrition Facts per serving: 225 cal., 4 g total fat (1 g sat. fat), 37 mg chol., 388 mg sodium, 29 g carbo., 6 g sugar, 3 g fiber, 17 g pro.
Daily Values: 7% vit. A, 33% vit. C, 8% calcium, 16% iron
Exchanges: 2 Starch, 1½ Very Lean Meat

Prep: 20 minutes
Cook: 10 minutes
Makes: 6 servings

	Nonstick cooking spray
1	medium onion, chopped (½ cup)
2	cloves garlic, minced
⅔	cup water
½	of a 6-ounce can (⅓ cup) tomato paste
2	tablespoons red wine vinegar
1	tablespoon brown sugar
1½	teaspoons chili powder
1	teaspoon dried oregano, crushed
1	teaspoon Worcestershire sauce
12	ounces pork tenderloin
¼	teaspoon salt
1	medium green sweet pepper, chopped (¾ cup)
6	whole wheat hamburger buns, split and toasted

Pork and Green Chile Stew

Today's pork is higher in protein and lower in fat. For this flavorful stew, you don't need to brown the meat first—this cuts out a step and a little extra fat too.

1 To roast poblano or sweet peppers, halve peppers and remove stems, seeds, and membranes. Place peppers, cut sides down, on a foil-lined baking sheet. Roast in a 425° oven about 20 minutes or until skin is bubbly and browned. Wrap peppers in the foil; let stand for 20 to 25 minutes or until cool enough to handle. Using a paring knife, pull the skin off gently and slowly. Coarsely chop peppers.

2 Trim fat from meat. Cut meat into bite-size pieces. In a Dutch oven combine roasted peppers, meat, onion, jalapeño peppers, salt, oregano, and garlic. Bake, covered, in a 325° oven for 45 minutes.

3 Stir in the potatoes. Bake, covered, for 30 minutes. Stir in zucchini and corn. Bake, covered, about 15 minutes more or until meat and vegetables are tender. Stir in cilantro. If desired, serve stew with lime wedges.

Nutrition Facts per serving: 269 cal., 6 g total fat (2 g sat. fat), 55 mg chol., 377 mg sodium, 34 g carbo., 3 g sugar, 5 g fiber, 22 g pro.
Daily Values: 19% vit. A, 251% vit. C, 6% calcium, 23% iron
Exchanges: 2 Vegetable, 1½ Starch, 2 Lean Meat

Prep: 35 minutes
Bake: 1½ hours
Oven: 425°F/325°F
Makes: 8 servings

4   fresh poblano peppers or 2 green
       sweet peppers
1½ pounds lean boneless pork shoulder
3   cups chopped onion
¼   cup finely chopped fresh jalapeño peppers
       (see tip, page 37)
1   teaspoon salt
½   teaspoon dried oregano, crushed
1   tablespoon bottled minced garlic
1½ pounds red potatoes, cut into 1-inch
       pieces
3   medium zucchini, halved lengthwise and
       cut into ½-inch slices
1   10-ounce package frozen whole kernel
       corn, thawed
½   cup snipped fresh cilantro
       Lime wedges (optional)

French Country Cassoulet

Traditionally, a cassoulet includes white beans and a variety of meats—such as sausage and pork—and is cooked slowly to meld flavors. Although this version eliminates the high-fat meat, it still cooks slowly to blend the flavors. It's worth the wait.

1 Rinse beans. In a 4-quart Dutch oven combine beans and 8 cups water. Bring to boiling; reduce heat. Simmer, uncovered, for 2 minutes. Remove from heat. Cover and let stand for 1 hour. (Or place beans in water in Dutch oven. Cover and let soak in a cool place for 6 to 8 hours or overnight.) Drain and rinse beans. Set aside.

2 Trim fat from meat. Cut meat into 1-inch pieces. In the same Dutch oven brown meat, half at a time, with the onion and garlic in hot oil. Drain fat. Add drained beans, chicken broth, wine, and bay leaves to the meat mixture. Bring to boiling; reduce heat. Simmer, covered, for 1 hour, stirring occasionally.

3 Remove bay leaves. Stir in carrots, celery root, celery, rosemary, salt, and pepper. Return to boiling; reduce heat. Simmer, covered, about 30 minutes or until beans are nearly tender. Uncover and boil gently about 30 minutes more or until beans are tender and liquid thickens, stirring occasionally.

Stand: 1 hour
Prep: 35 minutes
Cook: 2 hours
Makes: 6 servings

- 1 **pound dry navy, Great Northern, or white kidney (cannellini) beans**
- 1½ **pounds lamb stew meat**
- 1 **large onion, cut into chunks**
- 6 **cloves garlic, minced**
- 1 **tablespoon olive oil or cooking oil**
- 4 **cups reduced-sodium chicken broth**
- 2 **cups dry white wine**
- 3 **bay leaves**
- 4 **medium carrots, cut into 1-inch pieces**
- 6 **ounces celery root, peeled and cut into ½-inch pieces**
- 2 **stalks celery, cut into 1-inch pieces**
- 1½ **teaspoons dried rosemary, crushed**
- ½ **teaspoon salt**
- ¼ **teaspoon coarsely ground black pepper**

Nutrition Facts per serving: 519 cal., 8 g total fat (2 g sat. fat), 73 mg chol., 722 mg sodium, 57 g carbo., 9 g sugar, 21 g fiber, 44 g pro.
Daily Values: 205% vit. A, 14% vit. C, 15% calcium, 36% iron
Exchanges: 2 Vegetable, 3 Starch, 4½ Very Lean Meat, 1½ Fat

Minted Lamb Chops

The classic flavor combination of lamb with mint gets a new twist. Rather than topping lamb with mint jelly, the lamb chops are marinated in the aromatic fresh mint and other flavorings before cooking. You'll love the way the meat picks up the flavors.

1 Trim fat from chops. Place chops in a plastic bag set in a shallow dish. For the marinade, in a small bowl combine snipped mint, lemon juice, oil, water, ginger, paprika, cumin, salt, ground red pepper, and garlic. Pour over chops; seal bag. Marinate in the refrigerator for 4 to 24 hours, turning bag occasionally. Drain chops, discarding marinade.

2 Place chops on the rack of an uncovered grill directly over medium coals. Grill for 12 to 14 minutes for medium rare (145°F) or 15 to 17 minutes for medium (160°F), turning once. Transfer chops to a serving platter. Sprinkle with the shredded mint.

Broiler Method: Place chops on the unheated rack of a broiler pan. Broil 3 to 4 inches from the heat for 7 to 9 minutes for medium rare (145°F) or 10 to 15 minutes for medium (160°F), turning chops once.

Prep: 15 minutes
Marinate: 4 to 24 hours
Grill: 12 minutes
Makes: 4 servings

8	lamb rib chops, cut 1 inch thick (about 2½ pounds total)
¼	cup snipped fresh mint
¼	cup lemon juice
2	tablespoons cooking oil
2	tablespoons water
1	tablespoon grated fresh ginger
1½	teaspoons paprika
1	teaspoon ground cumin
½	teaspoon salt
⅛	teaspoon ground red pepper
1	large clove garlic, minced
1	to 2 tablespoons finely shredded fresh mint

Nutrition Facts per serving: 236 cal., 14 g total fat (4 g sat. fat), 80 mg chol., 234 mg sodium, 1 g carbo., 0 g sugar, 0 g fiber, 25 g pro.
Daily Values: 5% vit. A, 11% vit. C, 2% calcium, 15% iron
Exchanges: 3½ Lean Meat, 1 Fat

Poultry

Spring Chicken with Garlic

Garlic gets sweet and mellow when roasted. Squeeze the soft cloves from their skins, and eat them with the chicken or spread them on toasted bread.

1 Peel away outer leaves from garlic heads, leaving skin of cloves intact. Separate the cloves. (You should have about 40.) Peel and mince 4 cloves; reserve remaining garlic cloves.

2 In a small bowl combine minced garlic, 1 tablespoon of the oil, 1 tablespoon fresh thyme, the cracked black pepper, and ¼ teaspoon salt. Rub mixture over chicken.

3 Place 6 garlic cloves in cavity of chicken. Tie legs to tail; twist wing tips under back. Place onion wedges and remaining garlic cloves in bottom of a shallow roasting pan. Drizzle with remaining oil.

4 Place chicken, breast side up, on top of onion and garlic in roasting pan. Insert a meat thermometer into center of an inside thigh muscle. Roast in a 375° oven for 1¼ to 1½ hours or until drumsticks move easily in their sockets and meat thermometer registers 180°F.

5 Remove chicken from oven; transfer to a cutting board. Cover loosely with foil; let stand 15 minutes before carving. Remove onion and garlic from pan. Reserve 2 onion wedges.

6 For sauce, squeeze 10 of the roasted garlic cloves from skins into a blender container or food processor bowl. Add remaining onion wedges and ¼ cup of the half-and-half. Cover and blend or process until smooth; transfer to a small saucepan. Stir in flour. Add remaining

**Prep: 25 minutes • Roast: 1¼ hours
Stand: 15 minutes• Oven: 375°F
Makes: 6 servings**

- 3 heads garlic
- 2 tablespoons olive oil or cooking oil
- 1 tablespoon snipped fresh thyme or
       1 teaspoon dried thyme, crushed
- 1 teaspoon cracked black pepper
- ¼ teaspoon salt
- 1 3- to 3½-pound whole broiler-fryer chicken
- 1 medium onion, cut into wedges
- 2 cups fat-free half-and-half or half-and-half
- 2 tablespoons all-purpose flour
- 1 teaspoon snipped fresh thyme or
       ¼ teaspoon dried thyme, crushed
- ¼ teaspoon salt
- ⅛ teaspoon black pepper

half-and-half, the 1 teaspoon fresh thyme, ¼ teaspoon salt, and the ⅛ teaspoon black pepper. Cook and stir until slightly thickened and bubbly. Cook and stir 1 minute more. Serve chicken with sauce. Garnish with remaining roasted garlic cloves and reserved onion wedges.

Nutrition Facts per serving: 353 cal., 17 g total fat (4 g sat. fat), 79 mg chol., 351 mg sodium, 18 g carbo., 1 g sugar, 1 g fiber, 28 g pro.
Daily Values: 1% vit. A, 13% vit. C, 10% calcium, 10% iron
Exchanges: ½ Vegetable, 1 Starch, 3½ Lean Meat, 1½ Fat

Tarragon Chicken

This oven-baked chicken and potato dish requires very little preparation. Despite that, the dish delivers lots of flavor. All you have to do is steam a vegetable to complete the meal.

1 If desired, remove skin from chicken. In a small bowl combine dried tarragon, finely shredded lemon peel, salt, paprika, and ground red pepper; set aside.

2 Place potatoes and onion in an ovenproof Dutch oven; sprinkle with about half of the tarragon mixture. Place the chicken pieces on top of potatoes and onion. Sprinkle with remaining tarragon mixture.

3 Bake, covered, in a 375° oven for 45 to 50 minutes or until chicken is no longer pink (170°F for breasts; 180°F for thighs and drumsticks) and potatoes are tender. Drizzle with lemon juice. If desired, garnish with fresh tarragon and serve with lemon wedges.

Nutrition Facts per serving: 358 cal., 13 g total fat (4 g sat. fat), 104 mg chol., 537 mg sodium, 23 g carbo., 1 g sugar, 3 g fiber, 36 g pro.
Daily Values: 4% vit. A, 34% vit. C, 4% calcium, 17% iron
Exchanges: 1½ Starch, 4½ Lean Meat

Prep: 15 minutes
Bake: 45 minutes
Oven: 375°F
Makes: 4 servings

2 pounds meaty chicken pieces (breast halves, thighs, and drumsticks)
1 teaspoon dried tarragon, crushed
1 teaspoon finely shredded lemon peel
¾ teaspoon salt
½ teaspoon paprika
⅛ teaspoon ground red pepper
4 small potatoes (about 1 pound), cut into ¼-inch slices
1 large onion, cut into 8 wedges
1 tablespoon lemon juice
Snipped fresh tarragon (optional)
Lemon wedges (optional)

Oregano Chicken and Vegetables

This meal-in-a-skillet is bursting with Mediterranean flavors. Chicken, fresh sweet peppers, and chopped tomato simmer in a blend of white wine and broth seasoned with oregano and garlic. Serve the chicken and vegetables with steamed rice.

1 Sprinkle chicken with salt and black pepper. Lightly coat a large nonstick skillet with cooking spray. Heat skillet over medium heat. Add chicken and cook about 15 minutes or until light brown, turning once. Reduce heat to medium low.

2 Place half of the tomato, half of the lemon slices, the olives, parsley, onion, oregano, and garlic over chicken pieces. Sprinkle with ground red pepper. Add the broth and wine. Simmer, covered, for 15 minutes.

3 Add sweet peppers and the remaining tomato. Simmer, covered, 5 to 10 minutes more or until chicken is no longer pink (170°F for breasts, 180°F for thighs and drumsticks) and sweet peppers are crisp-tender. Transfer the chicken and vegetables to a serving platter. Garnish with remaining lemon slices.

Nutrition Facts per serving: 216 cal., 8 g total fat (2 g sat. fat), 69 mg chol., 508 mg sodium, 11 g carbo., 3 g sugar, 4 g fiber, 25 g pro.
Daily Values: 46% vit. A, 174% vit. C, 6% calcium, 14% iron
Exchanges: 2 Vegetable, 3 Lean Meat

Prep: 25 minutes
Cook: 20 minutes
Makes: 4 servings

1½ to 2 pounds meaty chicken pieces (breast halves, thighs, and drumsticks), skinned
¼ teaspoon salt
⅛ teaspoon black pepper
    Nonstick cooking spray
1 large tomato, peeled and chopped (¾ cup)
1 lemon, thinly sliced
½ cup pitted ripe olives
¼ cup snipped fresh parsley
¼ cup chopped onion
1 tablespoon snipped fresh oregano or 1 teaspoon dried oregano, crushed
1 clove garlic, minced
⅛ teaspoon ground red pepper
¾ cup chicken broth
¼ cup dry white wine or chicken broth
1 medium green sweet pepper, cut into strips
1 medium red sweet pepper, cut into strips

Chicken and Polenta

Ready-to-heat tubes of polenta have a fairly long shelf life in your refrigerator—but you may find they are such a convenient addition to weeknight dinners that they don't seem to last! The tubes are available in a variety of flavors, so experiment to find those you like best.

1 Sprinkle the chicken with salt. Lightly coat a 12-inch nonstick skillet with cooking spray. Heat skillet over medium-high heat. Add chicken and cook for 10 to 12 minutes or until no longer pink (180°F), turning once. Remove from skillet.

2 Add sweet peppers and onion to skillet. Cook and stir for 3 to 4 minutes or until sweet peppers are crisp-tender. Stir the cumin into undrained tomatoes; stir into pepper mixture. Bring to boiling. Return chicken to the skillet; heat through.

3 Meanwhile, in a 10-inch nonstick skillet heat oil over medium-high heat. Cook the polenta slices in hot oil for 10 to 12 minutes or until golden brown, turning once.

4 To serve, arrange chicken and polenta on dinner plates. Spoon pepper mixture over chicken and polenta. Sprinkle with fresh cilantro.

Start to Finish: 35 minutes
Makes: 4 servings

- 1½ **pounds skinless, boneless chicken thighs**
- ⅛ **teaspoon salt**
   Nonstick cooking spray
- 2 **medium green sweet peppers, coarsely chopped**
- 1 **medium onion, coarsely chopped**
- 2 **teaspoons ground cumin**
- 1 **14½-ounce can diced tomatoes**
- 1 **tablespoon olive oil**
- 1 **16-ounce tube refrigerated cooked polenta, cut into 8 slices**
- 2 **tablespoons snipped fresh cilantro**

Nutrition Facts per serving: 392 cal., 10 g total fat (2 g sat. fat), 136 mg chol., 802 mg sodium, 32 g carbo., 5 g sugar, 5 g fiber, 39 g pro.
Daily Values: 12% vit. A, 107% vit. C, 8% calcium, 14% iron
Exchanges: 2 Vegetable, 1½ Starch, 4 Lean Meat

Cheesy Chicken with Artichokes

You'll love the rich mushroom sauce that finishes this dish. Evaporated fat-free milk is a smart cook's trick for getting a creamy texture without adding a high-fat ingredient such as whipping cream or half-and-half.

1 In a large skillet bring chicken broth to boiling. Add chicken; reduce heat. Cover and simmer for 12 to 14 minutes or until chicken is no longer pink (170°F). Drain chicken, reserving ¾ cup broth. Cover chicken; keep warm.

2 Meanwhile, cook the artichoke hearts according to package directions; drain. Cover and keep warm.

3 For sauce, wipe out skillet with a paper towel; lightly coat skillet with cooking spray. Heat skillet over medium heat. Add mushrooms, onion, and garlic; cook and stir just until onion is tender. Stir in cornstarch. Add the reserved broth, evaporated milk, salt, and white pepper. Cook and stir until thickened and bubbly. Cook and stir for 2 minutes more. Stir in wine.

4 To serve, place chicken on dinner plates. Arrange artichokes around chicken. Spoon sauce over chicken and sprinkle with Parmesan cheese.

Start to Finish: 30 minutes
Makes: 4 servings

- 1 14-ounce can chicken broth
- 4 skinless, boneless chicken breast halves (about 1¼ pounds total)
- 1 9-ounce package frozen artichoke hearts
   Nonstick cooking spray
- 2 cups sliced fresh mushrooms
- ¼ cup chopped onion
- 1 clove garlic, minced
- 4 teaspoons cornstarch
- ¾ cup evaporated fat-free milk
- ⅛ teaspoon salt
- ⅛ teaspoon white pepper
- 2 tablespoons dry white wine or chicken broth
- ⅓ cup finely shredded or grated Parmesan cheese

Nutrition Facts per serving: 313 cal., 6 g total fat (3 g sat. fat), 92 mg chol., 664 mg sodium, 16 g carbo., 2 g sugar, 4 g fiber, 45 g pro.
Daily Values: 8% vit. A, 12% vit. C, 28% calcium, 11% iron
Exchanges: ½ Milk, 2 Vegetable, 5 Very Lean Meat, 1 Fat

Chicken Stuffed with Smoked Mozzarella

These impressive looking stuffed breasts seem more likely to be found on the table at an Italian restaurant than a home kitchen—unless you know the secret of how easy they are to make.

1 Place each chicken piece between 2 pieces of plastic wrap. Pound lightly with the flat side of a meat mallet into a rectangle about ⅛ inch thick. Remove plastic wrap. Sprinkle chicken with salt and pepper.

2 For filling, in a medium skillet cook shallots and garlic in the 2 teaspoons hot oil until tender. Remove from heat; stir in spinach, mozzarella cheese, and nuts.

3 In a shallow dish combine bread crumbs and Parmesan cheese. Place 2 to 3 tablespoons of filling in the center of each chicken breast. Fold in sides; roll up chicken. Secure with wooden toothpicks. Lightly brush chicken with the 1 tablespoon oil and coat with bread crumb mixture.

4 Place chicken rolls, seam sides down, in a shallow baking pan. Bake in a 400° oven about 25 minutes or until chicken is no longer pink (170°F). Remove toothpicks before serving.

Prep: 40 minutes
Bake: 25 minutes
Oven: 400°F
Makes: 6 servings

6   skinless, boneless chicken breast halves
       (about 2 pounds total)
¼   teaspoon salt
⅛   teaspoon black pepper
¼   cup finely chopped shallots or onion
1   clove garlic, minced
2   teaspoons olive oil
½   of a 10-ounce package frozen chopped
       spinach, thawed and well drained
¾   cup shredded smoked mozzarella cheese
       or mozzarella cheese (3 ounces)
3   tablespoons pine nuts or walnuts, toasted
¼   cup seasoned fine dry bread crumbs
¼   cup grated Parmesan cheese
1   tablespoon olive oil

Nutrition Facts per serving: 317 cal., 13 g total fat
(4 g sat. fat), 102 mg chol., 451 mg sodium, 7 g carbo.,
0 g sugar, 1 g fiber, 42 g pro.
Daily Values: 42% vit. A, 13% vit. C, 18% calcium,
12% iron
Exchanges: 1½ Vegetable, 5 Very Lean Meat, ½ High-
Fat Meat, 1½ Fat

Chicken with Red and Yellow Cherry Tomatoes

Fresh tarragon and colorful cherry tomatoes pair for this simply delicious chicken fix, perfect for a casual or last-minute gathering. Grape tomatoes work well in this dish too.

1 Sprinkle chicken with ¼ teaspoon of the salt and ⅛ teaspoon of the black pepper. In a large nonstick skillet heat oil over medium-high heat. Add chicken and cook for 10 to 12 minutes or until chicken is no longer pink (170°F), turning once. Transfer chicken to a serving platter; cover and keep warm.

2 Drain fat from skillet. Add tomatoes, water, tarragon, vinegar, the remaining ¼ teaspoon salt, and the remaining ⅛ teaspoon black pepper to skillet. Bring to boiling; reduce heat. Simmer, uncovered, for 3 to 4 minutes or until tomatoes begin to soften, stirring occasionally. Serve the tomato mixture over chicken.

Nutrition Facts per serving: 196 cal., 4 g total fat (1 g sat. fat), 82 mg chol., 373 mg sodium, 4 g carbo., 3 g sugar, 1 g fiber, 34 g pro.
Daily Values: 12% vit. A, 31% vit. C, 2% calcium, 8% iron
Exchanges: 1 Vegetable, 4½ Very Lean Meat, ½ Fat

Prep: 15 minutes
Cook: 10 minutes
Makes: 4 servings

- 4 skinless, boneless chicken breast halves (about 1¼ pounds total)
- ½ teaspoon salt
- ¼ teaspoon freshly ground black pepper
- 2 teaspoons olive oil
- 2 cups red and/or yellow cherry tomatoes, halved
- 2 tablespoons water
- 1 tablespoon snipped fresh tarragon or basil or ½ teaspoon dried tarragon or basil, crushed
- 1 tablespoon white wine vinegar

Cucumber-Yogurt Chicken

Spice up chicken with ground red pepper, then cool it down with yogurt-cucumber sauce. If the heat level isn't to your liking, adjust the amount of ground red pepper—or omit it and season the chicken with your favorite spice blend.

1 For sauce, in a small bowl combine yogurt, cucumber, radishes, mayonnaise, lemon peel, lemon juice, hot pepper sauce, and garlic. Cover and chill until ready to serve.

2 Sprinkle chicken with salt and ground red pepper. In a large nonstick skillet heat oil over medium-high heat. Add chicken and cook for 10 to 12 minutes or until chicken is no longer pink (170°F), turning once. Serve the chicken with sauce.

Nutrition Facts per serving: 307 cal., 11 g total fat (2 g sat. fat), 104 mg chol., 321 mg sodium, 6 g carbo., 4 g sugar, 1 g fiber, 43 g pro.
Daily Values: 4% vit. A, 15% vit. C, 13% calcium, 7% iron
Exchanges: 1 Vegetable, 5 Very Lean Meat, 1½ Fat

Prep: 15 minutes
Cook: 10 minutes
Makes: 4 servings

- 1   8-ounce carton plain low-fat yogurt
- 1   cup chopped, peeled seedless cucumber
- ½   cup finely chopped radishes
- 2   tablespoons mayonnaise or salad dressing
- ¼   teaspoon finely shredded lemon peel
- 1   tablespoon lemon juice
- ¼   teaspoon bottled hot pepper sauce
- 1   small clove garlic, minced
- 4   skinless, boneless chicken breast halves (about 1½ pounds total)
- ¼   teaspoon salt
- ¼   teaspoon ground red pepper
- 2   teaspoons cooking oil

Lemon Chicken

This delectable chicken dish boasts the flavor of the Asian restaurant favorite of the same name—without the mess or the added calories of deep frying.

1 Place each chicken breast half between 2 pieces of plastic wrap. Pound lightly with the flat side of a meat mallet to about ¼ inch thick. Remove plastic wrap.

2 In a shallow dish stir together flour and pepper. Coat chicken with flour mixture, shaking off any excess.

3 In a large skillet heat margarine over medium heat. Add chicken and cook for 4 to 6 minutes or until chicken is no longer pink (170°F), turning once. Remove from skillet; cover and keep warm.

4 For sauce, in a small bowl stir together chicken broth, lemon juice, and cornstarch. Add to skillet. Cook and stir until thickened and bubbly. Cook and stir for 2 minutes more. Stir in green onions. If desired, top chicken with lemon slices. Spoon sauce over chicken.

Start to Finish: 25 minutes
Makes: 4 servings

- 4   skinless, boneless chicken breast halves (about 1¼ pounds total)
- ⅓   cup all-purpose flour
- ¼   teaspoon black pepper
- 2   tablespoons margarine or butter
- 1   cup chicken broth
- ¼   cup lemon juice
- 1   tablespoon cornstarch
- ¼   cup sliced green onions
     Lemon slices, cut in half (optional)

Nutrition Facts per serving: 269 cal., 8 g total fat (2 g sat. fat), 82 mg chol., 339 mg sodium, 11 g carbo., 1 g sugar, 1 g fiber, 35 g pro.
Daily Values: 6% vit. A, 16% vit. C, 3% calcium, 9% iron
Exchanges: ½ Starch, 4½ Very Lean Meat, 1½ Fat

Italian-Style Chicken Cutlets

A savory blend of Parmesan cheese, rosemary, and bread crumbs creates a crispy golden coating for these chicken cutlets.

1 Place each chicken piece between 2 pieces of plastic wrap. Pound lightly with the flat side of a meat mallet to ½ inch thick. Remove plastic wrap. Sprinkle chicken with salt and black pepper.

2 In a shallow dish combine bread crumbs, Parmesan cheese, parsley, and rosemary. Place whole egg and egg white in another shallow dish; beat slightly. Dip chicken in beaten egg and coat with crumb mixture.

3 In a large skillet heat oil over medium-high heat. Add chicken and cook for 10 to 12 minutes or until chicken is no longer pink (170°F), turning once. If desired, serve chicken with lemon wedges.

Prep: 15 minutes
Cook: 10 minutes
Makes: 4 servings

- 4 skinless, boneless chicken breast halves (about 1¼ pounds total)
- ¼ teaspoon salt
- ¼ teaspoon freshly ground black pepper
- ¾ cup fine dry bread crumbs
- 2 tablespoons freshly grated Parmesan cheese
- 1 tablespoon snipped fresh Italian flat-leaf parsley
- 1 teaspoon snipped fresh rosemary
- 1 egg
- 1 egg white
- 2 tablespoons olive oil
  Lemon wedges (optional)

Nutrition Facts per serving: 312 cal., 12 g total fat (3 g sat. fat), 137 mg chol., 698 mg sodium, 11 g carbo., 1 g sugar, 1 g fiber, 38 g pro.
Daily Values: 4% vit. A, 4% vit. C, 9% calcium, 12% iron
Exchanges: 1 Starch, 5 Very Lean Meat, 1½ Fat

16 g
carb

Tortilla-Crusted Chicken

Crushed tortilla chips make an irresistible crunchy coating for oven-fried chicken. Although chips are a high-calorie food, they lend lots of flavor and crunch, so you need only a few.

1 Coat a 15×10×1-inch baking pan with cooking spray; set aside. In a shallow dish combine tortilla chips, oregano, cumin, and pepper. Place egg in another shallow dish; beat slightly. Dip chicken in beaten egg and coat with tortilla chip mixture.

2 Arrange chicken in the prepared baking pan. Bake in a 375° oven about 25 minutes or until chicken is no longer pink (170°F). If desired, serve the chicken with salsa.

Nutrition Facts per serving: 305 cal., 10 g total fat (2 g sat. fat), 135 mg chol., 225 mg sodium, 16 g carbo., 0 g sugar, 2 g fiber, 36 g pro.
Daily Values: 3% vit. A, 2% vit. C, 7% calcium, 9% iron
Exchanges: 1 Starch, 4½ Very Lean Meat, 1½ Fat

Prep: 10 minutes
Bake: 25 minutes
Oven: 375°F
Makes: 4 servings

Nonstick cooking spray
1 cup finely crushed tortilla chips
½ teaspoon dried oregano, crushed
¼ teaspoon ground cumin
¼ teaspoon freshly ground black pepper
1 egg
4 boneless, skinless chicken breast halves
   (about 1¼ pounds total)
Salsa (optional)

Spinach-Chicken Bake

To quick-thaw the spinach, place it in a colander and run cold water over it. Press spinach with a wooden spoon against the colander to remove as much water as possible or use your hands to squeeze out the excess liquid.

1 In a shallow dish combine bread crumbs and Parmesan cheese. Lightly coat chicken pieces with some of the crumb mixture. Arrange in a 3-quart rectangular baking dish. Reserve the remaining crumb mixture.

2 In a large saucepan cook green onions in hot margarine until tender. Stir in flour. Add milk all at once. Cook and stir until thickened and bubbly. Cook and stir for 1 minute more. Stir in spinach and ham.

3 Spoon spinach mixture over chicken; sprinkle with remaining crumb mixture. Bake in a 350° oven for 40 to 45 minutes or until chicken is no longer pink (170°F).

Nutrition Facts per serving: 243 cal., 6 g total fat (2 g sat. fat), 90 mg chol., 474 mg sodium, 8 g carbo., 1 g sugar, 1 g fiber, 38 g pro.
Daily Values: 39% vit. A, 9% vit. C, 10% calcium, 10% iron
Exchanges: ½ Vegetable, ½ Starch, 5 Very Lean Meat, ½ Fat

Prep: 25 minutes
Bake: 40 minutes
Oven: 350°F
Makes: 12 servings

- ¾ cup seasoned fine dry bread crumbs
- ¼ cup grated Parmesan cheese
- 12 skinless, boneless chicken breast halves (about 3¾ pounds total)
- ½ cup sliced green onions
- 2 tablespoons margarine or butter
- 2 tablespoons all-purpose flour
- 1 cup milk
- 1 10-ounce package frozen chopped spinach, thawed and well drained
- 1 4-ounce package boiled ham slices, chopped

Creamy Chicken Enchiladas

Take a shortcut and buy roasted chicken breast instead of cooking it yourself. The light sour cream works better for baking than the fat-free version, which tends to separate when heated.

1 In a large saucepan combine chicken and enough water to cover. Bring to boiling; reduce heat. Simmer, covered, for 12 to 14 minutes or until chicken is no longer pink (170°F). Remove from saucepan. When cool enough to handle, shred chicken with a fork into bite-size pieces. (You should have about 3 cups.) Set aside.

2 If using fresh spinach, place in a steamer basket over boiling water; reduce heat. Cover and steam for 3 to 5 minutes or until tender. (Or cover and cook in a small amount of boiling water for 3 to 5 minutes.) Drain well.

3 In a large bowl combine shredded chicken, spinach, and green onions; set aside. For sauce, in a medium bowl combine sour cream, yogurt, flour, cumin, and salt. Stir in milk and chile peppers.

4 For filling, pour half of the sauce over chicken mixture; stir to combine. Divide filling among tortillas; roll up tortillas. Place, seam sides down, in a 2-quart rectangular baking dish. Spoon remaining sauce over tortillas.

5 Bake in a 350° oven about 40 minutes or until heated through. Sprinkle with cheese; let stand 5 minutes. Transfer to a serving platter. If desired, garnish with tomato and additional sliced green onions.

Prep: 40 minutes
Bake: 40 minutes
Stand: 5 minutes
Oven: 350°F
Makes: 6 servings

1 pound skinless, boneless chicken breast halves
8 cups torn spinach or one 10-ounce package frozen chopped spinach, thawed and well drained
½ cup thinly sliced green onions
2 8-ounce cartons light dairy sour cream
½ cup plain fat-free yogurt
¼ cup all-purpose flour
½ teaspoon ground cumin
¼ teaspoon salt
1 cup fat-free milk
2 4-ounce cans diced green chile peppers, drained
12 7-inch flour tortillas
⅔ cup shredded reduced-fat cheddar or Monterey Jack cheese (about 3 ounces)
Chopped tomato (optional)

Nutrition Facts per serving: 465 cal., 15 g total fat (7 g sat. fat), 79 mg chol., 721 mg sodium, 44 g carbo., 9 g sugar, 5 g fiber, 36 g pro.
Daily Values: 58% vit. A, 42% vit. C, 50% calcium, 32% iron
Exchanges: 3 Vegetable, 2 Starch, 4 Very Lean Meat

Moroccan-Style Grilled Chicken Skewers

These sweet and spicy chicken skewers have an exotic aroma that's an enticing hint of their intoxicating flavor. Use this same marinade on roasted bone-in chicken breasts.

1 Cut each chicken breast half lengthwise into 4 strips. Thread chicken, accordion-style, onto eight 8-inch skewers, leaving ¼ inch between strips. (If using wooden skewers, soak in water for 30 minutes before grilling.) Place in a 3-quart rectangular dish.

2 For marinade, in a small bowl combine vinegar, honey, oil, cumin, paprika, ground red pepper, salt, cinnamon, and garlic. Pour over chicken skewers. Cover and marinate in the refrigerator for 2 to 4 hours, turning skewers occasionally. Drain the chicken skewers, reserving marinade.

3 Place the chicken skewers on the rack of an uncovered grill directly over medium-hot coals. Grill for 8 to 10 minutes or until chicken is no longer pink, turning and brushing once halfway through grilling with reserved marinade.

Broiler Method: Place skewers on the unheated rack of a broiler pan. Broil 4 to 5 inches from the heat for 8 to 10 minutes or until chicken is no longer pink, turning and brushing once with reserved marinade.

Nutrition Facts per serving: 200 cal., 5 g total fat (1 g sat. fat), 66 mg chol., 137 mg sodium, 9 g carbo., 9 g sugar, 0 g fiber, 26 g pro.
Daily Values: 5% vit. A, 3% vit. C, 2% calcium, 6% iron
Exchanges: ½ Other Carbo., 3½ Very Lean Meat, 1 Fat

Prep: 15 minutes
Marinate: 2 hours
Grill: 8 minutes
Makes: 4 servings

- 4 skinless, boneless chicken breast halves (about 1 pound total)
- ⅓ cup white wine vinegar
- 2 tablespoons honey
- 1 tablespoon olive oil
- ½ teaspoon ground cumin
- ½ teaspoon paprika
- ¼ teaspoon ground red pepper
- ⅛ teaspoon salt
- ⅛ teaspoon ground cinnamon
- 1 large clove garlic, minced

Quick Caribbean Chicken

Sweet and savory flavors dance a rhythmic duet in this Caribbean-inspired dish. To keep cooking time to a minimum, use quick-cooking brown rice.

1 Sprinkle chicken with salt and ground red pepper. In a large nonstick skillet heat oil over medium-high heat. Add chicken; cook and stir for 3 minutes.

2 Add sweet potato and banana pepper. Cook and stir for 5 to 6 minutes more or until chicken is no longer pink and sweet potato is tender.

3 In a small bowl stir together pineapple juice and cornstarch; stir into chicken mixture. Cook, stirring gently, until bubbly. Add banana pieces; cook, stirring gently, for 2 minutes more. Serve chicken mixture over hot cooked brown rice.

Nutrition Facts per serving: 334 cal., 4 g total fat (1 g sat. fat), 49 mg chol., 203 mg sodium, 52 g carbo., 15 g sugar, 5 g fiber, 24 g pro.
Daily Values: 122% vit. A, 38% vit. C, 4% calcium, 8% iron
Exchanges: 1½ Fruit, 2 Starch, 2½ Very Lean Meat

Start to Finish: 20 minutes
Makes: 4 servings

12 ounces chicken breast tenderloins
¼ teaspoon salt
⅛ to ¼ teaspoon ground red pepper
1 teaspoon cooking oil
1 medium sweet potato, peeled, halved lengthwise, and thinly sliced
1 small fresh banana pepper, seeded and chopped (see tip, page 37)
¾ cup unsweetened pineapple juice
1 teaspoon cornstarch
2 unripe bananas, quartered lengthwise and cut into ¾-inch pieces
2 cups hot cooked brown rice

Spicy Orange Chicken

A perfect pair! The vitamin C in oranges helps your body better absorb the iron in the spinach. If you need a little rice to soak up every drop of this flavorful dish, add 15 grams of carbohydrate for ⅓ cup cooked long grain rice.

1 Remove peel and white membrane from one orange. Slice orange crosswise; halve slices. Set aside. Squeeze enough juice from the remaining orange to measure ⅓ cup; set aside. In a 4-quart Dutch oven heat 1 teaspoon of the oil over medium heat. Add the spinach; cover and cook for 4 to 5 minutes or just until wilted, stirring occasionally. Drain and transfer to a serving platter. Cover and keep warm.

2 Meanwhile, in a small bowl combine the ⅓ cup orange juice, the soy sauce, honey, ginger, cornstarch, and crushed red pepper. Set aside.

3 Sprinkle chicken with salt and black pepper. Wipe out Dutch oven with a paper towel. In Dutch oven heat the remaining 2 teaspoons oil over medium-high heat. Add garlic; cook and stir for 30 seconds. Add chicken; cook and stir for 2 to 3 minutes or until chicken is no longer pink. Stir orange juice mixture; add to chicken in Dutch oven. Cook and stir until thickened and bubbly. Cook and stir for 1 minute more.

4 To serve, arrange orange slices on top of spinach. Spoon chicken mixture over oranges and spinach.

Start to Finish: 30 minutes
Makes: 4 servings

2	oranges
1	tablespoon cooking oil
2	10-ounce packages baby spinach
1	tablespoon reduced-sodium soy sauce
1	teaspoon honey
1	teaspoon grated fresh ginger
½	teaspoon cornstarch
⅛ to ¼	teaspoon crushed red pepper
1	pound skinless, boneless chicken breast strips
¼	teaspoon salt
¼	teaspoon freshly ground black pepper
3	cloves garlic, minced

Nutrition Facts per serving: 207 cal., 6 g total fat (1 g sat. fat), 66 mg chol., 521 mg sodium, 8 g carbo., 5 g sugar, 13 g fiber, 31 g pro.
Daily Values: 158% vit. A, 93% vit. C, 14% calcium, 58% iron
Exchanges: 2 Vegetable, 4 Very Lean Meat, ½ Fat

34 g
carb

Curried Chicken and Potato Packets

Your family will love the Indian flavors of chicken and vegetables cooked in a velvety sour cream sauce. Individual serving packets give this dish flair; precooked chicken strips make it fast.

1 Tear off four 24×18-inch pieces of heavy foil. Fold each piece in half to make a double thickness of foil that measures 18×12 inches; set aside.

2 In a large bowl combine frozen chicken, potatoes, carrots, and onion; set aside. In a small bowl combine sour cream, curry powder, mustard, salt, paprika, and crushed red pepper. Pour over chicken mixture; toss to coat.

3 Divide chicken mixture among the foil pieces. Bring up opposite long edges of foil and seal with a double fold. Fold ends to completely enclose chicken mixture, leaving space for steam to build.

4 Place chicken packets on the rack of an uncovered grill directly over medium coals. Grill about 25 minutes or until vegetables are tender, turning once or twice. To serve, carefully and slowly open packets to allow steam to escape.

Prep: 15 minutes
Grill: 25 minutes
Makes: 4 servings

- 1   9-ounce package frozen cooked chicken breast strips
- 4   medium potatoes, cut into ¾-inch cubes
- 1½ cups packaged peeled baby carrots
- 1   small onion, thinly sliced
- ½   cup light dairy sour cream or plain low-fat yogurt
- 1   teaspoon curry powder
- 1   teaspoon Dijon-style mustard
- ½   teaspoon salt
- ½   teaspoon paprika
- ⅛   teaspoon crushed red pepper

Nutrition Facts per serving: 270 cal., 6 g total fat (2 g sat. fat), 55 mg chol., 720 mg sodium, 34 g carbo., 5 g sugar, 4 g fiber, 22 g pro.
Daily Values: 238% vit. A, 39% vit. C, 10% calcium, 14% iron
Exchanges: 1 Vegetable, 2 Starch, 2 Very Lean Meat, ½ Fat

Chicken Manicotti with Red Pepper Cream Sauce

Roasted red peppers, reduced-fat cream cheese, and fat-free milk combine to make a rich, creamy sauce that envelops these chicken- and broccoli-filled manicotti. It's sure to satisfy.

1 Cook pasta according to package directions; drain. Rinse with cold water; drain again.

2 Meanwhile, for sauce, in a small heavy saucepan cook and stir cream cheese and ¼ cup of the milk over medium-low heat until smooth. Stir in the remaining milk. In a blender container or food processor bowl combine cream cheese mixture, roasted sweet peppers, Parmesan cheese, salt, and ¼ teaspoon black pepper. Cover and blend or process until smooth.

3 For filling, in a large bowl stir together ¾ cup of the sauce, the broccoli, chicken, green onion, and ¼ teaspoon black pepper. Using a small spoon, stuff each manicotti shell with about ¼ cup filling or each jumbo shell with 2 to 3 tablespoons filling. Place in a 3-quart rectangular baking dish. Bake, covered, in a 350° oven for 30 minutes or until heated through.

4 To serve, reheat the remaining sauce. Arrange manicotti or jumbo shells on dinner plates. Spoon sauce over shells.

Prep: 40 minutes
Bake: 30 minutes
Oven: 350°F
Makes: 6 servings

- **12** manicotti shells or 18 jumbo pasta shells
- **1** 8-ounce package reduced-fat cream cheese (Neufchâtel), cut up
- **¾** cup fat-free milk
- **½** of a 7-ounce jar roasted red sweet peppers (½ cup), drained and chopped, or one 4-ounce jar diced pimiento, drained
- **3** tablespoons grated Parmesan cheese
- **¼** teaspoon salt
- **¼** teaspoon black pepper
- **1** 10-ounce package frozen chopped broccoli, thawed and drained
- **1** 9-ounce package frozen diced cooked chicken, thawed (2 cups)
- **2** tablespoons thinly sliced green onion
- **¼** teaspoon black pepper

Nutrition Facts per serving: 344 cal., 13 g total fat (7 g sat. fat), 69 mg chol., 350 mg sodium, 31 g carbo., 3 g sugar, 3 g fiber, 24 g pro.
Daily Values: 27% vit. A, 97% vit. C, 14% calcium, 11% iron
Exchanges: 1½ Vegetable, 1½ Starch, 2½ Lean Meat, 1 Fat

3 g
carb

Prosciutto-Stuffed Turkey Breast

This dish calls for a special occasion. Classic Italian ingredients such as prosciutto, pine nuts, and Parmesan combine for a knock-your-socks-off savory roast.

1 For stuffing, in a medium saucepan cook leek in 2 teaspoons of the hot oil until tender. Stir in bread crumbs, nuts, Parmesan cheese, 2 tablespoons of the fresh sage, and the parsley. Set aside.

2 Remove skin from turkey breast in one piece; set aside. Remove bone; split breast into 2 equal pieces. Place breast halves, skinned sides down, on plastic wrap so the two halves form a square. Cover with plastic wrap. Pound with the flat side of a meat mallet into a rectangle about ½ inch thick.

3 To stuff, place prosciutto on top of turkey. Spoon stuffing on top of prosciutto. Starting from a side that is parallel to the turkey seam, roll up turkey. Wrap skin around turkey; secure with 100-percent-cotton string.

4 Place turkey roll on a rack in a shallow roasting pan. Brush with remaining oil. Insert a meat thermometer into center of turkey roll. Roast in a 375° oven for 1¼ to 1½ hours or until turkey is no longer pink and meat thermometer registers 170°F. Remove from oven. Transfer turkey roll to a cutting board; reserve pan drippings. Cover turkey loosely with foil; let stand for 10 minutes before slicing.

5 For gravy, spoon 2 tablespoons drippings into a medium saucepan. Stir in flour. Stir in chicken broth and wine. Add the remaining sage. Cook and stir until thickened and

Prep: 30 minutes
Roast: 1¼ hours
Stand: 10 minutes
Oven: 375°F
Makes: 12 servings

- 1 large leek, thinly sliced (½ cup)
- 4 teaspoons olive oil or cooking oil
- ½ cup soft bread crumbs, toasted
- ⅓ cup pine nuts, toasted
- ¼ cup grated Parmesan cheese
- 3 tablespoons snipped fresh sage or 1 tablespoon dried sage, crushed
- 2 tablespoons snipped fresh parsley
- 1 4½- to 5-pound whole turkey breast
- 4 ounces thinly sliced prosciutto or cooked ham
- 2 tablespoons all-purpose flour
- 1⅓ cups reduced-sodium chicken broth
- ¼ cup dry white wine or reduced-sodium chicken broth

bubbly. Cook and stir for 2 minutes more. Serve the turkey with gravy.

Nutrition Facts per serving: 303 cal., 15 g total fat (4 g sat. fat), 101 mg chol., 435 mg sodium, 3 g carbo., 0 g sugar, 0 g fiber, 37 g pro.
Daily Values: 1% vit. A, 2% vit. C, 6% calcium, 13% iron
Exchanges: 5½ Lean Meat

Nut-Crusted Turkey Breast

It doesn't have to be Thanksgiving to cook a turkey, and you needn't bother with the fuss of a whole bird when it's the breast that makes those great healthful leftovers for sandwiches.

1 Remove skin from turkey breast. Place turkey breast on a lightly greased rack in a shallow roasting pan. Combine oil, salt, and garlic; brush over breast. Insert a meat thermometer into thickest part of breast, not touching bone. Roast in a 375° oven for 30 minutes.

2 Meanwhile, in a blender container or food processor bowl combine almonds and pine nuts. Cover and blend or process until finely chopped. In a small bowl combine the finely chopped nuts, coriander, cinnamon, and pepper.

3 Remove turkey breast from oven. Brush surface with orange marmalade. Sprinkle with nut mixture; press gently so nuts adhere. Roast for 30 to 45 minutes more or until meat thermometer registers 170°F. Remove from oven. Cover loosely with foil; let stand for 15 minutes before slicing.

Nutrition Facts per serving: 245 cal., 10 g total fat (2 g sat. fat), 72 mg chol., 130 mg sodium, 9 g carbo., 6 g sugar, 1 g fiber, 31 g pro.
Daily Values: 4% calcium, 13% iron
Exchanges: ½ Other Carbo., 4½ Very Lean Meat, 1½ Fat

Prep: 15 minutes
Roast: 1 hour
Stand: 15 minutes
Oven: 375°F
Makes: 8 to 10 servings

1　3- to 3½-pound turkey breast half with bone
1　tablespoon olive oil or cooking oil
¼　teaspoon salt
1　clove garlic, minced
⅓　cup slivered almonds
⅓　cup pine nuts or slivered almonds
1　teaspoon ground coriander
¼　teaspoon ground cinnamon
¼　teaspoon coarsely ground black pepper
¼　cup orange marmalade

Asian-Style Turkey

This versatile and tasty dish is great to serve to kids of all ages (teenagers love 'em) who prefer not to use a knife and fork. Be sure to soak the wooden skewers before broiling so they don't catch fire.

1 Cut turkey lengthwise into thin strips. Place turkey in a plastic bag set in a shallow dish.

2 For marinade, in a small bowl combine white wine, orange juice, soy sauce, water, rice vinegar, oil, garlic powder, and ginger. Pour over turkey; seal bag. Marinate in the refrigerator for 4 hours, turning the bag occasionally. Drain turkey, discarding marinade.

3 Thread turkey, accordion-style, onto skewers, leaving ¼ inch between strips. (If using wooden skewers, soak in water for 30 minutes before broiling.) Place skewers on the unheated rack of a broiler pan. Broil 4 to 5 inches from the heat for 8 to 10 minutes or until turkey is no longer pink, turning occasionally to brown evenly.

Prep: 20 minutes
Marinate: 4 hours
Broil: 8 minutes
Makes: 4 servings

1	pound turkey breast tenderloin or skinless, boneless chicken breast halves
¼	cup dry white wine
¼	cup orange juice
¼	cup soy sauce
2	tablespoons water
1	tablespoon rice vinegar
1	tablespoon cooking oil
1	teaspoon garlic powder
1	teaspoon ground ginger

Nutrition Facts per serving: 161 cal., 3 g total fat (1 g sat. fat), 68 mg chol., 514 mg sodium, 1 g carbo., 1 g sugar, 0 g fiber, 28 g pro.
Daily Values: 7% vit. C, 2% calcium, 8% iron
Exchanges: 4 Very Lean Meat, ½ Fat

Savory Mushroom Burgers

These grilled turkey burgers are a mushroom lover's fantasy. Mushrooms are heaped on top as a tasty tease and packed into the juicy patties too.

1 Remove stems from mushrooms. Finely chop half of the mushrooms (you should have about 1 cup); slice the remaining mushrooms and set aside. In a small saucepan cook finely chopped mushrooms and garlic in ½ cup of the chicken broth for 4 to 5 minutes or until tender. Stir in bulgur. Bring to boiling; reduce heat. Simmer, covered, about 10 minutes or until bulgur is tender and liquid is absorbed. Remove from heat; cool slightly.

2 In a large bowl combine ground turkey, green onion, Worcestershire sauce, and black pepper. Add bulgur mixture; mix well. Shape into four ¾-inch-thick patties.

3 Place patties on the greased rack of an uncovered grill directly over medium coals. Grill for 14 to 18 minutes or until turkey is no longer pink (165°F), turning once.

4 Meanwhile, in a covered small saucepan cook the sliced mushrooms in the remaining broth for 4 to 5 minutes or until tender.

5 If desired, spread mustard on bottom halves of buns. Serve burgers and sliced mushrooms in buns.

Prep: 25 minutes
Grill: 14 minutes
Makes: 4 servings

7 ounces fresh mushrooms (such as chanterelle, porcini, shiitake, and/or button)
2 cloves garlic, minced
¾ cup chicken broth
3 tablespoons bulgur
12 ounces uncooked ground turkey breast
2 tablespoons thinly sliced green onion
2 teaspoons Worcestershire sauce
¼ teaspoon black pepper
Dijon-style mustard (optional)
4 hamburger buns or Kaiser rolls, split and toasted

Nutrition Facts per serving: 303 cal., 9 g total fat (2 g sat. fat), 55 mg chol., 456 mg sodium, 29 g carbo., 4 g sugar, 3 g fiber, 26 g pro.
Daily Values: 2% vit. C, 9% calcium, 17% iron
Exchanges: 1 Vegetable, 1½ Starch, 3 Lean Meat

Pasta with Arugula and Smoked Sausage

Lean, smoked turkey or chicken sausage adds lots of flavor punch to this hearty pasta entrée without overloading it with fat.

1 Cut sausage lengthwise into quarters; cut into ¼-inch slices. Set aside. In a large skillet cook leek and garlic in hot oil until tender. Stir in sausage, chicken broth, and roasted sweet peppers. Bring to boiling; reduce heat. Add arugula and cook for 1 to 2 minutes or until arugula is wilted, stirring frequently. Remove from heat.

2 Meanwhile, cook pasta according to package directions; drain. Add cooked pasta, basil, Parmesan cheese, and black pepper to sausage mixture; toss gently to combine.

Nutrition Facts per serving: 266 cal., 6 g total fat (2 g sat. fat), 25 mg chol., 442 mg sodium, 38 g carbo., 1 g sugar, 2 g fiber, 14 g pro.
Daily Values: 23% vit. A, 88% vit. C, 15% calcium, 16% iron
Exchanges: 1½ Vegetable, 2 Starch, 1 Lean Meat

Start to Finish: 30 minutes
Makes: 4 servings

- 4 ounces smoked turkey or chicken sausage
- 1 large leek, cut into ¼-inch slices (½ cup)
- 2 cloves garlic, minced
- 1 teaspoon olive oil
- ⅔ cup reduced-sodium chicken broth
- ½ of a 7-ounce jar (½ cup) roasted red sweet peppers, drained and cut into thin bite-size strips
- 8 cups torn arugula or spinach leaves
- 6 ounces dried medium bow tie pasta
- ¼ cup snipped fresh basil
- ¼ cup finely shredded Parmesan cheese
- ½ teaspoon cracked black pepper

Skillet-Style Lasagna

Lasagna, traditionally a time-consuming, calorie-laden recipe, gets updated with a lighter fat and calorie profile and a no-fuss top-of-the-range method. Never fear—all the traditional flavors of this family favorite are still delightfully present.

1 Remove casings from sausage, if present. In a large skillet cook sausage and onion until meat is brown, breaking up meat during cooking. Drain fat. Stir in spaghetti sauce and water. Bring to boiling. Stir in noodles and zucchini. Return to boiling; reduce heat. Simmer, covered, about 12 minutes or until noodles are tender, stirring occasionally.

2 Meanwhile, in a small bowl stir together ricotta cheese, Parmesan cheese, and parsley. Using a spoon, drop cheese mixture into 6 mounds on top of sausage mixture. Sprinkle the mounds with mozzarella cheese.

3 Cook, covered, over low heat for 4 to 5 minutes or until the cheese mixture is heated through. Let stand for 10 minutes before serving.

Prep: 20 minutes
Cook: 16 minutes
Stand: 10 minutes
Makes: 6 servings

8	ounces uncooked turkey sausage
½	cup chopped onion
2	cups light bottled spaghetti sauce
1	cup water
2	cups dried wide noodles
1½	cups coarsely chopped zucchini
½	cup fat-free ricotta cheese
2	tablespoons grated Parmesan or Romano cheese
1	tablespoon snipped fresh parsley
½	cup shredded reduced-fat mozzarella cheese (2 ounces)

Nutrition Facts per serving: 214 cal., 7 g total fat (3 g sat. fat), 35 mg chol., 670 mg sodium, 20 g carbo., 8 g sugar, 2 g fiber, 17 g pro.
Daily Values: 9% vit. A, 13% vit. C, 22% calcium, 12% iron
Exchanges: 1 Vegetable, 1 Starch, 2 Lean Meat

Turkey Noodle Soup

The tangy flavor of lemon lends a delightfully brisk lift to a classic turkey noodle soup. It's a perfect way to use leftover cooked turkey or chicken that is tucked away in your freezer.

1 In a large saucepan combine chicken broth, water, turkey, carrots, onion, celery, and, if using, dried thyme. Bring to boiling; reduce heat. Simmer, covered, for 15 minutes.

2 Stir in the noodles and squash. Cook, uncovered, for 10 to 12 minutes or until noodles are tender. Stir in lemon juice and, if using, fresh thyme. Cook, uncovered, for 1 minute more.

Nutrition Facts per serving: 165 cal., 3 g total fat (1 g sat. fat), 46 mg chol., 428 mg sodium, 18 g carbo., 3 g sugar, 2 g fiber, 17 g pro.
Daily Values: 125% vit. A, 17% vit. C, 4% calcium, 10% iron
Exchanges: 1 Vegetable, 1 Starch, 1½ Very Lean Meat

Start to Finish: 45 minutes
Makes: 5 servings

3 cups reduced-sodium chicken broth
2¼ cups water
1½ cups chopped cooked turkey or chicken
1 cup thinly sliced carrots
1 medium onion, cut into thin wedges
½ cup thinly sliced celery
2 teaspoons snipped fresh thyme or
　　1 teaspoon dried thyme, crushed
2 cups dried wide noodles
1 medium yellow summer squash,
　　quartered lengthwise and sliced
　　(1⅓ cups)
2 tablespoons lemon juice

Fish & Shellfish

12 g
carb

Citrus Sole

The slightly sweet, creamy sauce lends rich flavor and the oranges bring pizzazz to the delicate sole. You'll be surprised by how much the orange slices intensify in flavor as they cook.

1 Thaw fish, if frozen. Prepare Citrus Sauce. Cover and chill until ready to serve. Remove peel and white membrane from oranges; cut each orange into 4 slices. Set aside.

2 Rinse fish; pat dry with paper towels. Place fish on the greased unheated rack of a broiler pan, tucking under any thin edges. In a small bowl combine margarine, salt, paprika, and pepper; brush over fish. Arrange orange slices around fish on broiler rack. Broil about 4 inches from the heat for 4 to 6 minutes or until fish flakes easily when tested with a fork and orange slices are heated through. To serve, drizzle Citrus Sauce over the fish and orange slices.

Citrus Sauce: In a small bowl stir together ½ cup light dairy sour cream, 2 tablespoons orange marmalade, and ¼ teaspoon dried thyme or herbes de Provence, crushed.

Prep: 15 minutes
Broil: 4 minutes
Makes: 4 servings

- **4** 3-ounce fresh or frozen sole or whitefish fillets, about ½ inch thick
- **1** recipe Citrus Sauce
- **2** oranges
- **2** teaspoons margarine or butter, melted
- **¼** teaspoon salt
- **¼** teaspoon paprika
  Dash black pepper

Nutrition Facts per serving: 175 cal., 5 g total fat (2 g sat. fat), 51 mg chol., 257 mg sodium, 12 g carbo., 11 g sugar, 1 g fiber, 18 g pro.
Daily Values: 9% vit. A, 28% vit. C, 9% calcium, 2% iron
Exchanges: ½ Fruit, ½ Other Carbo., 2 Very Lean Meat, ½ Fat

Ginger-Marinated Sea Bass

You'll love the ease with which you can throw together this sweet-spicy-salty marinade. The bold flavors infused into the fish may even convert those who typically won't eat fish.

1 Thaw fish, if frozen. Rinse fish; pat dry with paper towels. Place fish in a shallow, nonmetallic dish. For marinade, in a small bowl combine teriyaki sauce, lemon juice, ginger, brown sugar, ground red pepper, and garlic. Pour over fish; turn fish to coat. Cover and marinate in the refrigerator for 1 to 2 hours, turning the fish occasionally. Drain fish, reserving marinade.

2 Coat the unheated rack of a broiler pan with cooking spray. Place fish on the prepared rack. Broil about 4 inches from the heat for 8 to 12 minutes or until fish flakes easily when tested with a fork, turning and brushing once with reserved marinade. Discard any remaining marinade. If desired, garnish the fish with cilantro.

Prep: 15 minutes
Marinate: 1 hour
Broil: 8 minutes
Makes: 4 servings

- **4** 6-ounce fresh or frozen sea bass or halibut steaks, cut 1 inch thick
- **¼** cup light teriyaki sauce
- **2** tablespoons lemon juice
- **1** tablespoon grated fresh ginger
- **2** teaspoons brown sugar
- **⅛** teaspoon ground red pepper
- **2** cloves garlic, minced
  Nonstick cooking spray
  Fresh cilantro sprigs (optional)

Nutrition Facts per serving: 193 cal., 3 g total fat (1 g sat. fat), 69 mg chol., 556 mg sodium, 6 g carbo., 4 g sugar, 0 g fiber, 33 g pro.
Daily Values: 6% vit. A, 7% vit. C, 2% calcium, 6% iron
Exchanges: ½ Other Carbo., 4 Very Lean Meat

Halibut with Strawberry Salsa

Strawberries make the basis of this wonderful salsa. Like most salsas, this is a balance of sweet and spicy. It's especially tasty spooned over snow-white halibut.

1 For strawberry salsa, in a small bowl stir together plum sauce, lime juice, and ginger. Remove 3 tablespoons of the mixture and combine with the salt and black pepper; set aside. Stir strawberries, cucumber, green onion, cilantro, and jalapeño pepper into the remaining mixture. Cover and chill for up to 1 hour.

2 Thaw fish, if frozen. Rinse fish; pat dry with paper towels. Coat the unheated rack of a broiler pan with cooking spray. Place fish on the prepared rack. Brush with the reserved 3 tablespoons plum sauce mixture. Sprinkle with sesame seeds.

3 Broil about 4 inches from the heat for 6 to 9 minutes or until fish flakes easily when tested with a fork. Serve the fish with strawberry salsa.

Nutrition Facts per serving: 175 cal., 3 g total fat (0 g sat. fat), 36 mg chol., 270 mg sodium, 12 g carbo., 8 g sugar, 1 g fiber, 24 g pro.
Daily Values: 8% vit. A, 66% vit. C, 8% calcium, 9% iron
Exchanges: ½ Fruit, ½ Other Carbo., 3 Very Lean Meat

Prep: 20 minutes
Broil: 6 minutes
Makes: 4 servings

3 tablespoons bottled plum sauce
3 tablespoons lime juice
½ teaspoon grated fresh ginger
¼ teaspoon salt
⅛ teaspoon black pepper
1 cup coarsely chopped strawberries
½ cup chopped, seeded cucumber
2 tablespoons thinly sliced green onion
2 tablespoons snipped fresh cilantro
½ of a small fresh jalapeño pepper, seeded and finely chopped (see tip, page 37)
4 4- to 5-ounce fresh or frozen halibut steaks, cut ¾ inch thick
   Nonstick cooking spray
1 teaspoon sesame seeds

Grilled Salmon with Herb Crust

The herb crust adds incomparable flavor to the salmon without a lot of effort. It also works beautifully with other grilled fish, such as tuna, halibut, and cod.

1 Thaw fish, if frozen. Rinse fish; pat dry with paper towels. Cut into 4 serving-size pieces; set aside.

2 In a food processor bowl combine oregano, cilantro, green onions, lemon juice, oil, salt, pepper, and garlic. Cover and process until chopped. Transfer to a shallow dish. (Or use a sharp knife to finely chop oregano, cilantro, green onions, and garlic. Transfer to a shallow dish. Stir in lemon juice, oil, salt, and pepper.) Generously coat both sides of fish with herb mixture.

3 Place fish on the greased rack of an uncovered grill directly over medium coals. Grill for 6 to 9 minutes or until fish flakes easily when tested with a fork, turning once.

Prep: 15 minutes
Grill: 6 minutes
Makes: 4 servings

12	ounces fresh or frozen skinless salmon fillets, about ¾ inch thick
⅓	cup coarsely snipped fresh oregano
⅓	cup coarsely snipped fresh cilantro
¼	cup sliced green onions
1	tablespoon lemon juice
2	teaspoons olive oil
¼	teaspoon salt
⅛	teaspoon black pepper
1	clove garlic

Nutrition Facts per serving: 126 cal., 5 g total fat (1 g sat. fat), 44 mg chol., 207 mg sodium, 2 g carbo., 0 g sugar, 0 g fiber, 17 g pro.
Daily Values: 11% vit. A, 11% vit. C, 3% calcium, 5% iron
Exchanges: 2½ Lean Meat

3 g
carb

Grilled Swordfish with Tomato Chutney

Once you taste this chutney, you'll find a million other uses for it. Go ahead and make a double batch and save the rest for later use with grilled pork chops or lamb.

1 Thaw fish, if frozen. For tomato chutney, in a medium saucepan heat 2 teaspoons olive oil over medium heat. Add leek; cook just until tender. Remove from heat. Stir in tomato, basil, capers, pepper, and salt. Cover and keep warm.

2 Rinse fish; pat dry with paper towels. Brush both sides of fish with 2 teaspoons olive oil. Place fish on the rack of an uncovered grill directly over medium coals. Grill for 8 to 12 minutes or until fish flakes easily when tested with a fork, turning once. Cut each fish steak in half. Serve the fish with tomato chutney.

Nutrition Facts per serving: 155 cal., 8 g total fat (2 g sat. fat), 32 mg chol., 218 mg sodium, 3 g carbo., 1 g sugar, 1 g fiber, 17 g pro.
Daily Values: 10% vit. A, 17% vit. C, 1% calcium, 7% iron
Exchanges: ½ Vegetable, 2½ Very Lean Meat, 1 Fat

Prep: 15 minutes
Grill: 8 minutes
Makes: 4 servings

- 2 6- to 8-ounce fresh or frozen swordfish or halibut steaks, cut 1 inch thick
- 2 teaspoons olive oil
- 1 small leek or 2 green onions, chopped (¼ cup)
- 1 cup chopped, seeded tomato
- ¼ cup snipped fresh basil
- 1 tablespoon drained capers
- ¼ teaspoon black pepper
- ⅛ teaspoon salt
- 2 teaspoons olive oil

Orange Roughy with Mustard Sauce

Orange roughy is often well-received because of its mild fish flavor. Don't hesitate to try this recipe with another type of fish fillet—just measure the thickness of the fillet and cook accordingly. The mustard sauce will complement anything you choose.

1 Prepare Mustard Sauce. Cover and chill for 1 hour.

2 Thaw fish, if frozen. Rinse fish; pat dry with paper towels. Cut into 4 serving-size pieces. In a small bowl stir together curry powder and cooking oil; brush on both sides of fish.

3 Coat the unheated rack of a broiler pan with cooking spray. Place fish on prepared rack. Broil about 4 inches from the heat for 4 to 6 minutes per ½-inch thickness of fish or until fish flakes easily when tested with a fork. Serve the fish with the Mustard Sauce. Garnish with fresh ginger.

Mustard Sauce: In a small bowl stir together ⅓ cup plain fat-free yogurt, 1 tablespoon lime juice, and 2 teaspoons Dijon-style mustard.

Prep: 15 minutes
Chill: 1 hour
Broil: 4 minutes
Makes: 4 servings

1 recipe Mustard Sauce
1 pound fresh or frozen orange roughy or other fish fillets, ½ to ¾ inch thick
1 tablespoon curry powder
1 tablespoon cooking oil
   Nonstick cooking spray
1 ½-inch piece fresh ginger, peeled and cut into thin bite-size strips

Nutrition Facts per serving: 129 cal., 5 g total fat (1 g sat. fat), 23 mg chol., 102 mg sodium, 3 g carbo., 1 g sugar, 1 g fiber, 18 g pro.
Daily Values: 2% vit. A, 3% vit. C, 9% calcium, 4% iron
Exchanges: 2½ Very Lean Meat, 1 Fat

18 g carb

Crispy Orange Roughy with Dilled Yogurt Sauce

There's no need to fry in oil when you get great results like these crispy fillets with oven "frying." The simple dill sauce makes a nice accompaniment to the fish. If you like, change the herb for a different sauce every time.

1 Thaw fish, if frozen. Rinse fish; pat dry with paper towels. Cut into 4 serving-size pieces. Coat a shallow baking pan with cooking spray; set aside.

2 In a shallow dish combine cornmeal, thyme, and lemon-pepper seasoning. In another shallow dish beat egg white and water until frothy. In a third shallow dish combine bread crumbs, wheat germ, parsley, and paprika. Dip fish in cornmeal mixture, shaking off any excess. Dip in egg white mixture and coat with bread crumb mixture. Place in the prepared baking pan, tucking under any thin edges.

3 Bake in a 450° oven for 4 to 6 minutes per ½-inch thickness of fish or until fish flakes easily when tested with a fork.

4 Meanwhile, prepare Dilled Yogurt Sauce. Serve the fish with sauce and, if desired, lemon wedges.

Dilled Yogurt Sauce: In a small bowl stir together one 8-ounce container plain fat-free yogurt, ¼ cup lemon fat-free yogurt, 1 teaspoon dried dill, and a few dashes bottled hot pepper sauce.

Prep: 15 minutes
Bake: 4 minutes
Oven: 450°F
Makes: 4 servings

1 pound fresh or frozen orange roughy or other fish fillets, ½ to ¾ inch thick
  Nonstick cooking spray
¼ cup cornmeal
½ teaspoon dried thyme, crushed
¼ teaspoon lemon-pepper seasoning
1 egg white
2 tablespoons water
¼ cup fine dry bread crumbs
2 tablespoons toasted wheat germ
1 tablespoon snipped fresh parsley
½ teaspoon paprika
1 recipe Dilled Yogurt Sauce
  Lemon wedges (optional)

Nutrition Facts per serving: 190 cal., 2 g total fat (0 g sat. fat), 24 mg chol., 343 mg sodium, 18 g carbo., 4 g sugar, 1 g fiber, 24 g pro.
Daily Values: 8% vit. A, 4% vit. C, 20% calcium, 9% iron
Exchanges: 1 Starch, 3 Very Lean Meat

Red Snapper and Vegetable Packets

Cooking in packets is not only a great way to seal in flavor and moistness—it also reduces your cleanup time. Take care when opening the packets to avoid burns from the escaping steam.

1 Thaw fish, if frozen. If desired, remove and discard skin from fish. Rinse fish; pat dry with paper towels. Set aside.

2 In a medium microwave-safe bowl cover and microwave potatoes on 100 percent power (high) for 5 to 7 minutes or until nearly tender, stirring once. Add broccoli and about half the pesto; toss to coat.

3 Tear off four 12-inch squares of foil or parchment paper. Divide the vegetable mixture among foil squares. Top with fish, tucking under any thin edges. Spoon the remaining pesto over fish.

4 Bring up opposite edges of foil and seal with a double fold. Fold ends to completely enclose mixture, leaving space for steam to build. Place fish packets on a baking sheet.

5 Bake in a 400° oven about 15 minutes or until fish flakes easily when tested with a fork. To serve, carefully and slowly open packets to allow steam to escape.

Prep: 20 minutes
Bake: 15 minutes
Oven: 400°F
Makes: 4 servings

4	6-ounce fresh or frozen red snapper fillets (with skin), about ¾ inch thick
12	ounces tiny new potatoes, quartered
2	cups broccoli florets
⅓	cup purchased pesto

Nutrition Facts per serving: 376 cal., 12 g total fat (3 g sat. fat), 67 mg chol., 245 mg sodium, 25 g carbo., 2 g sugar, 3 g fiber, 42 g pro.
Daily Values: 16% vit. A, 80% vit. C, 18% calcium, 13% iron
Exchanges: 2 Vegetable, 1 Starch, 5 Very Lean Meat, 1 Fat

1 g
carb

Salmon Fillets in Garlic Broth

The salmon fillets bathe in a savory mixture of wine, fresh herbs, and garlic as they cook. Serve the fish and broth over cooked pasta, rice, or couscous to soak up every bit of the flavor.

1 Thaw fish, if frozen. Rinse fish; pat dry with paper towels. Sprinkle fish with salt and black pepper; set aside.

2 In a small bowl combine parsley, broth, wine, olive oil, red pepper, and garlic.

3 Place fish in a single layer in a 2-quart rectangular baking dish, tucking under any thin edges. Pour the parsley mixture evenly over fish.

4 Bake, uncovered, in a 425° oven for 8 to 12 minutes or until fish flakes easily when tested with a fork.

Nutrition Facts per serving: 163 cal., 6 g total fat (1 g sat. fat), 59 mg chol., 201 mg sodium, 1 g carbo., 0 g sugar, 0 g fiber, 23 g pro.
Daily Values: 5% vit. A, 7% vit. C, 2% calcium, 6% iron
Exchanges: 3 Lean Meat, 1 Fat

Prep: 15 minutes
Bake: 8 minutes
Oven: 425°F
Makes: 6 servings

6	4-ounce fresh or frozen skinless salmon fillets, about 1 inch thick
¼	teaspoon salt
⅛	teaspoon black pepper
¼	cup snipped fresh Italian flat-leaf parsley
¼	cup reduced-sodium chicken broth
¼	cup dry white wine
1	tablespoon olive oil
½	teaspoon crushed red pepper
4	large cloves garlic, minced

Salmon with Blackberry Sauce

The rich, velvetlike sauce of this showstopping dish contrasts with the flavor and color of the salmon. It's elegant and practical. Ready in just 30 minutes, serve it on a busy night or at your next summer dinner party.

1 Thaw fish, if frozen. For sauce, in a small saucepan combine jam, onion, thyme, mustard, and garlic. Bring just to boiling, stirring frequently; reduce heat. Simmer, uncovered, about 10 minutes or until sauce is slightly thickened. Remove from heat. Cover and keep warm.

2 Rinse fish; pat dry with paper towels. Coat the unheated rack of a broiler pan with cooking spray. Place fish on the prepared rack. Brush with about half of the melted margarine. Sprinkle with salt and, if desired, pepper.

3 Broil about 4 inches from the heat for 8 to 12 minutes or until fish flakes easily when tested with a fork, turning and brushing once with the remaining melted margarine.

4 To serve, spoon about 2 tablespoons of the sauce onto each dinner plate. Top with fish. Serve with lemon wedges and, if desired, fresh blackberries.

Start to Finish: 30 minutes
Makes: 4 servings

- **4** 6-ounce fresh or frozen salmon or halibut steaks, cut 1 inch thick
- **½** cup blackberry or apricot jam or preserves
- **2** tablespoons finely chopped onion
- **1** teaspoon snipped fresh thyme or ¼ teaspoon dried thyme, crushed
- **1** teaspoon Dijon-style mustard
- **1** small clove garlic, minced
- **2** tablespoons margarine or butter, melted
- **¼** teaspoon salt
- **⅛** teaspoon black pepper (optional)
  Lemon wedges
  Blackberries (optional)

Nutrition Facts per serving: 363 cal., 12 g total fat (2 g sat. fat), 88 mg chol., 346 mg sodium, 28 g carbo., 20 g sugar, 1 g fiber, 34 g pro.
Daily Values: 9% vit. A, 7% vit. C, 4% calcium, 9% iron
Exchanges: 2 Other Carbo., 4½ Lean Meat, 1½ Fat

Seared Tuna with Grapefruit-Orange Relish

Tuna steak stays moist and flavorful when cooked as quickly as possible. Pan-searing over high heat is ideal—it seals the juices on the inside and gives the outside an irresistible caramel-colored crust.

1 Thaw fish, if frozen. For citrus relish, in a small mixing bowl combine vinegar, soy sauce, and ginger. Whisk in the 1 tablespoon olive oil. Cut grapefruit sections into thirds and orange sections in half. Stir fruit, red onion, and cilantro into vinegar mixture. Set aside.

2 Rinse fish; pat dry with paper towels. In a large skillet heat the 2 teaspoons olive oil over medium-high heat. Add fish and cook for 6 to 9 minutes or until fish flakes easily when tested with a fork, turning once. Serve the fish with citrus relish. If desired, garnish with additional fresh cilantro.

Nutrition Facts per serving: 244 cal., 11 g total fat (2 g sat. fat), 43 mg chol., 199 mg sodium, 7 g carbo., 5 g sugar, 1 g fiber, 27 g pro.
Daily Values: 48% vit. A, 48% vit. C, 2% calcium, 7% iron
Exchanges: ½ Fruit, 4 Very Lean Meat, 1½ Fat

Prep: 20 minutes
Cook: 6 minutes
Makes: 4 servings

4   4-ounce fresh or frozen tuna steaks, cut ¾ inch thick
2   teaspoons sherry vinegar or white wine vinegar
2   teaspoons soy sauce
½   teaspoon grated fresh ginger
1   tablespoon olive oil
1   medium grapefruit, peeled and sectioned
1   medium orange, peeled and sectioned
2   tablespoons finely chopped red onion
2   tablespoons snipped fresh cilantro
2   teaspoons olive oil
     Fresh cilantro (optional)

Lemon-Thyme Fish Kabobs

When days warm up and you feel the urge to grill, try these fish and veggie skewers. Leave a little room on each side of the fish when you thread the skewers to help it cook evenly.

1 Thaw fish, if frozen. For marinade, in a medium bowl combine lemon juice, 1 tablespoon of the oil, the salt, thyme, and black pepper. Rinse fish; pat dry with paper towels. Cut into 1-inch cubes. Add fish to marinade; toss gently to coat. Cover and marinate at room temperature for 30 minutes. Drain fish, discarding the marinade.

2 In a large bowl combine the remaining 1 tablespoon oil and the lemon-pepper seasoning. Add mushrooms, squash, and sweet pepper; toss to coat. Alternately thread fish, mushrooms, squash, and sweet pepper onto eight 12-inch skewers, leaving ¼ inch between pieces. (If using wooden skewers, soak in water for 30 minutes before broiling.)

3 Coat the unheated rack of a broiler pan with cooking spray. Place fish skewers on the prepared rack. Broil about 4 inches from the heat for 8 to 10 minutes or until fish flakes easily when tested with a fork, turning once. Place a cherry tomato on the end of each skewer the last 2 minutes of broiling. If desired, serve the kabobs with hot cooked rice.

Grilling Method: Place skewers on the greased rack of an uncovered grill directly over medium coals. Grill for 8 to 12 minutes or until the fish flakes easily when tested with a fork, turning once. Place a cherry tomato on the end of each skewer the last 2 minutes of grilling.

Prep: 25 minutes
Marinate: 30 minutes
Broil: 8 minutes
Makes: 4 servings

12 ounces fresh or frozen skinless swordfish, tuna, or shark steaks, cut 1 inch thick
¼ cup lemon juice
2 tablespoons olive oil
½ teaspoon salt
½ teaspoon dried thyme, crushed, or 1 tablespoon fresh snipped thyme
⅛ teaspoon black pepper
¼ teaspoon lemon-pepper seasoning
12 medium fresh whole mushrooms
2 small zucchini or yellow summer squash, cut into 1-inch slices
1 medium yellow, green, or red sweet pepper, cut into 1-inch pieces
 Nonstick cooking spray
8 cherry tomatoes
3 cups hot cooked rice or orzo pasta (rosamarina) (optional)

Nutrition Facts per serving: 192 cal., 10 g total fat (2 g sat. fat), 32 mg chol., 369 mg sodium, 8 g carbo., 4 g sugar, 2 g fiber, 19 g pro.
Daily Values: 12% vit. A, 147% vit. C, 2% calcium, 9% iron
Exchanges: 1½ Vegetable, 2½ Very Lean Meat, 1½ Fat

43 g
carb

Salmon Tacos with Citrus Cucumber Slaw

Let the market guide your selection of fresh fish for these tacos and your choice of vegetables for the slaw. Any fresh, crunchy vegetable can replace the cucumber and cabbage—try broccoli, carrots, asparagus, zucchini, or pea pods.

1 For slaw, in a large bowl combine cabbage, cucumber, orange juice, onion, tomato, jalapeño pepper, grapefruit juice, and lime juice. Cover and chill for 2 to 8 hours.

2 Thaw fish, if frozen. Rinse fish; pat dry with paper towels. Place fillets in a shallow nonmetallic dish. Pour the Honey Marinade over fish; turn fish to coat. Cover and marinate in the refrigerator for 2 hours, turning fish occasionally. Drain fish, discarding the marinade.

3 Place fish on the greased rack of an uncovered grill directly over medium coals. Grill for 8 to 12 minutes or until fish flakes easily when tested with a fork, turning once. Remove from grill. Cut into 6 serving-size pieces.

4 To assemble tacos, divide fish among flour tortillas. Top with slaw; roll up tortillas. Garnish with cilantro sprigs.

Honey Marinade: In a small bowl combine ¼ cup honey, 1 tablespoon balsamic vinegar, 1 tablespoon cooking oil, 1 tablespoon water, 2 teaspoons ground cumin, 1 teaspoon ground coriander, and 1 teaspoon ground red Chimayo or New Mexico-style chile pepper.

Prep: 30 minutes
Chill: 2 hours
Grill: 8 minutes
Makes: 6 servings

2½ cups shredded green cabbage or other cabbage
1 medium cucumber, peeled (if desired), seeded, and cut into thin bite-size strips
½ cup orange juice
¼ cup thinly sliced red onion
1 medium Roma tomato, seeded and chopped
1 large fresh jalapeño pepper, seeded and finely chopped (see tip, page 37)
2 tablespoons grapefruit juice
2 tablespoons lime juice
1½ pounds fresh or frozen salmon fillets, about 1 inch thick
1 recipe Honey Marinade
6 10-inch flour tortillas, warmed
Fresh cilantro sprigs

Nutrition Facts per serving: 399 cal., 13 g total fat (2 g sat. fat), 62 mg chol., 240 mg sodium, 43 g carbo., 18 g sugar, 3 g fiber, 27 g pro.
Daily Values: 9% vit. A, 73% vit. C, 10% calcium, 16% iron
Exchanges: 2 Vegetable, ½ Fruit, 1 Starch, ½ Other Carbo., 3 Lean Meat, ½ Fat

Fish Cakes with Green Goddess Sauce

This sauce was originally developed in the 1920s in honor of an actor starring in a play called "The Green Goddess" and is frequently served both as a salad dressing and a sauce for fish. This enlightened version is every bit as good as the original from the San Francisco Palace Hotel.

1 Thaw fish, if frozen. Rinse fish; pat dry with paper towels. Cut into ½-inch pieces. In a medium bowl combine egg, bread crumbs, onion, mayonnaise dressing, parsley, mustard, lime peel, and salt. Add fish; mix well. Shape into 12 patties, about ½ inch thick. Place cornmeal in a shallow dish; coat the fish cakes with cornmeal.

2 In a large nonstick skillet or on a griddle heat oil over medium heat. Cook cakes, half at a time, in hot oil for 4 to 6 minutes or until golden brown, turning once. Drain on paper towels. Cover and keep warm in a 300°F oven while cooking the remaining cakes.

3 To serve, place 3 fish cakes on each dinner plate and top with 2 tablespoons of the Green Goddess Sauce. Cover and chill remaining sauce for another use.

Green Goddess Sauce: In a blender container or food processor bowl combine ¼ cup plain fat-free yogurt, ¼ cup light dairy sour cream, and 3 tablespoons snipped fresh tarragon. Cover and blend or process until smooth. Transfer to a small bowl. Stir in ¼ cup light dairy sour cream, 2 tablespoons snipped fresh chives, 2 teaspoons lime juice, and 1 clove garlic, minced. Makes ¾ cup.

Nutrition Facts per serving: 232 cal., 10 g total fat (3 g sat. fat), 113 mg chol., 436 mg sodium, 12 g carbo., 3 g sugar, 1 g fiber, 22 g pro.
Daily Values: 9% vit. A, 6% vit. C, 15% calcium, 10% iron
Exchanges: 1 Starch, 2½ Very Lean Meat, 1 Fat

Prep: 25 minutes
Cook: 4 minutes per batch
Makes: 4 servings

12 ounces fresh or frozen skinless haddock or cod fillets
1 beaten egg
¼ cup fine dry bread crumbs
2 tablespoons finely chopped onion
4 teaspoons light mayonnaise dressing or salad dressing
1 tablespoon snipped fresh Italian flat-leaf parsley
1 tablespoon Dijon-style mustard
1 teaspoon finely shredded lime peel
¼ teaspoon salt
2 tablespoons cornmeal
1 tablespoon cooking oil
1 recipe Green Goddess Sauce

Creamy Fish Chowder

In 30 minutes, you can have this tasty milk-based chowder on the table.
Add some zip by seasoning it with a few dashes of bottled hot pepper sauce.

1 Thaw fish, if frozen. Rinse fish; pat dry with paper towels. Cut fish into bite-size pieces. In a large saucepan cook onion in hot margarine over medium heat about 5 minutes or until tender.

2 Stir in flour. Add water all at once; stir until smooth. Stir in the potato, celery, sweet pepper, bay leaf, salt, and black pepper. Bring just to boiling; reduce heat. Simmer, covered, for 15 to 20 minutes or until potato is nearly tender.

3 Stir in milk and fish. Bring just to boiling; reduce heat. Simmer, uncovered, about 5 minutes or until fish flakes easily when tested with a fork. Stir in parsley. Remove bay leaf before serving.

Nutrition Facts per serving: 255 cal., 7 g total fat (1 g sat. fat), 51 mg chol., 484 mg sodium, 21 g carbo., 7 g sugar, 2 g fiber, 26 g pro.
Daily Values: 13% vit. A, 29% vit. C, 19% calcium, 6% iron
Exchanges: ½ Milk, 1 Starch, 2½ Very Lean Meat, ½ Fat

Prep: 20 minutes
Cook: 20 minutes
Makes: 4 servings

- 1 pound fresh or frozen skinless, boneless cod, haddock, or orange roughy fillets
- 1 cup chopped onion
- 2 tablespoons margarine or butter
- 3 tablespoons all-purpose flour
- 1½ cups water
- 1 cup peeled, cubed potato
- ½ cup chopped celery
- ¼ cup chopped green sweet pepper
- 1 bay leaf
- ½ teaspoon salt
- ¼ teaspoon black pepper
- 2 cups fat-free milk
- 1 tablespoon snipped fresh parsley

Spicy Shrimp Gazpacho

You may have had gazpacho before, but sweet shrimp and fragrant fruit give this version of summer's favorite soup a definite edge.

1 In a large bowl stir together the tomatoes, tomato juice, peaches, broth, cucumber, green onions, cilantro, jalapeño peppers, lime juice, sugar, hot pepper sauce, and garlic. Cover and chill for 2 to 24 hours. Just before serving, stir in shrimp.

Nutrition Facts per serving: 152 cal., 1 g total fat (0 g sat. fat), 124 mg chol., 334 mg sodium, 20 g carbo., 13 g sugar, 4 g fiber, 16 g pro.
Daily Values: 43% vit. A, 175% vit. C, 6% calcium, 21% iron
Exchanges: 2 Vegetable, ½ Fruit, 2 Very Lean Meat

Prep: 20 minutes
Chill: 2 to 24 hours
Makes: 4 to 6 servings

2 cups chopped, peeled tomatoes
2 cups low-sodium tomato juice
2 medium peaches or nectarines, peeled and chopped (1½ cups)
1 cup beef broth or vegetable broth
½ cup chopped, seeded cucumber
¼ cup sliced green onions
¼ cup snipped fresh cilantro
2 medium fresh jalapeño peppers, seeded and finely chopped (see tip, page 37)
2 tablespoons lime juice
1 teaspoon sugar
   Several dashes bottled hot pepper sauce
1 clove garlic, minced
1 8-ounce package frozen peeled, cooked shrimp, thawed

7 g
carb

Zucchini with Shrimp

When your garden is laden with zucchini, take advantage of this light dish. The zucchini and asparagus are steamed to retain the most nutrients and that fresh-from-the-garden flavor.

1 Thaw shrimp, if frozen. Rinse shrimp; pat dry with paper towels. Halve each zucchini lengthwise. Place each half, cut side down, on a cutting board; cut into long, thin strips. Set aside. Snap off and discard the woody bases from asparagus. Cut asparagus diagonally into bite-size pieces.

2 Place asparagus in a steamer basket over gently boiling water. Cover and steam for 2 minutes. Add zucchini and steam for 1 to 3 minutes more or just until vegetables are crisp-tender (do not overcook). Drain well; cover and keep warm.

3 Meanwhile, in a large skillet cook jalapeño pepper, ginger, and garlic in hot oil over medium-high heat for 30 seconds. Add shrimp. Cook and stir for 2 to 3 minutes or until shrimp are opaque.

4 Stir cilantro, sesame seeds, sesame oil, salt, and black pepper into shrimp mixture. Add steamed asparagus and zucchini; toss gently to coat. Transfer to a serving platter. If desired, sprinkle with additional snipped cilantro and/or toasted sesame seeds.

Start to Finish: 30 minutes
Makes: 4 servings

8 ounces fresh or frozen, peeled, deveined medium shrimp
5 medium zucchini (about 1¼ pounds)
8 ounces asparagus
1 fresh jalapeño pepper, seeded and finely chopped (see tip, page 37)
1 tablespoon grated fresh ginger
2 cloves garlic, minced
2 tablespoons cooking oil
2 tablespoons snipped fresh cilantro
1 tablespoon sesame seeds, toasted
2 teaspoons toasted sesame oil
¼ teaspoon salt
¼ teaspoon black pepper

Nutrition Facts per serving: 184 cal., 11 g total fat (2 g sat. fat), 86 mg chol., 241 mg sodium, 7 g carbo., 4 g sugar, 3 g fiber, 15 g pro.
Daily Values: 15% vit. A, 47% vit. C, 6% calcium, 14% iron
Exchanges: 1½ Vegetable, 1½ Very Lean Meat, 1½ Fat

Garlicky Shrimp and Olives

Purchased shrimp in shells can save money, but they take time to devein. If you're in a hurry, buy 10 ounces of peeled and deveined shrimp. If you serve the shrimp over pasta, add 20 grams of carbohydrate per ½ cup hot cooked pasta.

1 Thaw shrimp, if frozen. Peel and devein shrimp, leaving tails intact. Rinse shrimp; pat dry with paper towels. Set aside.

2 In a large skillet combine pimiento, olives, sherry, parsley, orange juice, capers, tomato paste, pepper, and garlic. Bring to boiling. Add shrimp. Cook and stir over medium-high heat for 1 to 3 minutes or until shrimp are opaque. If desired, serve the shrimp mixture over hot cooked pasta.

Nutrition Facts per serving: 118 cal., 2 g total fat (0 g sat. fat), 97 mg chol., 240 mg sodium, 6 g carbo., 2 g sugar, 1 g fiber, 14 g pro.
Daily Values: 18% vit. A, 49% vit. C, 6% calcium, 15% iron
Exchanges: 1 Vegetable, 1½ Very Lean Meat, ½ Fat

Start to Finish: 20 minutes
Makes: 4 servings

12 ounces fresh or frozen medium shrimp in shells
2 2-ounce jars diced pimiento, drained
10 pitted ripe olives, halved
¼ cup dry sherry or orange juice
2 tablespoons snipped fresh parsley
2 tablespoons orange juice
2 teaspoons drained capers
2 teaspoons tomato paste
⅛ teaspoon coarsely ground black pepper
2 cloves garlic, minced
Hot cooked fusilli pasta (optional)

BowTie Seafood Skillet

Shapes and colors balance harmoniously in this chic and lovely dish. The Basil Sauce is similar to pesto but far healthier and more subtle; it won't compete with the flavors of the seafood.

1 Thaw shrimp and scallops, if frozen. For marinade, in a medium bowl combine lemon peel, lemon juice, olive oil, salt, pepper, and garlic. Peel and devein shrimp. Rinse shrimp and scallops; pat dry with paper towels. Add shrimp and scallops to marinade; toss gently to coat. Cover and marinate in the refrigerator for 30 to 60 minutes. Drain shrimp and scallops, discarding marinade.

2 Meanwhile, prepare Basil Sauce; set aside. Cook pasta according to package directions; drain. Cover and keep warm.

3 Coat a large nonstick skillet with cooking spray. Heat skillet over medium heat. Add shrimp and scallops; cook and stir for 3 to 5 minutes or until shrimp and scallops are opaque. Remove from heat. Add the sauce and cooked pasta to shrimp mixture; toss gently to coat. Sprinkle with additional pepper.

Basil Sauce: In a blender container combine 2 cups packed fresh basil leaves, 2 tablespoons olive oil, 1 tablespoon lemon juice, ¾ teaspoon salt, and 2 cloves garlic, minced. Cover; blend until smooth.

Nutrition Facts per serving: 291 cal., 9 g total fat (1 g sat. fat), 113 mg chol., 516 mg sodium, 30 g carbo., 2 g sugar, 2 g fiber, 21 g pro.
Daily Values: 13% vit. A, 15% vit. C, 7% calcium, 16% iron
Exchanges: 2 Starch, 2 Very Lean Meat, 1½ Fat

Prep: 20 minutes
Marinate: 30 minutes
Cook: 3 minutes
Makes: 6 servings

12 ounces fresh or frozen medium shrimp in shells
8 ounces fresh or frozen sea scallops
1 teaspoon finely shredded lemon peel
2 tablespoons lemon juice
1 tablespoon olive oil
¼ teaspoon salt
¼ teaspoon freshly ground black pepper
2 cloves garlic, minced
1 recipe Basil Sauce
8 ounces dried bow tie pasta
Nonstick cooking spray

Pan-Seared Scallops with Lemon Vinaigrette

The oil in which the scallops cook is first infused with flavor, thanks to the addition (and removal) of lemon peel and fresh basil while the oil is warming. Use this same method to season oil for other dishes—change the herbs to create your own delicious combinations.

1 Thaw scallops, if frozen. Rinse scallops; pat dry with paper towels. Set aside.

2 Using a sharp knife, score lemon into 4 lengthwise sections; remove peel from lemon. Scrape white portion from peel; discard. Cut peel into very thin strips; set aside. Squeeze enough juice from lemon to measure 2 tablespoons; set aside.

3 In a large skillet cook asparagus and onion in 1 tablespoon of the hot oil over medium-high heat for 2 to 3 minutes or until crisp-tender, stirring frequently. Sprinkle with salt and pepper. Transfer asparagus mixture to a serving platter. Cover and keep warm.

4 In the same skillet combine the reserved lemon peel strips, the remaining 2 table-spoons oil, and the basil sprigs. Cook for 30 to 60 seconds or until heated through. Using a slotted spoon, remove lemon peel and basil sprigs, reserving oil in skillet. Discard lemon peel and basil sprigs.

5 Cook scallops in the reserved oil for 2 to 3 minutes or until scallops are opaque, stirring occasionally. Stir in the reserved lemon juice. Season to taste with salt and pepper.

6 Arrange the scallop mixture on top of asparagus mixture. If desired, garnish with fresh basil; serve with lemon wedges.

Start to Finish: 30 minutes
Makes: 4 servings

12	ounces fresh or frozen sea scallops
1	lemon
1	pound asparagus, trimmed and cut into 2-inch pieces
1	medium red onion, cut into wedges
3	tablespoons olive oil
¼	teaspoon salt
⅛	teaspoon black pepper
2	or 3 fresh basil sprigs
	Snipped fresh basil (optional)
	Lemon wedges (optional)

Nutrition Facts per serving: 189 cal., 11 g total fat (1 g sat. fat), 28 mg chol., 284 mg sodium, 7 g carbo., 2 g sugar, 2 g fiber, 16 g pro. **Daily Values:** 8% vit. A, 25% vit. C, 4% calcium, 5% iron **Exchanges:** 1 Vegetable, 2 Very Lean Meat, 1½ Fat

12 g
carb

Crab and Pasta Cakes with Cilantro-Lime Mayonnaise

Serrano peppers are slightly hotter than jalapeños, so use them sparingly if you prefer to keep the heat mild. If you prefer to skip the heat, substitute green sweet pepper.

1 Prepare Cilantro-Lime Mayonnaise. Cover and chill until ready to serve. Carefully clean lump crabmeat, removing any shell or cartilage pieces. Using kitchen shears, cut the cooked spaghetti into 1-inch pieces; set aside.

2 In a large bowl combine the eggs, green onions, bread crumbs, cilantro, serrano peppers, the 2 teaspoons oil, the salt, and black pepper. Add crabmeat and spaghetti pieces; mix well. Shape into 12 patties, about ½ inch thick.

3 In a large heavy skillet heat the 2 tablespoons oil over medium heat. Cook patties, a few at a time, in hot oil about 6 minutes or until golden brown, turning once. Drain on paper towels. Cover and keep warm in a 300°F oven while cooking the remaining patties.

4 Serve the crab cakes with Cilantro-Lime Mayonnaise and, if desired, lime and/or lemon wedges.

Cilantro-Lime Mayonnaise: In a small bowl combine ¼ cup light mayonnaise dressing or salad dressing, 1 tablespoon finely snipped fresh cilantro, ½ teaspoon finely shredded lime peel, and 1 tablespoon lime juice. Makes ½ cup.

Nutrition Facts per serving: 199 cal., 12 g total fat (2 g sat. fat), 112 mg chol., 375 mg sodium, 12 g carbo., 1 g sugar, 1 g fiber, 12 g pro.
Daily Values: 6% vit. A, 20% vit. C, 7% calcium, 7% iron
Exchanges: 1 Starch, 1 Very Lean Meat, 2 Fat

Prep: 25 minutes
Cook: 6 minutes per batch
Makes: 6 servings (12 crab cakes)

- **1** recipe Cilantro-Lime Mayonnaise
- **8** ounces cooked lump crabmeat, flaked, or flake-style imitation crabmeat
- **1** cup cooked spaghetti or linguine
- **2** beaten eggs
- **3** green onions, finely chopped
- **¼** cup fine dry bread crumbs
- **2** tablespoons snipped fresh cilantro
- **2** fresh serrano peppers, finely chopped, or 2 tablespoons chopped green sweet pepper (see tip, page 37)
- **2** teaspoons olive oil or cooking oil
- **¼** teaspoon salt
- **¼** teaspoon black pepper
- **2** tablespoons cooking oil
  Lime and/or lemon wedges (optional)

Meatless

Barley-Stuffed Cabbage Rolls

Your family is sure to love these slightly nutty, wonderfully savory cabbage rolls. Make a double batch on the weekend—one for this week and one to freeze!

1 Rinse wild rice with cold water; drain. In a medium saucepan combine the 1¾ cups water and the broth. Bring to boiling. Stir in rice and barley. Return to boiling; reduce heat. Simmer, covered, for 30 minutes. Stir in fennel, carrot, and thyme. Simmer, covered, for 10 to 15 minutes more or until rice and barley are tender; drain. Stir in walnuts.

2 Meanwhile, fill a large Dutch oven with water. Bring to boiling. Cut out center veins from cabbage leaves, keeping each leaf in one piece. Immerse leaves, 4 at a time, into the boiling water for 2 to 3 minutes or until leaves are limp. Drain well.

3 Place about ½ cup of the rice mixture on each cabbage leaf; fold in sides. Starting from an unfolded edge, carefully roll up each leaf. For sauce, in a medium bowl stir together the tomato sauce, brown sugar, and hot pepper sauce. Spoon about ¾ cup of the sauce into a 2-quart square baking dish. Place cabbage rolls in dish. Spoon remaining sauce over cabbage rolls.

4 Bake, covered, in a 400° oven about 25 minutes or until heated through. If desired, sprinkle with Parmesan cheese.

Prep: 55 minutes
Bake: 25 minutes
Oven: 400°F
Makes: 4 servings

⅓ cup uncooked wild rice
1¾ cups water
1 cup vegetable broth or chicken broth
½ cup regular barley
1 small fennel bulb, chopped (about ¾ cup)
½ cup shredded carrot
1 tablespoon snipped fresh thyme or
    ½ teaspoon dried thyme, crushed
¼ cup chopped walnuts, toasted
8 large cabbage leaves
2 8-ounce cans low-sodium tomato sauce
1 tablespoon brown sugar
  Few dashes bottled hot pepper sauce
  Grated Parmesan cheese (optional)

Nutrition Facts per serving: 304 cal., 6 g total fat (1 g sat. fat), 0 mg chol., 342 mg sodium, 57 g carbo., 22 g sugar, 14 g fiber, 7 g pro.
Daily Values: 80% vit. A, 92% vit. C, 8% calcium, 17% iron
Exchanges: 3 Vegetable, 2½ Starch, ½ Fat

Ravioli with Garbanzo Beans and Spinach

A popular pasta—cheese ravioli—gets an exciting and healthful update when tossed with unexpected ingredients. The garbanzo beans, spinach, and other vegetables contribute a generous amount of fiber—9 grams per serving.

1 Cook ravioli according to the package directions; drain. Cover and keep warm.

2 Meanwhile, in a large skillet heat oil over medium-high heat. Add garlic; cook and stir for 15 seconds. Add garbanzo beans, squash, tomatoes, thyme, and pepper. Cook and stir for 4 to 5 minutes or just until squash is tender.

3 Add the cooked ravioli to bean mixture; toss gently to combine. To serve, arrange the shredded spinach on a serving platter. Top with the ravioli mixture.

Nutrition Facts per serving: 386 cal., 9 g total fat (3 g sat. fat), 26 mg chol., 691 mg sodium, 60 g carbo., 2 g sugar, 9 g fiber, 19 g pro.
Daily Values: 47% vit. A, 56% vit. C, 38% calcium, 33% iron
Exchanges: 2½ Vegetable, 3 Starch, 1 Lean Meat, ½ Fat

Start to Finish: 20 minutes
Makes: 4 servings

1   9-ounce package refrigerated light
    cheese-filled ravioli
2   teaspoons olive oil
2   cloves garlic, minced
1   15-ounce can garbanzo beans, rinsed
    and drained
1   medium yellow summer squash, thinly
    sliced (about 1¼ cups)
4   Roma tomatoes, quartered
2   teaspoons snipped fresh thyme or
    ½ teaspoon dried thyme, crushed
¼   teaspoon coarsely ground black pepper
4   cups shredded spinach

Ziti with Ricotta and Vegetables

This is a dish to make when the tomato vines are laden with ripe red juicy tomatoes. The lovely seedless fresh sauce has no trace of bitterness—the vegetables sing in the sweet creamy flavor of the ricotta and fresh basil.

1 Cook pasta according to package directions, omitting any oil or salt and adding broccoli and asparagus the last 3 minutes of cooking; drain. Return pasta mixture to saucepan; cover and keep warm.

2 Meanwhile, place a fine-mesh sieve over a large bowl. Cut tomatoes in half; squeeze seeds and juice into sieve. Using the back of a spoon, press seeds to extract juice. Reserve tomatoes and juice; discard seeds.

3 Add ricotta cheese, basil, thyme, vinegar, oil, salt, pepper, and garlic to tomato juice in bowl; mix well. Chop the reserved tomatoes; stir into ricotta mixture. Add the cooked pasta mixture to ricotta mixture; toss to combine. Serve immediately. Sprinkle each serving with Parmesan cheese.

Nutrition Facts per serving: 368 cal., 8 g total fat (3 g sat. fat), 17 mg chol., 420 mg sodium, 57 g carbo., 11 g sugar, 5 g fiber, 17 g pro.
Daily Values: 38% vit. A, 115% vit. C, 20% calcium, 18% iron
Exchanges: 2 Vegetable, 3 Starch, 1 Lean Meat, ½ Fat

Start to Finish: 25 minutes
Makes: 4 servings

8	ounces dried ziti or penne pasta
2½	cups broccoli florets
1½	cups asparagus or green beans cut into 1-inch pieces
2	large ripe tomatoes
1	cup light ricotta cheese
¼	cup snipped fresh basil or 1 tablespoon dried basil, crushed
4	teaspoons snipped fresh thyme or 1 teaspoon dried thyme, crushed
4	teaspoons balsamic vinegar
1	tablespoon olive oil
½	teaspoon salt
½	teaspoon freshly ground black pepper
1	clove garlic, minced
2	tablespoons grated Parmesan or Romano cheese

Fettuccine with Eggplant Sauce

A little like tofu, the eggplant takes on the flavors of the remaining ingredients and lends this dish body, making it a highly satisfying meatless main course.

1 If desired, peel eggplant. Cut eggplant into ½-inch cubes.

2 In a large saucepan cook eggplant in hot oil about 7 minutes or until nearly tender. Add onion and garlic; cook and stir for 3 minutes more. Stir in tomato sauce, undrained tomatoes, sweet pepper, basil, and oregano. Bring to boiling; reduce heat. Simmer, covered, for 30 minutes. Add salt and pepper.

3 Meanwhile, cook pasta according to package directions; drain and return to saucepan. Pour the eggplant mixture over cooked pasta; toss gently to coat.

Nutrition Facts per serving: 324 cal., 6 g total fat (1 g sat. fat), 0 mg chol., 573 mg sodium, 57 g carbo., 10 g sugar, 5 g fiber, 9 g pro.
Daily Values: 4% vit. A, 29% vit. C, 5% calcium, 16% iron
Exchanges: 2½ Vegetable, 3 Starch, ½ Fat

Prep: 25 minutes
Cook: 30 minutes
Makes: 6 servings

- 1 small eggplant (12 ounces)
- 2 tablespoons olive oil
- ½ cup chopped onion
- 1 clove garlic, minced
- 1 15-ounce can tomato sauce
- 1 14½-ounce can Italian-style stewed tomatoes
- 1 medium green sweet pepper, cut into strips
- 2 teaspoons dried basil, crushed
- 1 teaspoon dried oregano, crushed
- ¼ teaspoon salt
- ⅛ teaspoon black pepper
- 12 ounces dried fettuccine

Mushroom Stroganoff

Here's a family-pleasing stroganoff in a healthy, meatless version. Experiment with any combination of mushrooms, all of which have their own unique taste.

1 Cook pasta according to package directions, except omit any oil or salt; drain. Return pasta to saucepan; cover and keep warm.

2 Meanwhile, in a small bowl stir together the sour cream and flour. In another small bowl stir together the water and bouillon cube until cube is dissolved. Stir bouillon and pepper into sour cream mixture. Set aside.

3 Remove stems from mushrooms. Thinly slice mushroom caps; set aside.

4 Coat a large skillet with cooking spray. Add margarine and heat over medium-high heat until melted. Add mushrooms, onions, and garlic; cook and stir until vegetables are tender. Stir in the sour cream mixture. Cook and stir until thickened and bubbly. Cook and stir for 1 minute more.

5 Pour the mushroom mixture over cooked pasta; toss gently to coat. Sprinkle with snipped parsley.

Start to Finish: 35 minutes
Makes: 4 servings

- 8 ounces dried fettuccine
- 1 8-ounce carton light dairy sour cream
- 2 tablespoons all-purpose flour
- ¾ cup warm water
- 1 large vegetable bouillon cube (enough for 2 cups broth)
- ¼ teaspoon black pepper
- 12 ounces assorted fresh mushrooms (such as shiitake, baby portobello, crimini, and/or button mushrooms) (5 cups)
  Nonstick cooking spray
- 1 tablespoon margarine or butter
- 2 medium onions, cut into thin wedges
- 1 clove garlic, minced
  Snipped fresh parsley

Nutrition Facts per serving: 363 cal., 10 g total fat (4 g sat. fat), 18 mg chol., 324 mg sodium, 55 g carbo., 8 g sugar, 3 g fiber, 15 g pro.
Daily Values: 11% vit. A, 6% vit. C, 14% calcium, 14% iron
Exchanges: 2 Vegetable, 3 Starch, 1½ Fat

Smoky Macaroni and Cheese

Watch those elbows disappear from the table when this creamy version of a timeless favorite is served. It has half the fat and calories of the typical homemade combo and twice the flavor—thanks to the smoked cheddar cheese.

1 Cook macaroni according to the package directions; drain. Return macaroni to saucepan. If desired, remove any darker outer layer from smoked cheese with a vegetable peeler. Shred cheese (you should have about ¾ cup); set aside.

2 For sauce, in a medium saucepan combine broth and onion. Bring to boiling; reduce heat to medium. Cook, covered, about 5 minutes or until onion is tender. In a screw-top jar combine half-and-half, flour, mustard, and pepper; cover and shake well. Add to onion mixture. Cook and stir just until bubbly. Remove from heat. Add smoked cheese, stirring until most of the cheese is melted. Pour the sauce over cooked macaroni; toss to combine. Pour into a 1½-quart casserole.

3 Bake, covered, in a 350° oven for 10 minutes. Uncover and bake about 10 minutes more or until bubbly. Let stand for 5 minutes. Top with chopped apple and Parmesan cheese.

Prep: 20 minutes
Bake: 20 minutes
Stand: 5 minutes
Oven: 350°F
Makes: 4 servings

- 8 ounces dried large elbow macaroni
- 3 ounces smoked cheddar cheese or smoked Gouda cheese
- 1 cup reduced-sodium chicken broth
- ½ cup chopped onion
- ¾ cup fat-free half-and-half
- 1 tablespoon all-purpose flour
- ½ teaspoon dry mustard
- ¼ teaspoon black pepper
- 1 medium tart apple, cored and coarsely chopped (⅔ cup)
- 1 tablespoon finely shredded Parmesan cheese

Nutrition Facts per serving: 373 cal., 9 g total fat (5 g sat. fat), 24 mg chol., 353 mg sodium, 56 g carbo., 8 g sugar, 3 g fiber, 16 g pro.
Daily Values: 5% vit. A, 5% vit. C, 21% calcium, 11% iron
Exchanges: 3½ Starch, 1 High-Fat Meat

Spinach Lasagna with Swiss Cheese Sauce

These lasagna rolls are a cross between lasagna and manicotti. The thick, cheesy sauce offers an interesting departure from classic lasagna.

1 Cook lasagna noodles according to package directions, except omit any oil or salt; drain. Rinse with cold water; drain again. Place noodles in a single layer on a sheet of foil; set aside.

2 For filling, in a large bowl combine the egg whites, ricotta cheese, spinach, half of the Swiss cheese, the Parmesan cheese, and, if desired, nutmeg.

3 Lightly coat a 2-quart rectangular baking dish with cooking spray; set aside. Spread about ⅓ cup of the filling on each lasagna noodle. Starting from a short end, roll up each noodle. Place the lasagna rolls, seam sides down, in the prepared baking dish; set aside.

4 For sauce, lightly coat a medium saucepan with cooking spray. Heat skillet over medium-high heat. Add mushrooms and green onions; cook and stir about 3 minutes or until vegetables are tender. In a medium bowl stir together ¼ cup of the evaporated milk and the flour until smooth; stir in the remaining evaporated milk and the salt. Stir the milk mixture into the mushroom mixture. Cook and stir until thickened and bubbly. Remove from heat. Stir in the remaining Swiss cheese until melted. Pour the sauce over the lasagna rolls.

5 Bake, covered, in a 350° oven about 35 minutes or until lasagna rolls are heated through. To serve, sprinkle with paprika.

Prep: 40 minutes
Bake: 35 minutes
Oven: 350°F
Makes: 8 servings

- 8 dried lasagna noodles
- 2 slightly beaten egg whites
- 1 15-ounce carton light ricotta cheese
- 1 10-ounce package frozen chopped spinach, thawed and well drained
- 6 ounces reduced-fat Swiss cheese, finely chopped
- ½ cup grated Parmesan cheese
- ¼ teaspoon ground nutmeg (optional)
  Nonstick cooking spray
- 1½ cups sliced fresh mushrooms
- ½ cup thinly sliced green onions
- 1 12-ounce can (1½ cups) evaporated fat-free milk
- 2 tablespoons all-purpose flour
- ¼ teaspoon salt
  Paprika

Nutrition Facts per serving: 250 cal., 6 g total fat (3 g sat. fat), 27 mg chol., 383 mg sodium, 27 g carbo., 4 g sugar, 2 g fiber, 21 g pro.
Daily Values: 63% vit. A, 17% vit. C, 55% calcium, 10% iron
Exchanges: 1 Vegetable, 1½ Starch, 2 Lean Meat

Cheese Calzones

It's easy to indulge in these cheese-stuffed Italian turnovers, even on a busy weeknight. Simply thaw the dough and spinach overnight in the refrigerator, then roll out and fill the calzones the next day.

1 Lightly coat a very large baking sheet with nonstick cooking spray; set aside. Divide bread dough into 8 equal pieces. Place dough on a floured surface and cover with a towel. Let dough rest while preparing filling.

2 For filling, in a small covered saucepan cook onion and garlic in a small amount of boiling water until onion is tender. Drain. Stir in spinach and the 1 teaspoon Italian seasoning. In a medium bowl stir together egg, ricotta, mozzarella, and Parmesan cheeses.

3 Roll each piece of dough into a 6-inch circle. Spread 2 tablespoons of the spinach mixture over half of each circle to within ½ inch of edge. Top with ¼ cup of the cheese mixture. Moisten edges of dough with water. Fold each circle in half, pinching edges or pressing edges together with tines of a fork to seal. Prick tops with a fork. Place calzones on the prepared baking sheet.

4 Bake in a 375° oven for 20 to 25 minutes or until golden. Meanwhile, in a small saucepan stir together tomato sauce, the ½ teaspoon Italian seasoning, and the 1 clove garlic; heat through. Serve with calzones.

Prep: 45 minutes
Bake: 20 minutes
Oven: 375°F
Makes: 8 servings

Nonstick cooking spray
1   16-ounce loaf frozen bread dough, thawed
½   cup chopped onion
2   cloves garlic, minced
1   10-ounce package frozen chopped spinach, thawed and well drained
1   teaspoon dried Italian seasoning, crushed
1   slightly beaten egg
1   15-ounce carton low-fat ricotta cheese
¾   cup shredded reduced-fat mozzarella cheese (3 ounces)
¼   cup grated Parmesan cheese
1   8-ounce can low-sodium tomato sauce
½   teaspoon dried Italian seasoning, crushed
1   clove garlic, minced

Nutrition Facts per calzone: 280 cal., 6 g total fat (3 g sat. fat), 43 mg chol., 542 mg sodium, 35 g carbo., 7 g sugar, 3 g fiber, 19 g pro.
Daily Values: 61% vit. A, 14% vit. C, 48% calcium, 16% iron
Exchanges: 1 Vegetable, 2 Starch, 1½ Lean Meat

Vegetarian Sloppy Joes

Ground meat substitutes made from soy beans are ideally suited for dishes that are highly seasoned—such as taco filling, chili, and sloppy Joes. It's sometimes called textured vegetable protein and is sold in health food stores and many grocery stores.

1 In a large skillet cook onion and sweet pepper in hot oil for 5 to 7 minutes or until tender. Stir in ground meat substitute, tomato puree, water, barbecue sauce, mustard, soy sauce (if desired), chili powder, and garlic.

2 Bring to boiling; reduce heat. Simmer, uncovered, for 20 minutes, stirring occasionally. Serve mixture in toasted buns.

Nutrition Facts per serving: 201 cal., 4 g total fat (1 g sat. fat), 0 mg chol., 431 mg sodium, 32 g carbo., 6 g sugar, 3 g fiber, 9 g pro.
Daily Values: 9% vit. A, 37% vit. C, 10% calcium, 14% iron
Exchanges: ½ Vegetable, 2 Starch, ½ Lean Meat

Prep: 20 minutes
Cook: 20 minutes
Makes: 8 to 10 servings

- 1 cup chopped onion
- 1 large green sweet pepper, chopped (1 cup)
- 1 tablespoon cooking oil
- 1½ cups refrigerated or frozen cooked and crumbled ground meat substitute (soy protein)
- 1 10¾-ounce can tomato puree
- 1 cup water
- ⅓ cup bottled barbecue sauce
- 1 tablespoon prepared mustard
- 1 tablespoon soy sauce (optional)
- 2 teaspoons chili powder
- 2 cloves garlic, minced
- 8 to 10 hamburger buns, split and toasted

Gazpacho Sandwich

Because these sandwiches must be made ahead to allow the flavors of the vegetables and herbs to meld together, they're perfect for a picnic lunch or an exceptional brown bag lunch.

1 Cut the French bread in half vertically. Cut a thin horizontal slice from the top of each portion; set aside. Using a paring knife, carefully remove bread from the center of each portion, leaving a ¼-inch shell. Reserve the center pieces of bread for another use.

2 Quarter the cherry tomatoes or halve the grape tomatoes. In a medium bowl stir together the tomatoes, mozzarella cheese, cucumber, onion, mint, vinegar, oil, salt, and white pepper. Line bottoms of bread shells with basil leaves. Fill with tomato mixture. Replace bread tops. Wrap each sandwich in plastic wrap and chill for 4 to 24 hours.

Nutrition Facts per serving: 284 cal., 10 g total fat (4 g sat. fat), 22 mg chol., 748 mg sodium, 36 g carbo., 5 g sugar, 3 g fiber, 12 g pro.
Daily Values: 22% vit. A, 31% vit. C, 22% calcium, 15% iron
Exchanges: 1 Vegetable, 2 Starch, 1 High-Fat Meat

Prep: 20 minutes
Chill: 4 to 24 hours
Makes: 2 servings

½ of an 8-ounce loaf baguette-style French bread
¾ cup yellow or red cherry tomatoes and/or grape tomatoes
2 ounces fresh mozzarella cheese, cubed
¼ cup coarsely chopped cucumber
2 thin slices red onion, separated into rings
1 tablespoon snipped fresh mint
1 tablespoon red wine vinegar
1 teaspoon olive oil
¼ teaspoon salt
⅛ teaspoon white pepper
½ cup fresh basil leaves

Pesto Bean Wraps

Bulgur, a whole grain that cooks quickly, can be used like rice or couscous. With an earthy taste and a tender, chewy texture, this Middle Eastern staple is simply wheat kernels that have been steamed, dried, and crushed.

1 In a large saucepan bring broth to boiling. Stir in bulgur. Return to boiling; reduce heat. Simmer, covered, for 10 minutes. Remove from heat. Stir in beans, sweet pepper, pesto, and green onions.

2 To serve, spoon the bean mixture onto centers of tortillas. Top with shredded lettuce. Roll up tortillas.

Test-Kitchen Tip: To cook your own beans, rinse ¾ cup dry beans. In a large Dutch oven combine beans and 5 cups water. Bring to boiling; reduce heat. Simmer, uncovered, for 2 minutes. Cover and let stand for 1 hour. Drain and rinse beans. In the same Dutch oven combine beans and 5 cups fresh water. Bring to boiling; reduce heat. Simmer, covered, for 1¼ to 1½ hours or until tender; drain.

Nutrition Facts per serving: 296 cal., 10 g total fat (2 g sat. fat), 4 mg chol., 407 mg sodium, 44 g carbo., 2 g sugar, 9 g fiber, 12 g pro.
Daily Values: 24% vit. A, 58% vit. C, 13% calcium, 21% iron
Exchanges: 3 Starch, ½ Very Lean Meat, 1 Fat

Start to Finish: 25 minutes
Makes: 6 servings

1⅓ cups vegetable broth or chicken broth
⅔ cup bulgur
2 cups cooked or canned red kidney beans, pinto beans, or other beans
1 medium red sweet pepper, chopped
⅓ cup purchased pesto
¼ cup thinly sliced green onions
6 8-inch tomato- or spinach-flavored flour tortillas
Shredded lettuce

Teriyaki Tempeh Pitas

You'll find tempeh, an Asian food staple (much the way tofu is, in some regions), in specialty markets and supermarkets with a large Asian foods section. Tempeh is a soy-based, meaty-textured protein full of phytonutrients.

1 Sprinkle tempeh slices with the five-spice powder. In a large skillet heat oil over medium heat. Cook tempeh slices in hot oil about 5 minutes or until light brown, turning once. Remove from heat. Sprinkle tempeh with soy sauce; set aside.

2 In a medium bowl stir together cabbage and hoisin sauce. Fill the pita halves with tempeh slices and cabbage mixture.

Nutrition Facts per serving: 395 cal., 17 g total fat (3 g sat. fat), 0 mg chol., 918 mg sodium, 38 g carbo., 4 g sugar, 2 g fiber, 26 g pro.
Daily Values: 88% vit. A, 27% vit. C, 20% calcium, 27% iron
Exchanges: ½ Vegetable, 2½ Starch, 2½ Medium-Fat Meat

Start to Finish: 15 minutes
Makes: 2 servings

- 1 8-ounce package tempeh, cut into thin slices
- 1 teaspoon five-spice powder
- 2 teaspoons roasted peanut oil or olive oil
- 2 tablespoons reduced-sodium soy sauce
- 1½ cups packaged shredded cabbage with carrot (coleslaw mix)
- 1 tablespoon bottled hoisin sauce
- 1 large pita bread round, halved crosswise

Vegetable Lo Mein

Lo mein is a healthful Chinese medley of veggies, noodles, and chicken or pork, coated with a stir-fry sauce and tossed together just before serving. In this meatless version, strips of fried egg "pancake" provide the protein.

1 In a small bowl combine mushrooms and the 1 cup boiling water. Cover and let stand for 20 minutes. Drain mushrooms, reserving ½ cup liquid. Chop mushrooms and set aside. Meanwhile, in a large saucepan cook noodles in additional boiling water for 5 minutes; drain. Return noodles to saucepan; cover and keep warm.

2 For egg strips, combine egg whites and whole egg. In a 10-inch nonstick skillet heat 1 teaspoon of the cooking oil and 1 teaspoon of the sesame oil over medium heat. Pour egg mixture into skillet. Lift and tilt skillet to form a thin layer of egg on the bottom. Cook, without stirring, for 2 to 3 minutes or just until set. Slide out onto a cutting board; cool slightly. Cut into 2×½-inch strips; set aside.

3 In the same skillet heat the remaining 1 teaspoon cooking oil and the remaining 1 teaspoon sesame oil over medium-high heat. Add mushrooms, ginger, crushed red pepper (if desired), and garlic. Cook and stir for 1 minute. Add snap peas and sweet pepper; cook and stir for 2 minutes more. Add the reserved mushroom liquid and the teriyaki sauce. Bring to boiling. Boil gently, uncovered, for 3 minutes.

4 Add the egg strips and vegetable mixture to cooked noodles; toss gently to combine. Serve immediately.

Start to Finish: 35 minutes
Makes: 4 servings

- 1 cup dried shiitake or Chinese black mushrooms (1 ounce)
- 1 cup boiling water
- 6 ounces dried udon noodles
- 2 egg whites
- 1 egg
- 2 teaspoons cooking oil
- 2 teaspoons toasted sesame oil
- 2 teaspoons finely chopped fresh ginger
- ½ teaspoon crushed red pepper (optional)
- 3 cloves garlic, minced
- 2 cups sugar snap peas or pea pods, halved
- 1 red sweet pepper, cut into thin bite-size strips
- ¼ cup light teriyaki sauce

Nutrition Facts per serving: 293 cal., 7 g total fat (1 g sat. fat), 53 mg chol., 434 mg sodium, 45 g carbo., 1 g sugar, 5 g fiber, 12 g pro.
Daily Values: 36% vit. A, 111% vit. C, 5% calcium, 17% iron
Exchanges: 1 Vegetable, 2½ Starch, ½ Lean Meat, 1 Fat

Vegetable and Tofu Stir-Fry

There are many types of tofu, so the uninitiated may find the supermarket shelf pretty confusing. Soft and silken tofu are delicate and work best in soups and gently cooked preparations. Firm tofu holds up well for stir-frying, scrambling, and other more robust handling.

1 Prepare rice according to package directions; keep warm.

2 For sauce, in a small bowl stir together the broth, dry sherry, cornstarch, soy sauce, sugar, ginger, and, if desired, crushed red pepper. Set aside.

3 Coat a wok or large skillet with cooking spray. Heat over medium-high heat. Add carrots and garlic to hot wok. Cook and stir for 2 minutes. Add broccoli; cook and stir for 3 to 4 minutes more or until vegetables are crisp-tender. Push vegetables from center of wok.

4 Stir the sauce. Add sauce to center of wok. Cook and stir until thickened and bubbly. Add tofu. Gently stir all ingredients together to coat with sauce. Cook, stirring gently, 1 minute more. Serve immediately over the hot cooked brown rice.

Start to Finish: 30 minutes
Makes: 4 servings

- 1½ cups instant brown rice
- ½ cup vegetable broth or chicken broth
- ¼ cup dry sherry
- 1 tablespoon cornstarch
- 1 tablespoon reduced-sodium soy sauce
- 1 teaspoon sugar
- 1 teaspoon grated fresh ginger
- ½ teaspoon crushed red pepper (optional)
  Nonstick cooking spray
- 1 cup thinly sliced carrots
- 3 cloves garlic, minced
- 3 cups broccoli florets
- 6 ounces extra-firm tofu (fresh bean curd), cut into ½-inch cubes

Nutrition Facts per serving: 216 cal., 3 g total fat (0 g sat. fat), 0 mg chol., 306 mg sodium, 39 g carbo., 5 g sugar, 5 g fiber, 9 g pro.
Daily Values: 174% vit. A, 108% vit. C, 6% calcium, 9% iron
Exchanges: 2 Vegetable, 2 Starch

Tabbouleh-Style Couscous with Tofu

Classic tabbouleh is a Middle Eastern dish of bulgur, tomatoes, onion, parsley, fresh mint, olive oil, and lemon juice. In this recipe, quick-cooking couscous is the main grain and tofu contributes enough protein to make it a main-dish meal. Serve it warm or chilled.

1 In a medium saucepan bring the broth to boiling. Stir in couscous. Remove from heat. Cover and let stand about 5 minutes or until liquid is absorbed.

2 Meanwhile, in a large nonstick skillet heat 1 tablespoon of the oil over medium-high heat. Add tofu, green onions, and garlic. Cook for 8 to 10 minutes or until tofu is light brown, turning carefully. (If necessary, reduce heat to medium to prevent overbrowning.)

3 In a large bowl combine the couscous, tofu mixture, the remaining 1 tablespoon oil, the tomatoes, basil, lemon juice, mint, and pepper; toss gently to coat. Sprinkle each serving with feta cheese.

Nutrition Facts per serving: 264 cal., 10 g total fat (3 g sat. fat), 8 mg chol., 257 mg sodium, 30 g carbo., 3 g sugar, 3 g fiber, 14 g pro.
Daily Values: 9% vit. A, 28% vit. C, 18% calcium, 11% iron
Exchanges: 2 Starch, 1 Medium-Fat Meat, ½ Fat

Start to Finish: 25 minutes
Makes: 6 servings

1⅓ cups reduced-sodium chicken broth or vegetable broth
1 cup quick-cooking couscous
2 tablespoons olive oil
1 16-ounce package extra-firm tofu (fresh bean curd), drained and cut into ½-inch cubes
⅔ cup sliced green onions
2 cloves garlic, minced
1½ cups chopped tomatoes
¼ cup snipped fresh basil
¼ cup lemon juice
1 tablespoon snipped fresh mint
¼ teaspoon black pepper
½ cup crumbled feta cheese (2 ounces)

Polenta with Broccoli

While the polenta stands after it cooks, it may get too thick. Add a tablespoon of water or broth and reheat the polenta until it reaches the desired consistency.

1 Prepare polenta according to package directions. Cover and keep warm. In a small bowl stir together broth and cornstarch; set aside.

2 In a large skillet cook onion in hot oil over medium heat for 4 to 5 minutes or until tender. Add garlic; cook and stir for 30 seconds more. Add broccoli. Cook and stir for 3 to 4 minutes or until crisp-tender. Stir in the roasted sweet peppers.

3 Stir broth mixture; add to vegetable mixture. Cook and stir until thickened and bubbly. Cook and stir 2 minutes more.

4 To serve, divide cooked polenta among 4 dinner plates. Spoon vegetable mixture over polenta. Sprinkle with pine nuts.

Start to Finish: 30 minutes
Makes: 4 servings

1 cup quick-cooking polenta mix
1 cup vegetable broth or chicken broth
1 tablespoon cornstarch
1 cup chopped onion
4 teaspoons olive oil
3 cloves garlic, minced
3 cups coarsely chopped broccoli florets
½ of a 7-ounce jar (½ cup) roasted red
    sweet peppers, drained and chopped
¼ cup pine nuts or slivered almonds,
    toasted

Nutrition Facts per serving: 390 cal., 11 g total fat (1 g sat. fat), 0 mg chol., 252 mg sodium, 67 g carbo., 2 g sugar, 10 g fiber, 11 g pro.
Daily Values: 20% vit. A, 192% vit. C, 6% calcium, 15% iron
Exchanges: 1½ Vegetable, 4 Starch, 1 Fat

Swiss Chard and Potato Frittata

A member of the beet family, Swiss chard contains carotenoids such as beta-carotene—those phytonutrients thought to play an anticancer role and to enhance immunity.

1 In a covered medium saucepan cook potatoes in a small amount of boiling lightly salted water for 10 to 12 minutes or until tender; drain. In a medium mixing bowl beat together the whole eggs, egg whites, chives, Parmesan cheese, milk, and pepper. Stir in potatoes; set aside.

2 In a large nonstick skillet cook onion in hot oil over medium heat about 5 minutes or until tender. Add Swiss chard. Cook about 15 minutes or until liquid is evaporated, stirring frequently.

3 Pour the egg mixture over Swiss chard mixture; do not stir. Cook over medium-low heat. As the egg mixture sets, run a spatula around edges of skillet, lifting egg mixture so the uncooked portion flows underneath. Continue cooking and lifting edges until the egg mixture is almost set (top will be wet). Cover and cook about 3 minutes more or just until top is set. Cut into wedges. Serve immediately.

Start to Finish: 25 minutes
Makes: 6 servings

3   medium red potatoes, peeled and cut into ½-inch cubes
4   eggs
3   egg whites
¼   cup snipped fresh chives
2   tablespoons finely shredded Parmesan cheese
2   tablespoons fat-free milk
¼   teaspoon freshly ground black pepper
1   medium onion, thinly sliced
1   tablespoon olive oil
4   cups chopped Swiss chard

Nutrition Facts per serving: 129 cal., 6 g total fat (2 g sat. fat), 144 mg chol., 151 mg sodium, 10 g carbo., 1 g sugar, 1 g fiber, 8 g pro.
Daily Values: 23% vit. A, 24% vit. C, 6% calcium, 7% iron
Exchanges: 1 Vegetable, ½ Starch, 1 Medium-Fat Meat

Southwestern Skillet

**One skillet is all you'll need to prepare this spicy egg combo.
If you top your eggs with sliced avocado, add 3 grams of carbohydrate.**

1 In a large skillet cook almonds over medium heat for 4 to 5 minutes or until lightly browned, stirring occasionally. Remove from skillet; set aside.

2 In the same skillet cook sweet pepper and jalapeño pepper in hot oil about 2 minutes or until tender. Stir in tomatoes, chili powder, cumin, and salt. Bring to boiling; reduce heat. Simmer, covered, for 5 minutes.

3 Break one of the eggs into a measuring cup. Carefully slide the egg into the simmering tomato mixture. Repeat with the remaining eggs. Sprinkle eggs lightly with salt and black pepper.

4 Cover and cook eggs over medium-low heat for 3 to 5 minutes or until whites are completely set and yolks begin to thicken but are not firm.

5 To serve, transfer eggs to serving plates with a slotted spoon. Stir tomato mixture; spoon around eggs on plates. Sprinkle with toasted almonds. If desired, serve with avocado slices.

Start to Finish: 25 minutes
Makes: 4 servings

- 2 tablespoons sliced almonds
- 1 yellow sweet pepper, cut into thin bite-size strips
- 1 fresh jalapeño pepper, seeded and chopped (see tip, page 37)
- 1 tablespoon olive oil or cooking oil
- 4 medium tomatoes, peeled and chopped
- 1 to 1½ teaspoons chili powder
- ½ teaspoon ground cumin
- ¼ teaspoon salt
- 4 eggs
- 1 medium ripe avocado, seeded, peeled, and sliced (optional)

Nutrition Facts per serving: 172 cal., 11 g total fat (2 g sat. fat), 213 mg chol., 228 mg sodium, 11 g carbo., 5 g sugar, 3 g fiber, 9 g pro.
Daily Values: 29% vit. A, 163% vit. C, 5% calcium, 10% iron
Exchanges: 2 Vegetable, 1 Medium-Fat Meat, 1 Fat

Crustless Feta and Cheddar Quiche

By omitting the pastry crust from this healthful quiche recipe, you can cut 9 grams of fat and 141 calories per serving. The feta and cheddar cheeses boost the flavor.

1 Lightly coat a 9-inch pie plate with cooking spray; set aside.

2 In a medium bowl combine egg product, flour, pepper, and salt. Stir in cottage cheese, broccoli, feta cheese, and cheddar cheese. Spoon into the prepared pie plate.

3 Bake in a 350° oven for 40 to 45 minutes or until a knife inserted near the center comes out clean. Cool on a wire rack for 5 to 10 minutes before serving.

Nutrition Facts per serving: 157 cal., 6 g total fat (4 g sat. fat), 26 mg chol., 523 mg sodium, 8 g carbo., 2 g sugar, 1 g fiber, 16 g pro.
Daily Values: 17% vit. A, 24% vit. C, 23% calcium, 6% iron
Exchanges: ½ Starch, 2 Lean Meat

Prep: 20 minutes
Bake: 40 minutes
Oven: 350°F
Makes: 8 servings

Nonstick cooking spray
1 cup refrigerated or frozen egg product, thawed
⅓ cup whole wheat pastry flour
¼ teaspoon black pepper
⅛ teaspoon salt
1½ cups low-fat cottage cheese (12 ounces), drained
1 10-ounce package frozen chopped broccoli, cooked and drained
1 cup crumbled feta cheese (4 ounces)
1 cup shredded reduced-fat cheddar cheese (4 ounces)

Tomato Polenta Pizza

Semolina is a type of wheat flour used in making pasta. Look for it in the baking section of your supermarket. If you are unable to find semolina, the quick-cooking polenta works just as well.

1 In a large saucepan bring milk just to boiling over medium heat. Sprinkle the semolina flour over milk, stirring constantly. Cook and stir for 2 minutes (mixture will be very stiff). Remove from heat and cool for 5 minutes. Stir in eggs, Asiago cheese, salt, and pepper.

2 Coat a 12-inch pizza pan with cooking spray. Spread the semolina mixture in the prepared pizza pan. Cover and chill for 2 to 24 hours. Arrange the tomato slices over semolina mixture. Top with mozzarella cheese.

3 Bake in a 400° oven about 20 minutes or until cheese is melted and beginning to brown. Sprinkle with fresh basil and/or oregano. Serve immediately.

Nutrition Facts per serving: 319 cal., 9 g total fat (5 g sat. fat), 94 mg chol., 376 mg sodium, 39 g carbo., 8 g sugar, 2 g fiber, 19 g pro.
Daily Values: 16% vit. A, 17% vit. C, 34% calcium, 13% iron
Exchanges: ½ Milk, ½ Vegetable, 2 Starch, 1 Medium-Fat Meat, ½ Fat

Prep: 25 minutes
Chill: 2 to 24 hours
Bake: 20 minutes
Oven: 400°F
Makes: 6 servings

3	cups fat-free milk
1½	cups semolina pasta flour or quick-cooking polenta mix
2	beaten eggs
½	cup finely shredded Asiago or Parmesan cheese (2 ounces)
¼	teaspoon salt
⅛	teaspoon black pepper Nonstick cooking spray
4	Roma tomatoes, very thinly sliced
1	cup shredded mozzarella cheese (4 ounces)
2	tablespoons snipped fresh basil and/or oregano

31 g
carb

Corn and Tomato Bread Pudding

The proof of a delicious dinner is in this pudding, a classic baked custard dessert reinvented as a savory main course. Cut cubes from firm, day-old (or older) bread because fresh bread is too soft to hold its shape after soaking up all the eggs and milk.

1 Place dried tomatoes in a small bowl and cover with boiling water. Cover and let stand about 15 minutes or until softened; drain.

2 Meanwhile, in a medium mixing bowl beat together eggs, milk, and basil; set aside. In a 2-quart square baking dish combine torn English muffins, corn, cheese, and softened tomatoes; toss to combine. Carefully pour egg mixture evenly over English muffin mixture.

3 Bake in a 375° oven about 30 minutes or until a knife inserted near the center comes out clean. Cool slightly.

4 If desired, arrange tomato wedges on dinner plates. Spoon the bread pudding on top of tomatoes.

Make-Ahead Tip: Prepare the mixture and the English muffin mixture as directed. Cover and chill separately for up to 24 hours. Continue as directed.

Prep: 20 minutes
Bake: 30 minutes
Oven: 375°F
Makes: 6 servings

- **3** tablespoons snipped dried tomatoes (not oil-packed)
- **4** eggs
- **1½** cups milk
- **1** tablespoon snipped fresh basil or 1 teaspoon dried basil, crushed
- **4** cups torn dry English muffins or French bread
- **1½** cups fresh or frozen whole kernel corn
- **1** cup shredded reduced-fat cheddar cheese or Monterey Jack cheese with jalapeño peppers (4 ounces)
- **1** tomato, cut into thin wedges (optional)

Nutrition Facts per serving: 272 cal., 9 g total fat (4 g sat. fat), 160 mg chol., 424 mg sodium, 31 g carbo., 3 g sugar, 3 g fiber, 16 g pro.
Daily Values: 10% vit. A, 7% vit. C, 29% calcium, 10% iron
Exchanges: 2 Starch, 1½ Medium-Fat Meat

Salad Meals

14 g
carb

Warm Fajita Salad

With lean beef, crisp vegetables, and salsa, this dish is a complete meal in itself. If you have room for dessert, try the Strawberries with Almond-Yogurt Cream, page 222.

1 For sauce, in a small bowl combine lime juice, broth, cilantro, cornstarch, and garlic. Set aside. Trim fat from meat. Cut meat into thin bite-size strips. Sprinkle with cumin, salt, and black pepper; toss to coat.

2 Lightly coat a large skillet with cooking spray. Heat skillet over medium-high heat. Add onions and sweet peppers; cook and stir for 3 to 4 minutes or until crisp-tender. Remove vegetables from skillet.

3 Add oil to hot skillet. Add meat; cook and stir for 2 to 3 minutes or until meat is slightly pink in center. Push meat from center of skillet.

4 Stir sauce. Add sauce to center of skillet. Cook and stir until thickened and bubbly. Return cooked vegetables to skillet. Stir all ingredients together to coat with sauce. Cook and stir until heated through.

5 To serve, arrange the salad greens and tomatoes on 4 dinner plates. Spoon meat mixture on top of greens. If desired, top with Baked Tortilla Strips; serve with salsa.

Baked Tortilla Strips: Cut 2 corn tortillas into ¼-inch strips. Place strips on an ungreased baking sheet. Coat with nonstick cooking spray. Combine ⅛ teaspoon each paprika and chili powder; sprinkle over tortilla strips. Bake in a 400° oven for 8 minutes or until golden and crisp, stirring once.

Start to Finish: 35 minutes
Oven: 400°F
Makes: 4 servings

¼ cup lime juice
¼ cup reduced-sodium chicken broth
1 tablespoon snipped fresh cilantro
1½ teaspoons cornstarch
2 cloves garlic, minced
12 ounces boneless beef top sirloin steak
½ teaspoon ground cumin
¼ teaspoon salt
¼ teaspoon black pepper
Nonstick cooking spray
2 small onions, cut into thin wedges
2 small green, red, and/or yellow sweet peppers, cut into thin strips
1 tablespoon cooking oil
1 10-ounce package torn mixed salad greens (about 8 cups)
12 cherry tomatoes, quartered
1 recipe Baked Tortilla Strips (optional)
Bottled salsa (optional)

Nutrition Facts per serving: 200 cal., 8 g total fat (2 g sat. fat), 52 mg chol., 246 mg sodium, 14 g carbo., 4 g sugar, 4 g fiber, 21 g pro.
Daily Values: 32% vit. A, 109% vit. C, 7% calcium, 18% iron
Exchanges: 2½ Vegetable, 2½ Lean Meat

Mango-Steak Salad with Cilantro Dressing

You'll love the sweet and spicy Latino flavors in this zippy salad. Make the steak salad as much as a day ahead, but save the dressing to drizzle over the greens just before serving.

1 Trim fat from steak. If using flank steak, score steak on both sides by making shallow diagonal cuts at 1-inch intervals in a diamond pattern. Sprinkle with salt and pepper.

2 Place steak on the rack of an uncovered grill directly over medium coals. Grill for 17 to 22 minutes for medium (160°F), turning once. Thinly slice the steak diagonally across the grain.

3 Meanwhile, for dressing, in a small mixing bowl whisk together the lime juice, oil, cilantro, honey, and garlic.

4 To serve, divide the romaine lettuce among 4 dinner plates. Top with steak slices, jicama, mango, and onion. Drizzle dressing over salads.

Broiler Method: Place steak on the unheated rack of a broiler pan. Broil 3 to 4 inches from the heat to medium doneness (160°F), turning once. (Allow 15 to 18 minutes for flank steak or 20 to 22 minutes for sirloin steak.)

Prep: 25 minutes
Grill: 17 minutes
Makes: 4 servings

- 12 ounces beef flank steak or boneless beef top sirloin steak, cut 1 inch thick
- ⅛ teaspoon salt
- ⅛ teaspoon black pepper
- ⅓ cup lime juice
- 2 tablespoons olive oil
- 2 tablespoons snipped fresh cilantro
- 1 tablespoon honey
- 2 cloves garlic, minced
- 6 cups torn romaine lettuce leaves
- 5 ounces jicama, peeled and cut into thin bite-size strips (1 cup)
- 1 medium mango, seeded, peeled, and sliced
- 1 small red onion, cut into thin wedges

Nutrition Facts per serving: 284 cal., 13 g total fat (4 g sat. fat), 34 mg chol., 128 mg sodium, 22 g carbo., 14 g sugar, 3 g fiber, 21 g pro.
Daily Values: 87% vit. A, 84% vit. C, 5% calcium, 16% iron
Exchanges: 1½ Vegetable, 1 Fruit, 2½ Lean Meat, 1 Fat

9 g
carb

Stir-Fried Beef and Apple Salad

Top round beef is very lean. If your market only carries it as larger roasts, freeze the extra portions for later use. Serve this salad warm or at room temperature— either way, it's sure to be a hit!

1 For dressing, in a screw-top jar combine rice vinegar, salad oil, chives, soy sauce, honey, cinnamon, and salt. Cover and shake well. Set aside.

2 Trim fat from meat. Cut meat into thin bite-size strips. Coat a large skillet with cooking spray. Add sesame oil to skillet. Heat skillet over medium-high heat. Add meat. Cook and stir in hot oil for 2 to 3 minutes or until meat is slightly pink in center. Add apple slices; cook and stir about 1 minute more or just until heated through. Sprinkle meat mixture with pepper.

3 To serve, divide the mixed greens among 4 dinner plates. Arrange meat mixture on top of greens. Shake dressing; drizzle over salads.

Start to Finish: 20 minutes
Makes: 4 servings

- ¼ cup rice vinegar
- 1 tablespoon salad oil
- 2 teaspoons snipped fresh chives
- 2 teaspoons reduced-sodium soy sauce
- 1 teaspoon honey or brown sugar
- ⅛ teaspoon ground cinnamon
   Dash salt
- 8 ounces beef top round steak
   Nonstick cooking spray
- 1 teaspoon toasted sesame oil
- 1 medium red apple, cored and thinly sliced
- ½ teaspoon coarsely cracked black pepper
- 6 cups torn mixed salad greens

Nutrition Facts per serving: 185 cal., 10 g total fat (3 g sat. fat), 33 mg chol., 164 mg sodium, 9 g carbo., 8 g sugar, 2 g fiber, 14 g pro.
Daily Values: 6% vit. A, 10% vit. C, 2% calcium, 10% iron
Exchanges: ½ Vegetable, ½ Fruit, 2 Lean Meat, 1 Fat

Pork and Pear Salad

Pork and pears combine in this perfect fall salad. Choose Red Bartlett pears and leave the pears unpeeled to add color and boost the fiber content. If the pears aren't ripe, place them in a paper bag and let them stand at room temperature for a few days.

1 Trim any fat from meat. Cut meat into thin bite-size strips. Sprinkle with sage and pepper. In a large skillet heat 1 tablespoon of the oil over medium-high heat. Add meat; cook and stir for 2 to 3 minutes or until meat is slightly pink in center. Add nuts; cook and stir for 30 seconds more. Remove meat mixture from skillet. Cover and keep warm.

2 For dressing, in the same skillet combine the remaining 1 tablespoon oil, the pineapple juice, honey, and mustard. Cook and stir just until bubbly, scraping up any brown bits on bottom of skillet.

3 Divide salad greens among 4 dinner plates. Arrange the pears on top of greens. Top with the meat mixture and drizzle with dressing. Serve immediately.

Start to Finish: 30 minutes
Makes: 4 servings

- 8 ounces boneless pork top loin roast or pork tenderloin
- ½ teaspoon dried sage, crushed
- ½ teaspoon black pepper
- 2 tablespoons olive oil
- ¼ cup coarsely chopped hazelnuts (filberts) or almonds, toasted
- ½ cup unsweetened pineapple juice
- 1 tablespoon honey
- 2 teaspoons Dijon-style mustard
- 1 8-ounce package torn mixed salad greens (about 7 cups)
- 2 medium pears, cored and sliced

Nutrition Facts per serving: 288 cal., 15 g total fat (2 g sat. fat), 31 mg chol., 47 mg sodium, 25 g carbo., 18 g sugar, 4 g fiber, 15 g pro.
Daily Values: 15% vit. A, 20% vit. C, 7% calcium, 9% iron
Exchanges: 2 Vegetable, 1 Fruit, 1½ Lean Meat, 2 Fat

30 g
carb

Roast Pork and Fruit Salad

Next time you roast a pork tenderloin, roast an extra! You'll be able to make and serve this irresistible salad in a jiffy.

1 For dressing, in a small bowl stir together the mayonnaise dressing, pineapple juice, the 1 tablespoon honey mustard, and the ginger. Cover and chill until ready to serve.

2 Trim any fat from meat. Place meat on a rack in a shallow roasting pan. Roast in a 425° oven for 20 minutes.

3 Spoon the 2 tablespoons honey mustard over meat. Roast for 5 to 10 minutes more or until juices run clear (160°F).

4 To serve, divide spinach, sliced fruit, and grapes among 4 dinner plates. Cut the meat into thin slices. Arrange meat slices on top of spinach mixture. Stir dressing; drizzle over salads. If desired, sprinkle with pepper.

Nutrition Facts per serving: 232 cal., 3 g total fat (1 g sat. fat), 50 mg chol., 202 mg sodium, 30 g carbo., 21 g sugar, 4 g fiber, 22 g pro.
Daily Values: 61% vit. A, 38% vit. C, 6% calcium, 15% iron
Exchanges: 1½ Vegetable, 1½ Fruit, 3 Very Lean Meat

Prep: 20 minutes
Roast: 25 minutes
Oven: 425°F
Makes: 4 servings

¼ cup fat-free mayonnaise dressing or salad dressing
¼ cup unsweetened pineapple juice or orange juice
1 tablespoon honey mustard
½ teaspoon grated fresh ginger
12 ounces pork tenderloin
2 tablespoons honey mustard
6 cups torn spinach and/or romaine lettuce leaves
2 cups sliced pears, apples, nectarines, and/or peeled peaches
1 cup green or red seedless grapes
Coarsely ground black pepper (optional)

Chicken Waldorf Salad

The original Waldorf Salad dates to the late 1800s and consisted only of apples, walnuts, and celery in a mayonnaise dressing. This updated, main-dish version adds chicken and dried cherries and substitutes pecans for the traditional walnuts.

1 In a medium bowl combine chicken, apples, dried cherries, pecans, and celery. For dressing, in a small bowl stir together mayonnaise dressing, sour cream, lemon juice, honey, and rosemary.

2 Pour dressing over chicken mixture; toss gently to coat. If desired, cover and chill for up to 24 hours. Serve the chicken mixture on lettuce leaves.

Nutrition Facts per serving: 336 cal., 10 g total fat (1 g sat. fat), 74 mg chol., 262 mg sodium, 34 g carbo., 24 g sugar, 4 g fiber, 29 g pro.
Daily Values: 8% vit. A, 14% vit. C, 7% calcium, 10% iron
Exchanges: 2 Fruit, 4 Very Lean Meat, 1½ Fat

Start to Finish: 20 minutes
Makes: 4 servings

12 ounces cooked skinless, boneless chicken breast halves, shredded or cubed (2 cups)
2 medium red and/or green apples, coarsely chopped (2 cups)
⅓ cup dried tart cherries
⅓ cup coarsely chopped pecans or peanuts
¼ cup thinly sliced celery
⅓ cup fat-free mayonnaise dressing or salad dressing
⅓ cup fat-free dairy sour cream
1 tablespoon lemon juice
1 tablespoon honey
1 to 1½ teaspoons dried rosemary, crushed
Lettuce leaves

29 g
carb

Chicken and Melon-Stuffed Shells

These impressive-looking cold stuffed shells make a memorable meal out of chicken salad. If you're short on time, purchase a roasted or rotisserie chicken breast from the grocery store or deli to substitute for the grilled chicken.

1 Cut each cantaloupe half into thirds. Cover and chill 4 of the wedges until ready to serve. Peel and chop the remaining 2 wedges; set aside.

2 Cook pasta shells according to package directions; drain. Rinse with cold water; drain again.

3 Meanwhile, in a large bowl combine chopped cantaloupe, chicken, honeydew melon, yogurt, lemon juice, chives, and mustard. Spoon about ¼ cup of the chicken mixture into each cooked pasta shell.

4 To serve, arrange 2 filled pasta shells and a cantaloupe wedge on each dinner plate. If desired, garnish with fresh thyme.

Start to Finish: 25 minutes
Makes: 4 servings

- 1 medium cantaloupe, halved and seeded
- 8 dried jumbo pasta shells
- 6 ounces chopped, cooked or grilled chicken (1 cup)
- ½ cup finely chopped, peeled honeydew melon
- ¼ cup plain low-fat yogurt
- 2 tablespoons lemon juice
- 1 tablespoon snipped fresh chives
- 1 teaspoon Dijon-style mustard
  Fresh thyme sprigs (optional)

Nutrition Facts per serving: 186 cal., 2 g total fat (0 g sat. fat), 26 mg chol., 55 mg sodium, 29 g carbo., 16 g sugar, 2 g fiber, 14 g pro.
Daily Values: 90% vit. A, 114% vit. C, 5% calcium, 7% iron
Exchanges: 1 Fruit, 1 Starch, 1½ Very Lean Meat

Chicken and Rice Salad

Ideal for everything from a ladies' luncheon to a Super Bowl party to a light summer supper, this salad is a complete meal all by itself. Jazz it up by serving the salad in a lettuce leaf or tomato halves .

1 In a medium saucepan bring water to boiling. Stir in uncooked rice. Return to boiling; reduce heat. Simmer, covered, about 15 minutes or until rice is tender. Place in a colander. Rinse with cold water; drain.

2 In a large bowl combine garbanzo beans, roasted sweet peppers, olives, and green onions. Drain artichokes, reserving the marinade. Chop artichokes; add to bean mixture. Stir in cooked rice.

3 Sprinkle chicken with chili powder and rosemary. In a large nonstick skillet heat 1 tablespoon of the reserved artichoke marinade over medium heat. Add chicken; cook and stir for 3 to 4 minutes or until chicken is no longer pink.

4 Stir the cooked chicken and the remaining artichoke marinade into rice mixture. Add feta cheese; toss gently to combine. Cover and chill for at least 6 to 24 hours.

Prep: 35 minutes
Chill: 6 to 24 hours
Makes: 6 servings

- 2 cups water
- 1 cup uncooked long grain rice
- ½ cup cooked or canned garbanzo beans, drained
- ½ of a 7-ounce jar (½ cup) roasted red sweet peppers, drained and chopped
- 1 2¼-ounce can sliced pitted ripe olives, drained
- ¼ cup thinly sliced green onions
- 1 6- or 6½-ounce jar marinated artichoke hearts
- 12 ounces skinless, boneless chicken breast halves, cut into bite-size strips
- 2 teaspoons chili powder
- ½ teaspoon dried rosemary, crushed
- ½ cup crumbled feta cheese with basil and tomato or plain feta cheese (2 ounces)

Nutrition Facts per serving: 265 cal., 6 g total fat (2 g sat. fat), 41 mg chol., 329 mg sodium, 34 g carbo., 1 g sugar, 3 g fiber, 19 g pro.
Daily Values: 8% vit. A, 71% vit. C, 9% calcium, 17% iron
Exchanges: 1 Vegetable, 2 Starch, 1½ Very Lean Meat, ½ Fat

13 g
carb

Curried Chicken Salad

Use a purchased deli-roasted chicken or the leftover poultry from last night's dinner as the main ingredient in this chilled salad. Crisp jicama and celery add snap to complement the juicy grapes. If you include the papaya, add 8 grams of carb.

1 Peel and section orange; halve or quarter each section. In a large bowl combine orange pieces, chicken, grapes, celery, and jicama.

2 For dressing, in a small bowl stir together mayonnaise dressing, yogurt, soy sauce, and curry powder. Pour dressing over chicken mixture; toss gently to coat. Cover and chill for 1 to 24 hours.

3 If desired, serve the chicken mixture in papaya halves and garnish with chives.

Nutrition Facts per serving: 220 cal., 9 g total fat (2 g sat. fat), 66 mg chol., 248 mg sodium, 13 g carbo., 10 g sugar, 2 g fiber, 22 g pro.
Daily Values: 3% vit. A, 22% vit. C, 5% calcium, 7% iron
Exchanges: 1 Fruit, 3 Very Lean Meat, 1½ Fat

Prep: 30 minutes
Chill: 1 to 24 hours
Makes: 6 servings

- 1 orange
- 3 cups cubed cooked chicken (about 1 pound)
- 1½ cups seedless red grapes, halved
- 1 cup thinly sliced celery
- ½ cup chopped, peeled jicama
- ¼ cup light mayonnaise dressing or salad dressing
- ¼ cup lemon low-fat yogurt
- 2 teaspoons soy sauce
- 1 teaspoon curry powder
- 3 small papayas, peeled, bias-sliced in half lengthwise, and seeded (optional)
  Fresh chives (optional)

Grilled Chicken Salad with Strawberry Dressing

Fresh berries, plums, and nectarines tossed with greens and grilled chicken make an ideal combination for a light summer dinner on the deck. Wait until the strawberries are at their best so the dressing has the sweetest flavor and brightest ruby red color.

1 Place chicken on the rack of an uncovered grill directly over medium coals. Grill for 12 to 15 minutes or until chicken is no longer pink (170°F), turning once. Cool slightly; cut chicken into pieces, about 2×1 inches in size.

2 Meanwhile, in a large bowl combine spinach, arugula, onion, and basil. To serve, divide the spinach mixture among 4 dinner plates. Arrange the plums, strawberries, and chicken on top of spinach mixture. Drizzle with the Strawberry Dressing.

Strawberry Dressing: In a food processor bowl or blender container combine ¾ cup cut-up strawberries, 2 tablespoons pourable strawberry all-fruit topping, 2 tablespoons olive oil, 4 teaspoons sherry vinegar or wine vinegar, ½ teaspoon grated fresh ginger, ¼ teaspoon salt, and ⅛ teaspoon black pepper. Cover and process or blend until smooth. Makes about ¾ cup.

Nutrition Facts per serving: 356 cal., 10 g total fat (1 g sat. fat), 82 mg chol., 240 mg sodium, 33 g carbo., 22 g sugar, 5 g fiber, 36 g pro.
Daily Values: 40% vit. A, 127% vit. C, 6% calcium, 12% iron
Exchanges: 1 Vegetable, 2 Fruit, 4½ Very Lean Meat, 1 Fat

Prep: 35 minutes
Grill: 12 minutes
Makes: 4 servings

4   skinless, boneless chicken breast halves
      (about 1¼ pounds total)
3   cups lightly packed, torn spinach leaves
1   cup lightly packed, torn arugula leaves
1   small red onion, thinly sliced and
      separated into rings
2   tablespoons snipped fresh basil
3   cups sliced golden plums and/or
      nectarines
2   cups sliced strawberries
1   recipe Strawberry Dressing

Dilled Tuna and Potato Salad

Purchase tuna packed in water instead of oil for this salad. Oil-packed tuna has significantly more fat and calories and less of the beneficial omega-3 fatty acids than the water-packed variety, which also has a milder flavor.

1 Scrub potatoes; cut into ½-inch cubes. In a covered medium saucepan cook potatoes in a small amount of boiling water for 10 to 12 minutes or just until tender. Drain and cool slightly.

2 Meanwhile, in a large bowl stir together mayonnaise dressing, yogurt, dill, milk, lemon peel, salt, and garlic. Stir in cucumber, green onions, and radishes. Add cooked potatoes, tuna, and chopped eggs; toss gently to coat. Cover and chill for 4 to 6 hours.

3 To serve, line 6 dinner plates with shredded lettuce. Gently stir tuna mixture and spoon on top of lettuce.

Nutrition Facts per serving: 227 cal., 10 g total fat (2 g sat. fat), 96 mg chol., 425 mg sodium, 19 g carbo., 3 g sugar, 2 g fiber, 16 g pro.
Daily Values: 17% vit. A, 32% vit. C, 10% calcium, 12% iron
Exchanges: ½ Vegetable, 1 Starch, 2 Lean Meat, 1 Fat

Prep: 30 minutes
Chill: 4 hours
Makes: 6 servings

3   medium red potatoes (about 1 pound)
½   cup light mayonnaise dressing or
        salad dressing
½   cup plain fat-free yogurt
1   tablespoon snipped fresh dill or
        1 teaspoon dried dill
1   tablespoon fat-free milk
½   teaspoon finely shredded lemon peel
¼   teaspoon salt
1   clove garlic, minced
1   cup chopped cucumber
¼   cup sliced green onions
¼   cup coarsely chopped radishes
1   9-ounce can chunk white tuna (water
        pack), drained and broken into chunks
2   hard-cooked eggs, chopped
6   cups shredded red-tipped leaf lettuce

Salmon Pinwheel Salad

Diners will marvel at these charming pinwheels—they look like they require more effort than they actually do. The salmon pinwheels can easily be poached the day before serving, and the Fresh Orange Dressing will keep in the refrigerator up to 3 days.

1 Thaw fish, if frozen. Rinse fish; pat dry with paper towels. Cut lengthwise into 6 even strips. Sprinkle lightly with the ⅛ teaspoon salt and ⅛ teaspoon pepper. Starting with the thick end of each strip, roll up into a pinwheel. Secure with a wooden toothpick or skewer.

2 In a medium skillet combine the white wine, bay leaf, the ¼ teaspoon salt, and ¼ teaspoon pepper. Bring to boiling. Add fish pinwheels. Return to boiling; reduce heat. Simmer, covered, for 6 to 8 minutes or until fish flakes easily when tested with a fork, turning once. Using a slotted spoon, remove fish from cooking liquid. Cover and chill for 2 to 12 hours. Discard cooking liquid.

3 To serve, divide the endive, leaf lettuce, orange sections, cucumber slices, and almonds among 6 dinner plates. Spoon the Fresh Orange Dressing over lettuce mixture. Top with the salmon pinwheels.

Fresh Orange Dressing: In a small bowl stir together ½ cup light dairy sour cream, ½ teaspoon finely shredded orange peel, 2 tablespoons orange juice, 2 teaspoons sugar, and ½ teaspoon poppy seeds. Stir in enough additional orange juice, 1 teaspoon at a time, to make dressing of desired consistency. Makes about ½ cup.

Prep: 30 minutes
Cook: 6 minutes
Chill: 2 hours
Makes: 6 servings

- 1 1½-pound fresh or frozen skinless salmon fillet, ½ to ¾ inch thick
- ⅛ teaspoon salt
- ⅛ teaspoon black pepper
- ½ cup dry white wine or water
- 1 bay leaf
- ¼ teaspoon salt
- ¼ teaspoon black pepper
- 4 cups torn curly endive
- 4 cups torn red-tipped leaf lettuce
- 2 medium oranges, peeled and sectioned
- 1 cup thinly sliced cucumber
- ¼ cup sliced almonds, toasted
- 1 recipe Fresh Orange Dressing

Nutrition Facts per serving: 227 cal., 9 g total fat (2 g sat. fat), 66 mg chol., 144 mg sodium, 9 g carbo., 5 g sugar, 3 g fiber, 26 g pro.
Daily Values: 34% vit. A, 39% vit. C, 11% calcium, 11% iron
Exchanges: 2 Vegetable, 3 Lean Meat, ½ Fat

45 g

carb

Noodle Salad with Shrimp

This cold noodle salad is fun for summertime dinners and makes a great totable picnic and lunch dish. It has plenty of refreshing crispy crunch.

1 For dressing, in a blender container combine vinegar, apricot preserves, honey, ginger, lemon peel, salt, oil, hot pepper sauce, and garlic. Cover and blend until smooth.

2 Place rice sticks in a medium bowl and cover with boiling water. Cover and let stand about 3 minutes or until softened; drain. Cut rice sticks into 2-inch pieces.

3 In a large bowl combine the rice sticks, shrimp, cabbage, cucumber, peas, and green onions. Pour the dressing over shrimp mixture; toss gently to coat.

4 To serve, arrange the shrimp mixture on 6 dinner plates. Sprinkle with peanuts and cilantro.

Nutrition Facts per serving: 303 cal., 4 g total fat (1 g sat. fat), 147 mg chol., 363 mg sodium, 45 g carbo., 19 g sugar, 4 g fiber, 20 g pro.
Daily Values: 17% vit. A, 36% vit. C, 8% calcium, 22% iron
Exchanges: 1 Vegetable, 1½ Starch, 1 Other Carbo., 2 Very Lean Meat, ½ Fat

Start to Finish: 30 minutes
Makes: 6 servings

⅔ cup rice vinegar
¼ cup apricot preserves
3 tablespoons honey
4 teaspoons grated fresh ginger
1 teaspoon finely shredded lemon peel
¼ teaspoon salt
¼ teaspoon toasted sesame oil
  Several dashes bottled hot pepper sauce
6 large cloves garlic, halved
4 ounces rice sticks
1 pound peeled, cooked shrimp
2 cups finely shredded savoy cabbage
1 seedless cucumber, halved lengthwise and sliced
1 cup frozen peas, thawed
6 green onions, sliced (⅔ cup)
¼ cup chopped dry roasted peanuts
2 tablespoons fresh cilantro leaves or small fresh cilantro sprigs

Mexican Crab Salad

This simple but elegant salad is easy to assemble—just the thing to serve when you are having guests for lunch. Serve the crab in hollowed-out tomatoes or over a bed of mixed greens.

1 Divide the salad greens among 6 dinner plates. Carefully clean lump crabmeat, removing any shell or cartilage pieces. Arrange the crabmeat, tomatoes, avocado, and chile peppers on top of salad greens. Sprinkle with onion and cilantro.

2 For dressing, in a screw-top jar combine the vinegar, oil, sugar, salt, and cumin. Cover and shake well. Pour the dressing over salads.

Nutrition Facts per serving: 168 cal., 11 g total fat (1 g sat. fat), 47 mg chol., 416 mg sodium, 8 g carbo., 4 g sugar, 3 g fiber, 11 g pro.
Daily Values: 21% vit. A, 37% vit. C, 9% calcium, 8% iron
Exchanges: 1½ Vegetable, 1½ Very Lean Meat, 2 Fat

Start to Finish: 25 minutes
Makes: 6 servings

- 6 cups mixed baby salad greens
- 2 cups cooked lump crabmeat or chunk-style imitation crabmeat
- 2 medium tomatoes, cut into wedges
- 1 medium ripe avocado, halved lengthwise, seeded, peeled, and sliced
- 1 4-ounce can diced green chile peppers, drained
- 2 tablespoons finely chopped red onion
- 2 tablespoons snipped fresh cilantro
- ¼ cup white vinegar
- 2 tablespoons olive oil or cooking oil
- 1 tablespoon sugar
- ½ teaspoon salt
- ½ teaspoon ground cumin

17 g

carb

Seafood Salad with Ginger-Cream Dressing

You'll love the interplay of piquant ginger, tangy sour cream, fruit, and seafood in this addictively delicious and deceptively simple salad.

1 In a large bowl combine the spinach, scallops, shrimp, peach slices, and mango slices. Pour the Ginger-Cream Dressing over scallop mixture; toss gently to coat.

2 To serve, divide the scallop mixture among 6 dinner plates. If desired, sprinkle with cashews.

Ginger-Cream Dressing: In a small bowl stir together ½ cup fat-free dairy sour cream, 2 tablespoons finely chopped crystallized ginger, 1 tablespoon sherry vinegar, ½ teaspoon finely shredded orange peel, and dash ground red pepper. Stir in enough orange juice (about 2 tablespoons) to make dressing of desired consistency. Season to taste with salt. Makes about ⅔ cup.

Make-Ahead Tip: Prepare Ginger-Cream Dressing as directed. Cover and chill for up to 3 days.

Nutrition Facts per serving: 182 cal., 3 g total fat (0 g sat. fat), 100 mg chol., 473 mg sodium, 17 g carbo., 9 g sugar, 2 g fiber, 22 g pro.
Daily Values: 90% vit. A, 46% vit. C, 10% calcium, 14% iron
Exchanges: 1½ Vegetable, ½ Fruit, 2½ Very Lean Meat, ½ Fat

Start to Finish: 25 minutes
Makes: 6 servings

8 cups torn spinach leaves or mixed salad greens
1 pound fresh or frozen scallops, cooked and chilled
8 ounces fresh or frozen peeled and deveined shrimp, cooked and chilled
1 large peach or nectarine or 2 apricots, pitted and sliced
1 large mango or small papaya, seeded, peeled, and sliced
1 recipe Ginger-Cream Dressing
2 tablespoons cashew halves or sliced almonds, toasted (optional)

Grilled Vegetable Salad

Tofu is a culinary chameleon—it picks up the flavors of the ingredients surrounding it. In this salad, the tofu absorbs the flavors of the dressing as it marinates. Quinoa, a grain that looks like rice, imparts a pleasing texture. Look for quinoa near the rice in your supermarket.

1 Cut the tofu lengthwise into 8 slices, ¼ to ½ inch thick. Place tofu in a shallow dish. Pour ¼ cup of the dressing over tofu; turn tofu to coat. Cover dish. Place vegetables in a plastic bag set in a deep bowl. Pour 3 tablespoons of the dressing over vegetables; seal bag. Marinate tofu and vegetables in the refrigerator for 4 to 24 hours, turning occasionally. Cover and chill the remaining dressing until ready to serve.

2 Place quinoa in a fine-mesh sieve and rinse with cold water. In a 2-quart saucepan bring the 2 cups water to boiling. Carefully stir in quinoa and barley. Return to boiling; reduce heat. Simmer, covered, about 15 minutes or until grains are tender and water is nearly absorbed; drain.

3 Meanwhile, drain tofu, discarding the marinade. Drain vegetables, reserving the marinade. Place vegetables on the rack of an uncovered grill directly over medium coals. Grill for 6 to 8 minutes or until vegetables are crisp-tender, turning occasionally. Remove from grill. Place tofu on the grill rack. Grill for 4 to 6 minutes or until lightly browned, turning once. Remove from grill. Cut tofu into triangles. Cover loosely with foil and keep warm.

4 In a large bowl combine the grilled vegetables and the reserved marinade; toss gently to coat. Set aside.

Prep: 20 minutes
Marinate: 4 to 24 hours
Cook: 15 minutes
Makes: 6 servings

- **1** 16-ounce package reduced-fat firm tofu (fresh bean curd), drained
- ¾ cup bottled reduced-fat Italian salad dressing
- **12** ounces yellow summer squash, halved lengthwise and cut into 2-inch pieces
- **4** large green, red, orange, and/or yellow sweet peppers, quartered and seeded
- ½ cup quinoa
- **2** cups water
- ½ cup quick-cooking barley
- ¼ cup shredded spinach leaves

5 In another large bowl combine shredded spinach, the cooked quinoa mixture, and the remaining dressing; toss gently to coat. Serve the tofu and vegetable mixture with quinoa mixture.

Nutrition Facts per serving: 232 cal., 7 g total fat (1 g sat. fat), 2 mg chol., 210 mg sodium, 32 g carbo., 2 g sugar, 7 g fiber, 13 g pro.
Daily Values: 51% vit. A, 181% vit. C, 7% calcium, 19% iron
Exchanges: 1½ Vegetable, 1½ Starch, 1 Lean Meat, ½ Fat

55 g
carb

Tangy Bulgur-Spinach Salad

Bulgur, also called cracked wheat, is a staple in many Middle Eastern cuisines. It is most often served as the key ingredient in tabbouleh salad.

1 In a medium bowl combine bulgur and boiling water. Cover and let stand about 10 minutes or until all of the water is absorbed. Let cool for 15 minutes.

2 Meanwhile, for dressing, in a small bowl stir together yogurt, vinaigrette salad dressing, parsley, and cumin.

3 In a large salad bowl combine the bulgur, spinach, beans, apple, and onion. Pour the dressing over spinach mixture; toss gently to coat.

Nutrition Facts per serving: 345 cal., 9 g total fat (2 g sat. fat), 3 mg chol., 670 mg sodium, 55 g carbo., 9 g sugar, 13 g fiber, 13 g pro.
Daily Values: 64% vit. A, 31% vit. C, 14% calcium, 19% iron
Exchanges: 2 Vegetable, 3 Starch, 1½ Fat

Start to Finish: 35 minutes
Makes: 4 servings

- 1 cup bulgur
- 1 cup boiling water
- ½ cup plain low-fat yogurt
- ¼ cup bottled red wine vinaigrette salad dressing
- 2 tablespoons snipped fresh parsley
- ½ teaspoon ground cumin
- 6 cups torn spinach leaves
- 1 15-ounce can garbanzo beans, rinsed and drained
- 1 cup coarsely chopped apple
- ½ of a medium red onion, thinly sliced and separated into rings

Spinach and Black Bean Salad

Dried apricots provide a flavor and nutrition boost to this pleasantly healthful black bean salad. If you find delectable fresh apricots in season, substitute 1 cup sliced fresh apricots and subtract 20 calories and 6 grams of carb from each serving.

1 In a large bowl combine the black beans, apricots, sweet pepper, green onion, cilantro, and garlic.

2 For dressing, in a screw-top jar combine apricot nectar, oil, vinegar, soy sauce, and ginger. Cover and shake well. Pour the dressing over the bean mixture; toss gently to coat. Cover and chill for 2 to 24 hours. To serve, add the spinach to bean mixture; toss to combine.

Nutrition Facts per serving: 195 cal., 7 g total fat (1 g sat. fat), 0 mg chol., 367 mg sodium, 30 g carbo., 9 g sugar, 8 g fiber, 9 g pro.
Daily Values: 93% vit. A, 81% vit. C, 9% calcium, 17% iron
Exchanges: 1½ Vegetable, ½ Fruit, 1 Starch, 1 Fat

Prep: 25 minutes
Chill: 2 to 24 hours
Makes: 4 servings

- 1 15-ounce can black beans, rinsed and drained
- ½ cup snipped dried apricots
- ½ cup chopped red and/or yellow sweet pepper
- 1 green onion, thinly sliced
- 1 tablespoon snipped fresh cilantro
- 1 clove garlic, minced
- ¼ cup apricot nectar
- 2 tablespoons salad oil
- 2 tablespoons rice vinegar
- 1 teaspoon soy sauce
- 1 teaspoon grated fresh ginger
- 4 cups shredded spinach

31 g
carb

Vegetable Salad with Chipotle Vinaigrette

You'll get a sensational surprise with each bite of this fresh veggie combo; the sweet-hot dressing wakes up your taste buds.

1 In a large bowl combine black beans, corn, jicama, sweet pepper, and onions. Set aside.

2 For vinaigrette, in a food processor bowl or blender container combine chipotle peppers, salad oil, lime juice, cilantro, oregano, salt, and garlic. Cover and process or blend until smooth.

3 Pour the vinaigrette over bean mixture; toss gently to coat. Cover and chill for 4 to 24 hours, stirring occasionally.

4 To serve, line 4 dinner plates with mixed greens. Spoon the bean mixture on top of greens. If desired, serve with chips.

Nutrition Facts per serving: 230 cal., 11 g total fat (2 g sat. fat), 0 mg chol., 383 mg sodium, 31 g carbo., 2 g sugar, 7 g fiber, 9 g pro.
Daily Values: 11% vit. A, 52% vit. C, 7% calcium, 12% iron
Exchanges: 1½ Vegetable, 1½ Starch, 1½ Fat

Prep: 25 minutes
Chill: 4 to 24 hours
Makes: 4 servings

1   15-ounce can black beans, rinsed and drained
1   cup frozen whole kernel corn, thawed
½   cup peeled jicama cut into thin bite-size strips
½   cup chopped green sweet pepper
4   red pearl onions, thinly sliced, or ¼ cup chopped red onion
1   to 2 canned chipotle peppers in adobo sauce
3   tablespoons salad oil
3   tablespoons lime juice
2   tablespoons snipped fresh cilantro or Italian flat-leaf parsley
2   teaspoons snipped fresh oregano or ½ teaspoon dried oregano, crushed
⅛   teaspoon salt
2   cloves garlic, minced
4   cups torn mixed salad greens
    Chipotle-flavored tostada chips or tortilla chips (optional)

Vegetables and Sides

9 g

carb

Buttermilk Biscuit Sticks

Hints of lemon and tarragon come through in every bite of these flaky, savory sticks. For variety, try rosemary and orange peel, or basil and lemon peel. If you're a purist when it comes to biscuits, omit the citrus peel and herb—the buttermilk flavor will be enough.

1 Lightly grease a baking sheet; set aside. In a medium bowl stir together flour, sugar, baking powder, lemon peel, tarragon, and baking soda. Using a pastry blender, cut in butter until mixture resembles coarse crumbs. Make a well in the center of flour mixture. Add the egg and buttermilk all at once. Using a fork, stir just until moistened.

2 Turn dough out onto a lightly floured surface. Quickly knead dough by gently folding and pressing for 10 to 12 strokes or until nearly smooth. Roll dough into a 12×6-inch rectangle. Cut into twenty-four 6×½-inch strips.

3 Place strips ½ inch apart on the prepared baking sheet. Brush strips with additional buttermilk. If desired, sprinkle with poppy seeds.

4 Bake in a 425° oven about 10 minutes or until golden brown. Remove from baking sheet and cool slightly on a wire rack. Serve warm.

Prep: 20 minutes
Bake: 10 minutes
Oven: 425°F
Makes: 24 biscuit sticks

2   cups all-purpose flour
2   tablespoons sugar
2   teaspoons baking powder
2   teaspoons finely shredded lemon peel
2   teaspoons snipped fresh tarragon or
     ½ teaspoon dried tarragon, crushed
¼   teaspoon baking soda
¼   cup butter
1   beaten egg
½   cup buttermilk
     Poppy seeds (optional)

Nutrition Facts per stick: 62 cal., 2 g total fat (1 g sat. fat), 15 mg chol., 75 mg sodium, 9 g carbo., 1 g sugar, 0 g fiber, 1 g pro.
Daily Values: 2% vit. A, 3% calcium, 3% iron
Exchanges: ½ Starch, ½ Fat

Pumpkin Crescent Rolls

These biscuitlike rolls will remind you of pumpkin pie. You don't have to wait for the holidays to enjoy them—make them the star of any meal.

1 Line a large baking sheet with foil; set aside. In a medium bowl stir together flour, baking powder, baking soda, nutmeg, and salt. Make a well in the center of flour mixture.

2 In a small bowl combine pumpkin, oil, and brown sugar. Add all at once to the flour mixture. Stir just until dough clings together.

3 Turn dough out onto a lightly floured surface. Quickly knead dough by gently folding and pressing for 10 to 12 strokes or until nearly smooth. Divide dough in half.

4 Roll each dough half into a 10-inch circle. Cut each circle into 8 wedges. Starting from the wide end of each wedge, loosely roll toward the point. Place, points down, 2 inches apart on the prepared baking sheet. Curve ends slightly to form a crescent shape.

5 In a small bowl combine the granulated sugar and cinnamon; sprinkle over rolls. Bake in a 400° oven for 9 to 11 minutes or until golden brown. Serve warm.

Prep: 20 minutes
Bake: 9 minutes
Oven: 400°F
Makes: 16 rolls

1¾	cups all-purpose flour
1	teaspoon baking powder
¼	teaspoon baking soda
¼	teaspoon ground nutmeg
⅛	teaspoon salt
¾	cup canned pumpkin
3	tablespoons cooking oil
2	tablespoons brown sugar
2	teaspoons granulated sugar
¼	teaspoon ground cinnamon

Nutrition Facts per roll: 79 cal., 3 g total fat (0 g sat. fat), 0 mg chol., 64 mg sodium, 12 g carbo., 2 g sugar, 1 g fiber, 1 g pro.
Daily Values: 51% vit. A, 1% vit. C, 2% calcium, 4% iron
Exchanges: 1 Starch

Cheese Batter Rolls

These golden, no-knead yeast rolls have a pleasant cornmeal crunch and are ever so easy— just spoon the dough into muffin cups, let rise, and bake.

1 In a large mixing bowl combine 2 cups of the flour and the yeast; set aside. In a medium saucepan heat and stir milk, sugar, shortening, and salt just until warm (120°F to 130°F) and shortening is almost melted. Add milk mixture to flour mixture; add egg.

2 Beat with an electric mixer on low to medium speed for 30 seconds, scraping sides of bowl constantly. Beat on high speed for 3 minutes. Using a wooden spoon, stir in cheese, cornmeal, and the remaining flour. Spoon batter into a lightly greased bowl. Cover and let rise in a warm place until double in size (50 to 60 minutes).

3 Generously grease twenty-four 2½-inch nonstick muffin cups. Stir dough down. Spoon into the prepared muffin cups, filling each about three-quarters full. Cover and let rise in a warm place until nearly double in size (30 to 40 minutes).

4 Bake in a 375° oven for 15 to 20 minutes or until golden brown. Cool in pans on wire racks for 5 minutes. Remove from muffin cups. Serve rolls warm or cool completely on wire racks.

Prep: 25 minutes
Rise: 1 hour 20 minutes
Bake: 15 minutes
Oven: 375°F
Makes: 24 rolls

3½ cups all-purpose flour
1 package active dry yeast
1¾ cups milk
¼ cup sugar
2 tablespoons shortening
1¼ teaspoons salt
1 beaten egg
4 ounces sliced sharp American
  cheese, chopped
½ cup cornmeal

Nutrition Facts per roll: 119 cal., 3 g total fat (2 g sat. fat), 15 mg chol., 201 mg sodium, 18 g carbo., 3 g sugar, 1 g fiber, 4 g pro.
Daily Values: 2% vit. A, 5% calcium, 5% iron
Exchanges: 1 Starch, ½ Fat

Shortcut Olive Flatbread

When baking both breads at once, switch placement of baking sheets in the oven halfway through the baking. Or bake one flatbread at a time, keeping the unbaked bread in the refrigerator.

1 Lightly grease 2 large baking sheets; set aside. Prepare hot roll mix according to package directions for basic dough, using the 1 egg and substituting the 2 tablespoons oil for margarine. Stir in 1 tablespoon of the fresh or ½ teaspoon of the dried basil.

2 Knead dough and let rest as directed. Divide dough in half. Roll each portion into a 12- or 13-inch circle. Place on the prepared baking sheets.

3 In a medium skillet cook onion and the remaining 3 tablespoons fresh basil in the 3 tablespoons hot oil until onion is tender. Using fingertips, press indentations every inch or so in dough rounds. Top dough evenly with onion mixture. Sprinkle with olives and cheese. Cover and let rise in a warm place until nearly double in size (30 to 40 minutes).

4 Bake in a 375° oven for 15 to 20 minutes or until golden brown. Transfer to wire racks; cool.

Prep: 40 minutes
Rise: 30 minutes
Bake: 15 minutes
Oven: 375°F
Makes: 16 servings

1	16-ounce package hot roll mix
1	egg
2	tablespoons olive oil or cooking oil
¼	cup snipped fresh basil or 2 teaspoons dried basil, crushed
⅔	cup finely chopped onion
3	tablespoons olive oil or cooking oil
¾	cup pitted kalamata olives, drained and chopped
½	cup crumbled feta cheese (2 ounces)

Nutrition Facts per serving: 168 cal., 7 g total fat (1 g sat. fat), 16 mg chol., 303 mg sodium, 21 g carbo., 2 g sugar, 1 g fiber, 4 g pro.
Daily Values: 1% vit. A, 1% vit. C, 2% calcium, 8% iron
Exchanges: 1½ Starch, 1 Fat

15 g
carb

Cucumber-Yogurt-Mint Soup

This refreshing soup makes a light first course that borrows its alluring combination of flavors from Greece. Be sure to use fresh, not dried, mint for the most intense flavor.

1 Peel the cucumber; cut in half lengthwise. Scoop out and discard seeds. Cut cucumber into ½-inch slices.

2 In a blender container or food processor bowl combine the cucumber, yogurt, lime juice, honey, cumin, and salt. Cover and blend or process until smooth. If desired, blend in milk to thin soup. Stir in fresh mint.

3 Transfer cucumber mixture to a storage container. Cover and chill for 2 to 24 hours. Stir before serving. If desired, garnish each serving with additional fresh mint.

Prep: 15 minutes
Chill: 2 to 24 hours
Makes: 4 servings

1   large cucumber
1   8-ounce carton plain low-fat yogurt
1   tablespoon lime juice
1   teaspoon honey
½   teaspoon ground cumin
¼   teaspoon salt
2   tablespoons milk (optional)
⅓   cup snipped fresh mint

Nutrition Facts per serving: 81 cal., 1 g total fat (1 g sat. fat), 3 mg chol., 185 mg sodium, 15 g carbo., 12 g sugar, 1 g fiber, 4 g pro.
Daily Values: 5% vit. A, 18% vit. C, 12% calcium, 8% iron
Exchanges: ½ Milk, 1 Vegetable

Tomato-Basil Bisque

This soothing soup combines the best of all worlds—the convenience of ready-made tomato sauce with the fresh taste of garden-grown tomatoes and basil. It's refreshing served chilled but just as delicious served steaming hot. Just heat it through on the stove top.

1 In a blender container combine tomatoes, broth, and tomato sauce. Cover and blend until smooth. Stir in basil. Cover and chill until ready to serve.

Nutrition Facts per serving: 43 cal., 1 g total fat (0 g sat. fat), 0 mg chol., 504 mg sodium, 10 g carbo., 5 g sugar, 2 g fiber, 2 g pro.
Daily Values: 18% vit. A, 43% vit. C, 1% calcium, 6% iron
Exchanges: 2 Vegetable

Start to Finish: 20 minutes
Makes: 4 servings

3 cups peeled, seeded, and coarsely chopped tomatoes
1 cup vegetable broth or chicken broth
1 8-ounce can tomato sauce
2 tablespoons snipped fresh basil or
1 teaspoon dried basil, crushed

15 g
carb

Vegetable-Barley Soup

Quick-cooking barley gives this soup unique texture and a sweet nuttiness. This is a nutritionally virtuous, soul-satisfying soup that fills the bill for a light lunch on a cool fall day.

1 In a large saucepan or Dutch oven combine beef broth, dried thyme (if using), salt, and black pepper. Add barley and carrot. Bring to boiling; reduce heat. Simmer, covered, for 5 minutes.

2 Stir in sweet pepper, sugar snap peas, and leek. Return to boiling; reduce heat. Simmer, covered, about 5 minutes more or until vegetables and barley are tender. Stir in undrained tomatoes and fresh thyme, if using; heat through.

*Test-Kitchen Tip: When slicing the leek, use the white portion and about 1 inch of the green tops of the leek.

Nutrition Facts per serving: 69 cal., 0 g total fat (0 g sat. fat), 0 mg chol., 363 mg sodium, 15 g carbo., 3 g sugar, 3 g fiber, 3 g pro.
Daily Values: 61% vit. A, 51% vit. C, 2% calcium, 4% iron
Exchanges: 1 Vegetable, ½ Starch

Start to Finish: 30 minutes
Makes: 8 servings

2   14-ounce cans reduced-sodium beef broth
1   tablespoon snipped fresh thyme or
      1 teaspoon dried thyme, crushed
½   teaspoon salt
⅛   teaspoon black pepper
⅔   cup quick-cooking barley
½   cup thinly sliced carrot
1   medium red or green sweet pepper, cut
      into ½-inch pieces
½   cup fresh or frozen sugar snap peas,
      halved crosswise, or frozen cut
      green beans
½   cup sliced leek*
1   14-ounce can reduced-sodium tomatoes,
      cut up

Winter Squash Soup

Winter squash—blessed with a velvety texture, a buttery taste, plus a good amount of dietary fiber—makes a nutrient-packed soup base. In addition, the golden hue is a clue that this soup is rich in vitamin A, which is crucial to maintaining the body's cells.

1 In a large saucepan heat oil over medium heat. Add onion, curry powder, and ginger. Cook and stir for 2 minutes. Stir in squash, chicken broth, apple juice, and salt. Heat through. Top each serving with yogurt.

Nutrition Facts per serving: 168 cal., 2 g total fat (0 g sat. fat), 1 mg chol., 330 mg sodium, 36 g carbo., 15 g sugar, 3 g fiber, 6 g pro.
Daily Values: 155% vit. A, 17% vit. C, 12% calcium, 11% iron
Exchanges: ½ Vegetable, 2 Starch

Start to Finish: 15 minutes
Makes: 4 servings

1½ teaspoons cooking oil
¼ cup finely chopped onion
1 to 2 teaspoons curry powder
½ teaspoon ground ginger
2 12-ounce packages frozen cooked winter squash, thawed
1 cup reduced-sodium chicken broth
1 cup apple juice or apple cider
¼ teaspoon salt
½ cup plain fat-free yogurt or fat-free dairy sour cream

Summer Fruit with Sesame Dressing

A simple three-ingredient dressing livens up a bowl of fresh fruit. We used peaches, papaya, strawberries, and raspberries, but feel free to create your own fruit combination.

1 In a large bowl combine the peaches, papaya, strawberries, and raspberries. Set aside.

2 For vinaigrette, in a small mixing bowl combine the vinegar, honey, and oil with a fork or wire whisk. Pour vinaigrette over fruit; toss gently to coat.

3 Divide the spinach among salad plates. Spoon the fruit mixture on top of spinach. Sprinkle with fresh mint.

Nutrition Facts per serving: 57 cal., 1 g total fat (0 g sat. fat), 0 mg chol., 39 mg sodium, 12 g carbo., 11 g sugar, 5 g fiber, 2 g pro.
Daily Values: 42% vit. A, 60% vit. C, 4% calcium, 15% iron
Exchanges: 1 Vegetable, ½ Fruit

Start to Finish: 25 minutes
Makes: 6 servings

2 cups sliced, peeled peaches or sliced nectarines
1 cup sliced, peeled papaya or mango
½ cup sliced strawberries
½ cup raspberries
¼ cup rice vinegar
1 teaspoon honey
½ teaspoon toasted sesame oil
6 cups spinach leaves
2 tablespoons snipped fresh mint

Fruit Verde

This beautiful fruit salad is a rainbow of greens, from pale to vibrant. Similarly, the flavors range from subtle to sweet to sophisticated. If you make the salad in advance, pour the syrup over the fruit just before serving.

1 In a large bowl combine honeydew melon, grapes, and pear. Peel and thinly slice 2 of the kiwifruits. Gently stir kiwi slices into melon mixture. Cover and chill until ready to serve.

2 For syrup, peel and cut up the remaining kiwi. In a blender container combine cut-up kiwi, mint, and grape juice. Cover and blend until smooth. Transfer to a bowl. Cover and chill for 1 hour.

3 To serve, pour the syrup over chilled melon mixture; toss gently to coat. If desired, garnish with additional fresh mint.

Prep: 15 minutes
Chill: 1 hour
Makes: 8 servings

- 1 cup honeydew melon balls or cubes
- 1 cup seedless green grapes
- 1 pear, cored and cut into ½-inch pieces
- 3 kiwifruits
- ½ cup loosely packed fresh mint leaves
- ½ cup white grape juice
  Fresh mint leaves (optional)

Nutrition Facts per serving: 61 cal., 0 g total fat (0 g sat. fat), 0 mg chol., 4 mg sodium, 14 g carbo., 12 g sugar, 2 g fiber, 1 g pro.
Daily Values: 1% vit. A, 76% vit. C, 2% calcium, 7% iron
Exchanges: 1 Fruit

17 g
carb

Apple and
Sweet Pepper Slaw

This delicious slaw is a snap to prepare, but you can make it even faster using preshredded cabbage or prepared veggies from the salad bar. Either way, you'll love the sweet crunch.

1 For dressing, in a small bowl stir together yogurt, salad dressing mix, and honey. If necessary, add a little water to reach desired consistency. Cover and chill until ready to serve.

2 In a large bowl combine cabbage, sweet pepper, apple, carrot, and celery. Pour the dressing over cabbage mixture; toss gently to coat.

Nutrition Facts per serving: 77 cal., 0 g total fat (0 g sat. fat), 0 mg chol., 230 mg sodium, 17 g carbo., 13 g sugar, 4 g fiber, 3 g pro.
Daily Values: 144% vit. A, 112% vit. C, 9% calcium, 4% iron
Exchanges: 2 Vegetable, ½ Fruit

Start to Finish: 20 minutes
Makes: 3 or 4 servings

⅓ cup plain fat-free yogurt or fat-free mayonnaise dressing or salad dressing

¼ of a 0.4-ounce envelope (about 1 teaspoon) buttermilk ranch dry salad dressing mix

1 teaspoon honey

2 cups shredded red and/or green cabbage

1 small red or green sweet pepper, cut into thin strips

1 apple, chopped

1 carrot, shredded

¼ cup thinly sliced celery

Spinach-Apricot Salad

The spinach is wilted and served warm in this beguiling salad. Cook it just until it wilts—it should still be bright green. Toast the almonds in a 350°F oven for 5 to 10 minutes or until they're golden.

1 If desired, remove stems from spinach. In a large bowl combine spinach and apricots; set aside.

2 In a 12-inch skillet heat oil over medium heat. Add garlic; cook and stir until golden brown. Stir in the vinegar. Bring to boiling; remove from heat.

3 Add spinach mixture to vinegar mixture. Return to heat; toss in skillet about 1 minute or just until spinach is wilted.

4 Transfer the spinach mixture to a serving dish. Season to taste with salt and pepper. Sprinkle with almonds. Serve immediately.

Start to Finish: 20 minutes
Makes: 4 servings

- 8 cups torn baby spinach leaves
- ⅓ cup dried apricots, snipped
- 1 tablespoon olive oil
- 1 clove garlic, thinly sliced or minced
- 4 teaspoons balsamic vinegar
  Dash salt and black pepper
- 2 tablespoons slivered almonds, toasted

Nutrition Facts per serving: 95 cal., 6 g total fat (1 g sat. fat), 0 mg chol., 113 mg sodium, 9 g carbo., 6 g sugar, 7 g fiber, 3 g pro.
Daily Values: 83% vit. A, 26% vit. C, 7% calcium, 28% iron
Exchanges: 1 Vegetable, ½ Fruit, 1 Fat

Curly Cukes and Radish Salad

You'll love the sophisticated, whimsical look of this crispy salad. It adds visual panache to your serving table, and the clean flavors offer the perfect accent for a broad range of dishes.

1 Trim ends of cucumbers. Using a sharp vegetable peeler, slice cucumbers lengthwise into wide, flat ribbons. Discard first and last slices. (You should have about 2 cups.)

2 In a medium bowl combine cucumber ribbons, radishes, jalapeño pepper, basil, sugar, and salt. Drizzle the olive oil and vinegar over cucumber mixture; toss gently to coat. Transfer to a serving bowl.

Nutrition Facts per serving: 38 cal., 2 g total fat (0 g sat. fat), 0 mg chol., 101 mg sodium, 4 g carbo., 3 g sugar, 1 g fiber, 1 g pro.
Daily Values: 5% vit. A, 14% vit. C, 2% calcium, 2% iron
Exchanges: 1 Vegetable, ½ Fat

Start to Finish: 20 minutes
Makes: 6 servings

- 2 medium seedless cucumbers
- 10 radishes, thinly sliced
- 1 fresh jalapeño pepper, seeded and sliced (see tip, page 37)
- 2 tablespoons snipped fresh basil
- ½ teaspoon sugar
- ¼ teaspoon salt
- 1 tablespoon olive oil
- 1 tablespoon white wine vinegar

Marinated Vegetable Salad

This salad is particularly delicious when made with ripe, just-picked summer tomatoes and fresh herbs. In the dead of winter, make it with the best tomatoes you can find, and let the flavor take you back to warm sunny days.

1 Cut tomatoes into wedges. Cut sweet pepper into small squares. In a medium bowl combine tomatoes, sweet pepper, squash, onion, and parsley; set aside.

2 For dressing, in a screw-top jar combine oil, vinegar, water, thyme, and garlic. Cover and shake well. Pour dressing over vegetable mixture; toss gently to coat.

3 Cover; let stand at room temperature for 30 to 60 minutes, stirring occasionally. (Or cover and chill for 4 to 24 hours, stirring once or twice. Let stand at room temperature about 30 minutes before serving.) Serve salad with a slotted spoon.

Nutrition Facts per serving: 68 cal., 5 g total fat (1 g sat. fat), 0 mg chol., 7 mg sodium, 6 g carbo., 4 g sugar, 1 g fiber, 1 g pro.
Daily Values: 11% vit. A, 49% vit. C, 1% calcium, 3% iron
Exchanges: 1 Vegetable, 1 Fat

Prep: 20 minutes
Stand: 30 minutes
Makes: 6 to 8 servings

2   medium tomatoes or 4 Roma tomatoes
1   medium green sweet pepper
1   small zucchini or yellow summer squash, thinly sliced
¼   cup thinly sliced red onion
2   tablespoons snipped fresh parsley
2   tablespoons olive oil
2   tablespoons balsamic vinegar or wine vinegar
2   tablespoons water
1   tablespoon snipped fresh thyme or basil or 1 teaspoon dried thyme or basil, crushed
1   clove garlic, minced

Tangy Potato Salad

A combination of the familiar red-skinned potatoes and the newer varieties of purple- or gold-fleshed potatoes gives this updated potato salad a colorful look. Avoid overcooking the potatoes—they should be tender but not mushy.

1 In a covered large saucepan cook potatoes in a small amount of boiling, lightly salted water for 10 to 12 minutes or until tender, adding beans the last 3 to 5 minutes of cooking; drain. Rinse with cold water; drain again.

2 In a medium bowl stir together the oil, vinegar, rosemary, salt, and pepper. Add potato mixture and green onions; toss gently to coat.

Nutrition Facts per serving: 130 cal., 7 g total fat (1 g sat. fat), 0 mg chol., 105 mg sodium, 15 g carbo., 1 g sugar, 3 g fiber, 2 g pro.
Daily Values: 5% vit. A, 25% vit. C, 3% calcium, 8% iron
Exchanges: 1 Starch, 1 Fat

Prep: 20 minutes
Cook: 10 minutes
Makes: 6 to 8 servings

8 ounces tiny new red potatoes, cut into ½-inch pieces
8 ounces purple potatoes or Yukon gold potatoes, cut into ½-inch pieces
8 ounces green beans, trimmed
3 tablespoons olive oil
3 tablespoons white wine vinegar
1 tablespoon snipped fresh rosemary or ½ teaspoon dried rosemary, crushed
¼ teaspoon salt
¼ teaspoon white pepper
¼ cup sliced green onions or 3 tablespoons snipped fresh chives

Potato-Fennel Salad

At first crunch, fennel may be mistaken for its slender cousin celery, but with each bite fennel's slightly sweet licoricelike flavor builds. During the September through April season, look for firm, smooth fennel bulbs without cracks or brown spots.

1 In a large saucepan bring water and salt to boiling. Add potatoes; cook, covered, for 8 minutes. Add asparagus and fennel; cook, covered, for 4 to 6 minutes more or just until potatoes are tender and asparagus and fennel are crisp-tender; drain. Arrange vegetables in a shallow serving dish. Cover and chill for 2 hours.

2 For dressing, in a small bowl stir together mayonnaise dressing, yogurt, green onions, vinegar, fennel leaves, and pepper. Cover and chill until ready to serve.

3 Just before serving, spoon dressing over vegetables; toss gently to coat. If desired, garnish with additional fennel leaves.

Nutrition Facts per serving: 122 cal., 1 g total fat (0 g sat. fat), 0 mg chol., 322 mg sodium, 23 g carbo., 4 g sugar, 5 g fiber, 6 g pro.
Daily Values: 5% vit. A, 61% vit. C, 8% calcium, 10% iron
Exchanges: 1½ Vegetable, 1 Starch

Prep: 25 minutes
Chill: 2 hours
Makes: 4 to 6 servings

1	cup water
¼	teaspoon salt
12	ounces tiny new potatoes, quartered
12	ounces asparagus, trimmed and cut into 1-inch pieces
1	medium fennel bulb, thinly sliced (1 cup)
¼	cup fat-free mayonnaise dressing or salad dressing
¼	cup plain fat-free yogurt
2	green onions, thinly sliced
1	tablespoon white wine vinegar
2	teaspoons snipped fresh fennel leaves
⅛	teaspoon coarsely ground black pepper
	Fresh fennel leaves (optional)

12 g
carb

Corn and Tomato Pasta Salad

This do-ahead salad captures the flavors—and attitude—of summer. Make it ahead for a casual weekend gathering using just-picked corn, tomatoes, and fresh basil from your farmer's market.

1 Cook pasta according to package directions; drain. Rinse with cold water; drain again. Cut corn kernels off the cobs (you should have 1 cup). In a covered small saucepan cook corn in a small amount of boiling water about 5 minutes or until tender. Drain and cool.

2 In a large bowl combine cooked pasta, cooked corn, chicken, and tomato. For dressing, in a screw-top jar combine vinegar, water, oil, pesto, salt, and pepper. Cover and shake well. Pour dressing over pasta mixture; toss gently to coat. If desired, cover and chill for 2 to 24 hours.

3 To serve, line a serving platter with romaine leaves. Spoon pasta mixture on top of greens. Sprinkle with fresh herbs.

Start to Finish: 25 minutes
Makes: 8 servings

- 1½   cups dried bow-tie pasta
- 2   fresh ears of corn, husked
- 1   cup shredded cooked chicken breast
- 1   large tomato, seeded and chopped
- 3   tablespoons vinegar
- 2   tablespoons water
- 1   tablespoon olive oil
- 1   tablespoon purchased pesto
- ¼   teaspoon salt
- ⅛   teaspoon black pepper
      Romaine lettuce leaves
      Snipped fresh herbs (such as basil, thyme, and/or marjoram)

Nutrition Facts per serving: 115 cal., 5 g total fat (1 g sat. fat), 16 mg chol., 108 mg sodium, 12 g carbo., 1 g sugar, 1 g fiber, 7 g pro.
Daily Values: 6% vit. A, 10% vit. C, 1% calcium, 4% iron
Exchanges: ½ Vegetable, ½ Starch, 1 Fat

Penne Salad with Italian Green Beans

This salad is at its best with crisp, fresh beans and radicchio, which is burgundy-red and has a slightly bitter taste. Choose radicchio heads with no signs of browning or wilting.

1 Cook pasta according to package directions, adding the fresh green beans the last 5 to 7 minutes of cooking or the thawed, frozen beans the last 3 to 4 minutes of cooking; drain. Rinse with cold water; drain again.

2 In a large bowl combine Italian dressing, tarragon, and pepper. Add pasta mixture and radicchio; toss gently to coat.

3 Divide the shredded spinach among salad plates. Spoon pasta mixture over spinach; sprinkle with Gorgonzola cheese.

Nutrition Facts per serving: 132 cal., 3 g total fat (1 g sat. fat), 5 mg chol., 199 mg sodium, 21 g carbo., 1 g sugar, 2 g fiber, 6 g pro.
Daily Values: 4% vit. A, 7% vit. C, 5% calcium, 6% iron
Exchanges: 1 Vegetable, 1 Starch, ½ Fat

Start to Finish: 35 minutes
Makes: 8 servings

- **6** ounces dried penne, cut ziti, elbow macaroni, or other short pasta
- **8** ounces Italian green beans, trimmed and bias-sliced 1 inch thick, or one 9-ounce package frozen Italian green beans, thawed
- **⅓** cup bottled fat-free Italian salad dressing
- **1** tablespoon snipped fresh tarragon or ½ teaspoon dried tarragon, crushed
- **½** teaspoon freshly ground black pepper
- **2** cups torn radicchio or 1 cup finely shredded red cabbage
- **4** cups spinach leaves, shredded
- **½** cup crumbled Gorgonzola or other blue cheese (2 ounces)

31 g
carb

Couscous-Artichoke Salad

This recipe makes a great warm salad too. Instead of chilling the couscous mixture, toss it immediately with the other ingredients.

1 In a medium saucepan bring chicken broth to boiling. Stir in couscous and onion; remove from heat. Cover and let stand about 5 minutes or until liquid is absorbed. Stir in jalapeño pepper, cinnamon, and black pepper. Cover and chill for 30 minutes.

2 In a large bowl combine the couscous mixture, artichoke hearts, tomato, sweet pepper, and raisins. For dressing, in a small mixing bowl whisk together the balsamic vinegar and olive oil. Pour the dressing over couscous mixture; toss gently to coat.

Nutrition Facts per serving: 194 cal., 6 g total fat (1 g sat. fat), 0 mg chol., 193 mg sodium, 31 g carbo., 6 g sugar, 4 g fiber, 6 g pro.
Daily Values: 7% vit. A, 39% vit. C, 3% calcium, 7% iron
Exchanges: 1 Vegetable, 1½ Starch, 1 Fat

Prep: 15 minutes
Chill: 30 minutes
Makes: 8 servings

1½ cups chicken broth
1 cup quick-cooking couscous
1 small onion, finely chopped
1 to 2 tablespoons finely chopped fresh
  jalapeño pepper (see tip, page 37)
¼ teaspoon ground cinnamon
¼ teaspoon black pepper
1 9-ounce package frozen artichoke hearts,
  thawed and cut up
1 large tomato, seeded and coarsely
  chopped
1 green sweet pepper, finely chopped
3 tablespoons raisins
¼ cup balsamic vinegar
3 tablespoons olive oil

Orange-Sauced Broccoli and Peppers

This vitamin C-rich, colorful combination tossed with a simple, slightly sweet sauce is sure to inspire everyone to eat more veggies!

1 In a medium saucepan cook broccoli and sweet pepper in a small amount of boiling, lightly salted water about 8 minutes or until broccoli is crisp-tender; drain. Return broccoli mixture to saucepan; cover and keep warm.

2 Meanwhile, for sauce, in a small saucepan cook onion and garlic in hot margarine until onion is tender. Stir in cornstarch. Add orange juice and mustard. Cook and stir until thickened and bubbly. Cook and stir 2 minutes more. Pour the sauce over broccoli mixture; toss gently to coat.

Start to Finish: 20 minutes
Makes: 6 servings

- 3½ cups broccoli florets
- 1 medium red or yellow sweet pepper, cut into 1-inch pieces
- 2 tablespoons finely chopped onion
- 1 clove garlic, minced
- 1 tablespoon margarine or butter
- 1½ teaspoons cornstarch
- ⅔ cup orange juice
- 2 teaspoons Dijon-style mustard

Nutrition Facts per serving: 55 cal., 2 g total fat (0 g sat. fat), 0 mg chol., 46 mg sodium, 8 g carbo., 4 g sugar, 2 g fiber, 2 g pro.
Daily Values: 38% vit. A, 142% vit. C, 3% calcium, 4% iron
Exchanges: 1½ Vegetable, ½ Fat

6 g
carb

Roasted Asparagus in Mustard-Dill Sauce

To choose asparagus in the market, look for closed spears and firm stalks. Whether you prefer the thick or pencil-thin spears is a matter of personal choice. The thicker the spear, the more mature the plant.

1 Snap off and discard woody bases from asparagus. Arrange asparagus in a shallow baking dish. In a small bowl combine broth and mustard. Pour over asparagus; turn asparagus to coat.

2 Roast in a 425° oven for 15 to 20 minutes or until asparagus is crisp-tender. Transfer to a serving dish. Sprinkle with pepper. If desired, top with lemon slices and dill.

*Test-Kitchen Tip: If dill mustard is not available, substitute 2 tablespoons Dijon-style mustard plus 1 teaspoon snipped fresh dill.

Prep: 10 minutes
Roast: 15 minutes
Oven: 425°F
Makes: 4 servings

2 pounds asparagus
¼ cup reduced-sodium chicken broth
2 tablespoons dill mustard*
   Freshly ground black pepper
   Lemon slices (optional)
   Fresh dill sprigs (optional)

Nutrition Facts per serving: 38 cal., 1 g total fat (0 g sat. fat), 0 mg chol., 84 mg sodium, 6 g carbo., 3 g sugar, 3 g fiber, 3 g pro.
Daily Values: 13% vit. A, 23% vit. C, 4% calcium, 7% iron
Exchanges: 1½ Vegetable

Basil Beets and Onion

You can't beat fresh beets—they provide twice the folate and potassium as their canned counterparts. Although fresh beets are usually plentiful year-round, the peak season runs from June to October. Look for small, smooth, firm beets with crisp, dark green leaves.

1 Cut off all but 1 inch of fresh beet stems and roots; wash. Do not peel. Cook, covered, in boiling water with fennel seeds and peppercorns for 35 to 45 minutes or until tender. Drain; discard fennel seeds and peppercorns. Cool slightly. Slip skins off beets and cube.

2 In a medium bowl, combine cubed beets, onion, basil, shallot, vinegar, oil, and salt. Serve warm or chilled.

Nutrition Facts per serving: 57 cal., 3 g total fat (0 g sat. fat), 0 mg chol., 162 mg sodium, 7 g carbo., 5 g sugar, 2 g fiber, 1 g pro.
Daily Values: 2% vit. A, 5% vit. C, 1% calcium, 3% iron
Exchanges: 1½ Vegetable, ½ Fat

Prep: 20 minutes
Cook: 35 minutes
Cool: 10 minutes
Makes: 5 servings

4	medium beets (about 1 pound)
½	teaspoon fennel seeds
5	whole black peppercorns
⅓	cup chopped red onion
2	tablespoons snipped fresh basil
1	tablespoon chopped shallot
2	tablespoons white wine vinegar
1	tablespoon olive oil
¼	teaspoon salt

11 g
carb

Braised Fall Vegetables

A touch of cardamom adds a spicy-sweet taste to this flavorful autumn side dish that's cooked in a skillet. This vegetable combination contributes loads of vitamin A and C, powerful antioxidants that help fight chronic disease.

1 In a large skillet heat margarine over medium heat until melted. Add cabbage wedges and carrots. Cook, covered, for 3 minutes, stirring once or twice with a wooden spoon. Gently stir in cauliflower, onion, water, vinegar, salt, cardamom, and pepper.

2 Bring to boiling; reduce heat. Simmer, covered, for 7 to 10 minutes or just until vegetables are crisp-tender.

Nutrition Facts per serving: 81 cal., 4 g total fat (1 g sat. fat), 0 mg chol., 179 mg sodium, 11 g carbo., 7 g sugar, 4 g fiber, 2 g pro.
Daily Values: 197% vit. A, 72% vit. C, 6% calcium, 5% iron
Exchanges: 2 Vegetable, ½ Fat

Start to Finish: 30 minutes
Makes: 6 to 8 servings

- 2 tablespoons margarine or butter
- ½ of a medium head red or green cabbage (about 1 pound), cut into 6 wedges
- 12 whole baby carrots or 3 medium carrots, quartered lengthwise and halved crosswise
- 2 cups cauliflower florets
- 1 medium red onion, cut into wedges
- ¼ cup water
- 2 tablespoons vinegar
- ¼ teaspoon salt
- ¼ teaspoon ground cardamom
- ¼ teaspoon black pepper

Brussels Sprouts with Lemon Sauce

People who say they don't like Brussels sprouts often change their minds when they try them cooked only until they are crisp-tender. This tangy lemon sauce makes them even more appealing.

1 Trim stems of Brussels sprouts and remove any wilted outer leaves. In a medium saucepan combine Brussels sprouts, the ¾ cup chicken broth, the margarine, and garlic. Bring to boiling; reduce heat. Simmer, covered, for 7 to 10 minutes or until Brussels sprouts are crisp-tender. Using a slotted spoon, transfer Brussels sprouts to a serving bowl. Cover and keep warm.

2 Meanwhile, in a small bowl combine the 2 tablespoons chicken broth, the lemon peel, lemon juice, cornstarch, and pepper. Gradually stir lemon mixture into hot broth in saucepan. Cook and stir over medium heat until thickened and bubbly. Cook and stir for 2 minutes more. Stir in fresh dill. Pour the sauce over Brussels sprouts.

Nutrition Facts per serving: 34 cal., 1 g total fat (0 g sat. fat), 0 mg chol., 132 mg sodium, 5 g carbo., 1 g sugar, 2 g fiber, 2 g pro.
Daily Values: 8% vit. A, 56% vit. C, 2% calcium, 4% iron
Exchanges: 1 Vegetable

Start to Finish: 20 minutes
Makes: 6 servings

3	cups Brussels sprouts (about 12 ounces)
¾	cup chicken broth
1	teaspoon margarine or butter
1	clove garlic, minced
2	tablespoons chicken broth
½	teaspoon finely shredded lemon peel
1	tablespoon lemon juice
1½	teaspoons cornstarch
⅛	teaspoon black pepper
2	teaspoons snipped fresh dill

8 g
carb

Roasted Vegetable Medley

Try this simple recipe when you have an abundance of veggies from your garden or from a recent trip to the farmer's market. Not only does the balsamic vinegar add a unique flavor, it glazes the colorful mixture too.

1 In a 13×9×2-inch baking pan combine onions, summer squash, zucchini, sweet peppers, and garlic.

2 In a screw-top jar combine parsley, vinegar, oil, oregano, salt, and black pepper; cover and shake well. Pour over vegetables; toss gently to coat.

3 Roast vegetables in a 425° oven about 25 minutes or until vegetables are crisp-tender, stirring twice.

Nutrition Facts per serving: 50 cal., 2 g total fat (0 g sat. fat), 0 mg chol., 150 mg sodium, 8 g carbo., 3 g sugar, 2 g fiber, 1 g pro.
Daily Values: 50% vit. A, 125% vit. C, 2% calcium, 4% iron
Exchanges: 1 Vegetable, ½ Fat

Prep: 15 minutes
Roast: 25 minutes
Oven: 425°F
Makes: 8 servings

2 medium red onions, cut into eighths
2 small yellow summer squash, cut into ½-inch slices
2 small zucchini, cut into ½-inch slices
3 red, yellow, and/or green sweet peppers, cut into ½-inch strips
4 cloves garlic, thinly sliced
2 tablespoons snipped fresh parsley
2 tablespoons balsamic vinegar
1 tablespoon olive oil
1 teaspoon dried oregano, crushed
½ teaspoon salt
¼ teaspoon black pepper

Cider-Roasted Squash

In the good old days winter squash was usually slathered with brown sugar and butter. Here, the golden vegetable goes upscale (and slims down), baked in an apple cider steam bath.

1 Coat a 3-quart rectangular baking dish with cooking spray. Add the squash and onion; toss to combine. In a small bowl combine apple juice, oil, brown sugar, salt, nutmeg, and pepper; pour over vegetables.

2 Roast vegetables in a 450° oven about 35 minutes or until vegetables are tender, stirring twice.

Nutrition Facts per serving: 85 cal., 4 g total fat (1 g sat. fat), 0 mg chol., 151 mg sodium, 13 g carbo., 5 g sugar, 2 g fiber, 2 g pro.
Daily Values: 89% vit. A, 21% vit. C, 4% calcium, 4% iron
Exchanges: 1 Starch

Prep: 25 minutes
Roast: 35 minutes
Oven: 450°F
Makes: 8 servings

Nonstick cooking spray
8 cups peeled, seeded winter squash (such as butternut or acorn), cut into 1-inch cubes
1 medium onion, cut into wedges
¼ cup apple juice or apple cider
2 tablespoons olive oil or cooking oil
1 tablespoon brown sugar
½ teaspoon salt
¼ teaspoon ground nutmeg or ginger
¼ teaspoon black pepper

Chipotle Grilled Potatoes

The smoky, spicy paste transforms simple grilled sweet and russet potatoes into a spectacular dish. Another time, mix up the addictive pepper and spice mixture (leaving out the olive oil) and brush on chicken or meat before grilling.

1 Scrub potatoes; pat dry with paper towels. Cut potatoes in half lengthwise; cut each half into 4 wedges.

2 In a covered large saucepan cook the potatoes in a small amount of boiling water about 15 minutes or just until tender. Drain and cool.

3 Meanwhile, place chipotle peppers in a blender container or food processor bowl. Cover and blend or process until peppers are ground. In a small bowl combine the ground chipotle peppers, oil, paprika, cumin, chili powder, salt, black pepper, and garlic. Stir in enough of the water to make a mixture of brushing consistency. Brush the chipotle mixture over potatoes.

4 Place the potatoes on the rack of an uncovered grill directly over medium coals. Grill for 4 to 6 minutes or until edges begin to brown, turning occasionally.

Prep: 25 minutes
Grill: 4 minutes
Makes: 6 servings

- 2 medium sweet potatoes (about 15 ounces)
- 2 medium russet potatoes (about 12 ounces)
- 3 dried chipotle peppers, seeded
- 2 teaspoons olive oil
- 1½ teaspoons paprika
- ½ teaspoon ground cumin
- ½ teaspoon chili powder
- ¼ teaspoon salt
- ¼ teaspoon black pepper
- 3 cloves garlic, minced
- 1 to 2 tablespoons water

Nutrition Facts per serving: 144 cal., 2 g total fat (0 g sat. fat), 0 mg chol., 191 mg sodium, 29 g carbo., 3 g sugar, 3 g fiber, 3 g pro.
Daily Values: 250% vit. A, 34% vit. C, 3% calcium, 8% iron
Exchanges: 2 Starch

Skinny Mashed Potatoes

Ranch-flavor sour cream adds pizzazz to these make-ahead spuds. To reduce calories and fat, choose light sour cream dip.

1 Coat a 1½-quart casserole with cooking spray; set aside. Peel and cut up potatoes. In a covered Dutch oven cook potatoes in boiling salted water for 20 to 25 minutes or until tender; drain. Transfer potatoes to a large mixing bowl.

2 Beat potatoes with an electric mixer on low speed. Add ranch dip, margarine, salt, and pepper. Fold in parsley. Spoon the potato mixture into the prepared casserole. If desired, cover and chill for up to 24 hours.

3 Bake in a 350° oven for 50 to 60 minutes or until heated through. If desired, garnish with additional parsley.

Nutrition Facts per serving: 151 cal., 4 g total fat (1 g sat. fat), 5 mg chol., 122 mg sodium, 26 g carbo., 3 g sugar, 2 g fiber, 3 g pro.
Daily Values: 6% vit. A, 26% vit. C, 4% calcium, 3% iron
Exchanges: 1½ Starch, ½ Fat

Prep: 30 minutes
Bake: 50 minutes
Oven: 350°F
Makes: 8 to 10 servings

Nonstick cooking spray
8   medium baking potatoes (such as russet, round white, or yellow) (about 2½ pounds)
½   cup light dairy sour cream ranch dip
2   tablespoons margarine or butter
¼   teaspoon salt
¼   teaspoon freshly ground black pepper
2   tablespoons snipped fresh parsley or chives

12 g
carb

Sautéed Peas and Celery

The simplicity and ease of this dish make it a perfect accompaniment for everything from holiday roasts to grilled chicken and baked fish.

1 In a large skillet heat oil over medium heat. Add onion and cook about 5 minutes or until tender. Add celery and cook about 3 minutes or just until tender.

2 Increase heat to medium high. Add peas and cook for 3 to 5 minutes more or until peas are heated through. Remove from heat. Stir in celery leaves, salt, and pepper.

Nutrition Facts per serving: 82 cal., 2 g total fat (0 g·sat. fat), 0 mg chol., 221 mg sodium, 12 g carbo., 5 g sugar, 5 g fiber, 4 g pro.
Daily Values: 13% vit. A, 19% vit. C, 3% calcium, 8% iron
Exchanges: 1 Starch

Start to Finish: 20 minutes
Makes: 8 servings

- 1 tablespoon olive oil
- ½ cup chopped red onion
- ½ cup chopped celery
- 2 10-ounce packages frozen peas, thawed
- ¼ cup chopped celery leaves
- ½ teaspoon salt
- ¼ teaspoon freshly ground black pepper

Ginger-Lime Peas and Carrots

You'll find a million uses for this ginger-lime butter—serve it over any vegetable, with grilled chicken, or drizzle it over fish before or after baking.

1 In a large saucepan cook carrots in a small amount of boiling water for 4 minutes. Add snap peas and cook for 2 to 3 minutes more or until vegetables are crisp-tender. Drain the vegetables in a colander.

2 In the same saucepan melt margarine. Stir in green onions, lime peel, lime juice, and ginger. Return cooked vegetables to saucepan. Cook and stir over medium-low heat until vegetables are heated through.

Nutrition Facts per serving: 77 cal., 3 g total fat (0 g sat. fat), 0 mg chol., 53 mg sodium, 11 g carbo., 3 g sugar, 3 g fiber, 2 g pro.
Daily Values: 208% vit. A, 31% vit. C, 4% calcium, 6% iron
Exchanges: 2 Vegetable, ½ Fat

Start to Finish: 15 minutes
Makes: 6 servings

2 cups packaged, peeled baby carrots
2 cups sugar snap peas or pea pods
4 teaspoons margarine or butter
2 medium green onions, sliced
1 teaspoon finely shredded lime peel
2 tablespoons lime juice
1 teaspoon grated fresh ginger

Three-Rice Pilaf

The nutty flavor of wild rice (which is actually a marsh grass), pleasant chewy texture of brown rice, and relative soft silkiness of white rice combine beautifully in this nutritious pilaf.

1 Rinse wild rice under cold water; drain and set aside. In a large saucepan or Dutch oven cook onion in hot margarine until tender. Carefully add water, bouillon granules, black pepper, and garlic.

2 Bring to boiling. Stir in wild rice and brown rice. Return to boiling; reduce heat. Simmer, covered, for 25 minutes.

3 Stir in long grain rice. Return to boiling; reduce heat. Simmer, covered, about 15 minutes more or until rice is tender. Stir in sweet pepper and chives.

Nutrition Facts per serving: 207 cal., 5 g total fat (1 g sat. fat), 0 mg chol., 488 mg sodium, 36 g carbo., 1 g sugar, 1 g fiber, 5 g pro.
Daily Values: 7% vit. A, 8% vit. C, 2% calcium, 8% iron
Exchanges: 2½ Starch

Prep: 20 minutes
Cook: 40 minutes
Makes: 8 servings

½ cup uncooked wild rice
¼ cup chopped onion
3 tablespoons margarine or butter
4 cups water
4 teaspoons instant chicken bouillon granules
⅛ teaspoon black pepper
1 clove garlic, minced
½ cup uncooked regular brown rice
1 cup uncooked long grain rice
2 tablespoons finely chopped red or green sweet pepper
1 tablespoon snipped fresh chives

Orzo-Broccoli Pilaf

Orzo (a rice-shaped pasta) and broccoli florets combine to make a double-duty side dish of a vegetable and a starch. To save time, use precut florets from the grocery store salad bar or produce department.

1 In a large saucepan heat oil over medium-high heat. Add mushrooms and onion; cook and stir until tender. Add orzo; cook and stir about 2 minutes or until orzo is lightly browned. Remove from heat.

2 Carefully stir broth, carrot, marjoram, and pepper into orzo mixture. Return to heat. Bring to boiling; reduce heat. Simmer, covered, about 15 minutes or until orzo is tender but still firm. Remove from heat. Stir in broccoli. Cover and let stand for 5 minutes.

Nutrition Facts per serving: 87 cal., 2 g total fat (0 g sat. fat), 0 mg chol., 184 mg sodium, 14 g carbo., 3 g sugar, 2 g fiber, 4 g pro.
Daily Values: 60% vit. A, 41% vit. C, 2% calcium, 5% iron
Exchanges: 1 Vegetable, ½ Starch, ½ Fat

Prep: 20 minutes
Cook: 15 minutes
Stand: 5 minutes
Makes: 6 servings

- 2   teaspoons olive oil
- 1   cup sliced fresh mushrooms
- ½   cup chopped onion
- ⅔   cup dried orzo pasta (rosamarina)
- 1   14-ounce can reduced-sodium chicken broth
- ½   cup shredded carrot
- 1   teaspoon dried marjoram, crushed
- ⅛   teaspoon black pepper
- 2   cups small broccoli florets

24 g carb

Mexicana Couscous

This dish gives you the flavors of Spanish rice in about one-third the time. Be sure to use a fork to fluff the couscous into separate grains before serving.

1 In a medium saucepan cook onion and garlic in hot oil over medium heat until tender. Stir in cumin; cook for 30 seconds. Carefully add broth, peas, tomatoes, and cilantro.

2 Bring to boiling. Stir in couscous. Remove from heat. Cover and let stand about 5 minutes or until liquid is absorbed. Fluff with a fork before serving. If desired, garnish with additional cilantro.

Nutrition Facts per serving: 139 cal., 3 g total fat (0 g sat. fat), 0 mg chol., 127 mg sodium, 24 g carbo., 2 g sugar, 3 g fiber, 5 g pro.
Daily Values: 6% vit. A, 13% vit. C, 2% calcium, 4% iron
Exchanges: ½ Vegetable, 1½ Starch

Prep: 20 minutes
Stand: 5 minutes
Makes: 6 servings

¾ cup chopped onion
2 cloves garlic, minced
1 tablespoon cooking oil
½ teaspoon ground cumin
1 cup reduced-sodium chicken broth
¾ cup frozen peas
¾ cup coarsely chopped fresh or canned tomatoes
2 tablespoons snipped fresh cilantro or 2 teaspoons dried cilantro, crushed
¾ cup quick-cooking couscous
   Fresh cilantro (optional)

Desserts

Apple-Cranberry Fruit Soup

As the first crisp, cool days usher in the fall season, this fruit soup will warm your soul. Make your own dried fruit mix to suit family preferences.

1 In a large saucepan combine apple cider and apricot nectar. Bring to boiling; remove from heat. Add tea bags. Cover and let stand for 3 minutes. Remove tea bags.

2 Meanwhile, cut up any large pieces of dried fruit. Add dried fruit and apple chunks to cider mixture. Return to boiling; reduce heat. Simmer, uncovered, about 5 minutes or just until apple chunks are tender. (Do not overcook fresh apples.)

Nutrition Facts per serving: 183 cal., 0 g total fat (0 g sat. fat), 0 mg chol., 7 mg sodium, 47 g carbo., 39 g sugar, 3 g fiber, 1 g pro.
Daily Values: 29% vit. A, 21% vit. C, 3% calcium, 7% iron
Exchanges: 3 Fruit

Prep: 20 minutes
Cook: 5 minutes
Makes: 8 servings

- **4 cups apple cider or apple juice**
- **1½ cups apricot nectar**
- **4 bags cranberry-flavored tea**
- **7 ounces mixed dried fruit [such as apples, pears, apricots, plums (prunes), and/or persimmons]**
- **3 medium cooking apples (such as Granny Smith, Jonathan, or Braeburn), cored and cut into large chunks**

Autumn Fruits with Cinnamon Custard

If lady apples and Seckel or Forelle pears aren't available, don't worry—this recipe works with any fall fruit. Try Anjou or Bartlett pears and a mix of cooking apples, but you may have to extend the cooking time slightly.

1 If desired, core pears and lady apples; set aside. In a large skillet bring apple cider just to boiling over low heat. Carefully add the pears, apples, and star anise. Sprinkle sugar over fruit. Cook, covered, about 5 minutes or just until fruit is tender.

2 Using a slotted spoon, carefully transfer the cooked fruit to dessert bowls. Discard the poaching liquid. Drizzle the fruit with Cinnamon Custard.

Cinnamon Custard: In a small heavy saucepan combine 1 beaten egg, ⅔ cup milk, and 4 teaspoons sugar. Cook and stir over medium heat just until mixture coats the back of a metal spoon. Stir in ½ teaspoon vanilla and a dash of ground cinnamon. Place the saucepan in a bowl of ice water for 10 minutes. Serve immediately.

Nutrition Facts per serving: 172 cal., 2 g total fat (1 g sat. fat), 37 mg chol., 25 mg sodium, 35 g carbo., 29 g sugar, 4 g fiber, 2 g pro.
Daily Values: 3% vit. A, 13% vit. C, 5% calcium, 3% iron
Exchanges: 1 Fruit, 1½ Other Carbo., ½ Fat

Start to Finish: 25 minutes
Makes: 6 servings

- 6 Seckel or Forelle pears, quartered lengthwise
- 6 lady apples, halved crosswise
- ⅔ cup apple cider or apple juice
- 3 whole star anise
- 3 tablespoons sugar
- 1 recipe Cinnamon Custard

Mango Parfait

If you don't have parfait glasses, assemble the parfaits in large wine glasses, champagne flutes, or margarita glasses. If fresh mangoes aren't available, substitute fresh papaya or cubed melon.

1 Combine soy milk, nectarine, and sugar in a blender container. Cover and blend until smooth; pour mixture into a medium bowl. Stir in sour cream. Cover and chill for 1 hour.

2 Remove seeds and peel mangoes. Cut fruit into ½-inch cubes (you should have 2 cups). For each serving, alternately layer mango pieces and sour cream mixture in a parfait glass or wine glass until glass is full, topping each serving with some of the sour cream mixture. If desired, garnish parfait with fresh fruit.

Nutrition Facts per serving: 128 cal., 1 g total fat (0 g sat. fat), 0 mg chol., 22 mg sodium, 29 g carbo., 21 g sugar, 3 g fiber, 3 g pro.
Daily Values: 86% vit. A, 51% vit. C, 6% calcium, 2% iron
Exchanges: 2 Fruit

Start to Finish: 20 minutes
Makes: 4 servings

¼ cup soy milk
1 nectarine, peeled, pitted, and chopped
2 tablespoons powdered sugar
1 4-ounce carton fat-free sour cream or light dairy sour cream
2 ripe mangoes
   Fresh fruit, such as sliced kiwifruit, raspberries, and/or strawberries (optional)

Peaches and Cherries

Like the lazy days of summer, this dessert is light and easy. It's the perfect recipe to help you take advantage of the abundance of cherries (available May to August) and peaches (available May to October).

1 In a 10-inch skillet bring wine and cinnamon just to boiling. Add peaches and cherries; reduce heat. Simmer, covered, for 10 minutes or just until peaches are tender. Using a slotted spoon, transfer peaches and cherries to a shallow serving dish.

2 Cook the remaining wine mixture, uncovered, over medium heat about 10 minutes or until reduced to ½ cup. Remove and discard cinnamon. Spoon the liquid over peaches and cherries.

3 In a small microwave-safe bowl microwave white baking bar and shortening on 100 percent power (high) for 1 to 1½ minutes or until melted, stirring once. Cool slightly.

4 Transfer cooled white baking bar to a self-sealing plastic bag; seal bag. Snip a ¼-inch corner off the bag. Squeezing gently, drizzle melted baking bar over peaches and cherries.

Prep: 15 minutes
Cook: 20 minutes
Makes: 6 servings

- 1½ cups white Zinfandel, rosé wine, or cranberry-apple drink
- 2 inches stick cinnamon
- 3 medium white or yellow peaches, halved and pitted
- ½ cup sweet cherries, pitted
- ⅓ of a 6-ounce package (2 ounces) white baking bar
- ½ teaspoon shortening

Nutrition Facts per serving: 124 cal., 4 g total fat (2 g sat. fat), 2 mg chol., 11 mg sodium, 14 g carbo., 12 g sugar, 1 g fiber, 1 g pro.
Daily Values: 5% vit. A, 5% vit. C, 3% calcium, 2% iron
Exchanges: 1 Fruit, 1½ Fat

22 g
carb

Strawberries with Almond-Yogurt Cream

For the yogurt "cream cheese," you'll get the best results if you purchase yogurt that does not contain gums, gelatin, or fillers. These ingredients prevent the curd and whey from separating.

1 Place a paper coffee filter in a small strainer or funnel set over a small bowl. Spoon yogurt into the filter. Cover and chill about 8 hours or until yogurt reaches the consistency of soft cream cheese. Spoon into a small bowl; discard the drained liquid. If desired, cover and chill for up to 3 days.

2 Gently stir brown sugar, amaretto, and lemon peel into the drained yogurt. If desired, cover and chill up to an additional 3 days.

3 Halve any large strawberries. Divide strawberries between dessert dishes. Gently stir yogurt mixture; spoon mixture on top of berries. If desired, sprinkle with almonds.

Prep: 10 minutes
Chill: 8 hours
Makes: 2 servings

1 8-ounce carton plain fat-free yogurt
1 tablespoon brown sugar
2 teaspoons amaretto or ¼ teaspoon almond extract
½ teaspoon finely shredded lemon peel
1½ cups strawberries, stems removed
   Sliced almonds, toasted (optional)

Nutrition Facts per serving: 126 cal., 1 g total fat (0 g sat. fat), 2 mg chol., 90 mg sodium, 22 g carbo., 18 g sugar, 3 g fiber, 7 g pro.
Daily Values: 1% vit. A, 105% vit. C, 25% calcium, 3% iron
Exchanges: ½ Milk, 1 Fruit

Angel Food Cake with Lemon Cream and Berries

This heavenly dessert is also angelically low in fat and calories. When fresh berries are out of season, thaw whole frozen strawberries and blueberries and sprinkle over the top.

1 Prepare cake mix, if using, and bake cake in a 10-inch tube pan or a 13×9×2-inch baking pan according to package directions. Cool cake completely according to package directions. (If using the 13-inch pan, turn cake in pan upside down, resting corners of pan on four cans of equal height; cool completely.)

2 For lemon cream, in a medium bowl stir together yogurt and one-fourth of the pudding mix until smooth. Gradually add remaining pudding mix to yogurt, stirring until smooth after each addition. Fold in the whipped topping. Serve the cake with lemon cream and berries.

<u>Test-Kitchen Tip:</u> Store any leftover lemon cream in the refrigerator up to 4 days.

Nutrition Facts per serving: 166 cal., 2 g total fat (2 g sat. fat), 0 mg chol., 322 mg sodium, 32 g carbo., 23 g sugar, 2 g fiber, 3 g pro.
Daily Values: 68% vit. C, 7% calcium, 3% iron
Exchanges: ½ Fruit, 1½ Other Carbo., ½ Fat

Prep: 15 minutes
Bake: per package directions
Makes: 16 servings

1 16-ounce package angel food cake mix or 1 15- to 16-ounce purchased angel food cake
2 8-ounce cartons lemon fat-free yogurt
1 4-serving-size package sugar-free instant vanilla pudding mix
1 8-ounce container frozen light whipped dessert topping, thawed
   Strawberries, raspberries, and/or blueberries

Carrot Snack Cake

All you need is a small serving of this spiced cake. The decorative powdered sugar replaces the traditional high-fat, high-calorie cream cheese frosting, making a lighter and more healthful cake.

1 Coat an 8×8×2-inch baking pan with cooking spray; set aside. In a medium mixing bowl beat butter with an electric mixer on medium to high speed for 30 seconds. Add granulated sugar. Beat until combined, scraping sides of the bowl occasionally. Beat in egg until combined. Using a wooden spoon, stir in carrot, milk, and vanilla.

2 In a small bowl combine flour, baking powder, cinnamon, salt, and nutmeg. Add to carrot mixture and stir until combined. Spread batter evenly in the prepared baking pan.

3 Bake in a 350° oven for 20 to 25 minutes or until a wooden toothpick inserted near the center comes out clean. Cool cake completely in pan on a wire rack. (Or cool cake in pan on a wire rack for 10 minutes; remove and cool completely.)

4 Place a paper doily on top of the cake. Lightly sift the powdered sugar evenly over doily. Carefully remove doily.

Prep: 15 minutes
Bake: 20 minutes
Oven: 350°F
Makes: 9 servings

Nonstick cooking spray
¼ cup butter
½ cup granulated sugar
1 egg
¾ cup finely shredded carrot
¼ cup fat-free milk
½ teaspoon vanilla
1 cup all-purpose flour
1¼ teaspoons baking powder
½ teaspoon ground cinnamon
⅛ teaspoon salt
⅛ teaspoon ground nutmeg
1 to 2 teaspoons sifted powdered sugar

Nutrition Facts per serving: 150 cal., 6 g total fat (3 g sat. fat), 38 mg chol., 161 mg sodium, 22 g carbo., 12 g sugar, 1 g fiber, 2 g pro.
Daily Values: 62% vit. A, 2% vit. C, 5% calcium, 4% iron
Exchanges: 1½ Other Carbo., 1 Fat

Gingerbread with Vanilla Sauce

A quick fix-up for a packaged mix, the crystallized ginger adds an extra boost of flavor to gingerbread. Look for crystallized ginger with the spices at your supermarket.

1 Lightly coat a 9×9×2-inch baking pan with cooking spray; set aside. In a medium bowl stir together gingerbread mix and water until combined. Stir in 1 tablespoon of the crystallized ginger. Spread batter in the prepared baking pan.

2 Bake in a 375° oven for 20 to 25 minutes or until a wooden toothpick inserted near the center comes out clean. Cool slightly in pan on a wire rack. Serve warm, topped with Vanilla Sauce and remaining crystallized ginger.

Vanilla Sauce: In a small bowl stir together ⅓ cup vanilla low-fat yogurt, ⅓ cup light dairy sour cream, and 1 teaspoon vanilla. Cover and chill until ready to serve. Makes ⅔ cup.

Nutrition Facts per serving: 166 cal., 4 g total fat (1 g sat. fat), 3 mg chol., 236 mg sodium, 29 g carbo., 16 g sugar, 0 g fiber, 3 g pro.
Daily Values: 1% vit. A, 5% calcium, 10% iron
Exchanges: 2 Other Carbo., ½ Fat

Prep: 10 minutes
Bake: 20 minutes
Oven: 375°F
Makes: 12 servings

Nonstick cooking spray
1 14½-ounce package gingerbread mix
1 cup water
2 tablespoons finely chopped crystallized ginger
1 recipe Vanilla Sauce

Cherry Trifle Cake

What an elegant fix-up! Take advantage of fresh cherry season to top this purchased sponge cake with the summer's sweet gems. Once cherry season is over, try halved strawberries or whole raspberries instead of cherries.

1 Place the cake on a serving platter; sprinkle with juice. Set aside. In a small mixing bowl stir together the whipped topping and yogurt; spread onto cake. Cover and chill for up to 2 hours.

2 Remove stems from cherries; halve and remove pits. To serve, arrange cherries, cut side down, on top of yogurt mixture.

Nutrition Facts per serving: 189 cal., 2 g total fat (1 g sat. fat), 47 mg chol., 122 mg sodium, 38 g carbo., 35 g sugar, 1 g fiber, 4 g pro.
Daily Values: 3% vit. A, 9% vit. C, 6% calcium, 8% iron
Exchanges: ½ Fruit, 2 Other Carbo.

Prep: 20 minutes
Chill: 2 hours
Makes: 10 servings

- 1 9½-inch tart-shaped sponge cake
- ½ cup cherry or orange juice
- ¼ of an 8-ounce container frozen light whipped dessert topping, thawed
- 1 6-ounce carton low-fat cherry-vanilla or desired flavor yogurt
- 2 cups fresh light or dark sweet cherries, such as Rainier or Bing

Chocolate-Raspberry Torte

You won't miss the butter in this sinfully delicious soufflé-style chocolate cake. Topped with fresh berries and dusted with a little powdered sugar, it makes an elegant statement.

1 In a medium mixing bowl allow egg whites to stand at room temperature for 30 minutes. Meanwhile, in a small saucepan combine milk and the ¼ cup cocoa powder. Cook and stir over medium heat about 5 minutes or until mixture is thickened. Remove from heat. Stir in unsweetened chocolate and vanilla until smooth. Cool to room temperature.

2 Lightly coat an 8×4×2-inch loaf pan with cooking spray. Coat bottom and sides with the 2 teaspoons cocoa powder; set aside. In a large bowl stir together flour, the ½ cup granulated sugar, the baking powder, baking soda, and salt. Stir cooled chocolate mixture into flour mixture until blended (batter will be thick); set aside.

3 Beat egg whites with an electric mixer on medium speed until soft peaks form. Gradually add the 2 tablespoons granulated sugar, beating on medium-high speed until stiff peaks form (tips stand straight). Gently fold one-third of the beaten egg whites into the chocolate mixture to lighten. Fold in the remaining beaten egg whites just until smooth. Spread batter in the prepared baking pan.

4 Bake in a 350° oven for 30 minutes or until a wooden toothpick inserted near the center comes out clean. Cool in pan on a wire rack for 15 minutes. Invert cake onto a serving plate; invert again onto wire rack and cool completely.

Prep: 30 minutes
Bake: 30 minutes
Stand: 30 minutes
Oven: 350°F
Makes: 12 servings

- 2 egg whites
- ½ cup fat-free milk
- ¼ cup unsweetened cocoa powder
- 1 ounce unsweetened chocolate, chopped
- 1 teaspoon vanilla
  Nonstick cooking spray
- 2 teaspoons unsweetened cocoa powder
- ½ cup all-purpose flour
- ½ cup granulated sugar
- ¼ teaspoon baking powder
- ¼ teaspoon baking soda
- ⅛ teaspoon salt
- 2 tablespoons granulated sugar
- 2 teaspoons sifted powdered sugar
- 2 tablespoons raspberry spreadable fruit
- ½ cup fresh raspberries

5 Sprinkle powdered sugar over torte. In a small saucepan heat spreadable fruit until melted and smooth. Drizzle over torte. Garnish with fresh raspberries.

Nutrition Facts per serving: 97 cal., 2 g total fat (1 g sat. fat), 0 mg chol., 74 mg sodium, 19 g carbo., 14 g sugar, 1 g fiber, 2 g pro.
Daily Values: 1% vit. A, 2% vit. C, 4% calcium, 4% iron
Exchanges: 1½ Other Carbo.

25 g
carb

Chocolate Decadence

Save this sinfully rich chocolate torte for any special occasion—a small serving will satisfy even the biggest chocolate craving. The torte is done when the top springs back when lightly touched. Don't be fooled—it will still be moist.

1 Lightly coat an 8×1½-inch round baking pan with cooking spray; line bottom with parchment paper. Set aside. In a small bowl combine the whole egg, egg yolk, and vanilla. In a medium mixing bowl combine the 2 egg whites and cream of tartar. Set both bowls aside.

2 In a saucepan combine the ⅔ cup granulated sugar, cocoa powder, and flour. Whisk in enough milk to form a paste; stir in remaining milk. Cook and stir over medium heat until mixture begins to simmer. Cook and stir 1½ minutes more; remove from heat. Stir in chocolate until smooth. Whisk in egg yolk mixture. Set aside.

3 Beat egg whites and cream of tartar with an electric mixer on medium speed until soft peaks form (tips curl). Gradually add the ¼ cup granulated sugar, beating on high speed until stiff peaks form (tips stand straight). Fold one-fourth of beaten egg whites into chocolate mixture. Fold in remaining beaten egg whites just until smooth. Spread batter in prepared pan.

4 Position oven rack in lower third of oven. Place the 8-inch round pan in a shallow roasting pan; place on oven rack. Pour enough boiling water into larger pan to come halfway up sides of the round pan.

5 Bake in a 350° oven about 30 minutes or until top springs back when lightly touched. Remove round pan from water. Cool torte in pan on a wire rack. Cover; chill for 24 hours.

Prep: 40 minutes • Bake: 30 minutes
Chill: 24 hours • Oven: 350°F
Makes: 12 servings

Nonstick cooking spray
1   egg
1   egg yolk
1   teaspoon vanilla
2   egg whites
⅛   teaspoon cream of tartar
⅔   cup granulated sugar
½   cup unsweetened cocoa powder
2   tablespoons all-purpose flour
¾   cup reduced-fat milk
5   ounces semisweet chocolate, finely chopped
¼   cup granulated sugar
2   teaspoons sifted powdered sugar
Fresh strawberries (optional)

6 To serve, run a thin knife around sides of pan to loosen torte. Place waxed paper on top of torte. Invert onto waxed paper; remove pan and parchment. Invert again onto a serving plate; remove waxed paper. Sprinkle with powdered sugar. Cut cake into wedges. Serve with fresh berries, if desired.

Nutrition Facts per serving: 158 cal., 5 g total fat (2 g sat. fat), 36 mg chol., 23 mg sodium, 25 g carbo., 21 g sugar, 1 g fiber, 4 g pro.
Daily Values: 2% vit. A, 6% calcium, 7% iron
Exchanges: 1½ Other Carbo., 1 Fat

Tiramisu

Treat your dinner guests to this reduced-fat knockoff of a classic Italian coffee-flavored dessert. This version will save you almost 100 calories and 15 grams of fat per serving.

1 In a large mixing bowl combine sour cream, cream cheese, sugar, milk, and vanilla. Beat with an electric mixer on high speed until smooth. In a small bowl combine coffee and coffee liqueur.

2 Arrange one package of the ladyfingers, cut sides up, in a 2-quart rectangular baking dish. Brush with half of the coffee mixture. Spread with half of the cream cheese mixture. Repeat with the remaining ladyfingers, coffee mixture, and cream cheese mixture. Sprinkle with sifted cocoa powder.

3 Cover and chill for 4 to 24 hours. If desired, sprinkle dessert plates with additional unsweetened cocoa powder. Cut dessert into squares to serve.

Prep: 30 minutes
Chill: 4 to 24 hours
Makes: 15 servings

- 2 8-ounce cartons fat-free dairy sour cream
- 2 8-ounce packages reduced-fat cream cheese (Neufchâtel), softened
- ½ cup sugar
- ¼ cup fat-free milk
- ½ teaspoon vanilla
- ½ cup strong coffee
- 2 tablespoons coffee liqueur
- 2 3-ounce packages ladyfingers, split
- 2 tablespoons sifted unsweetened cocoa powder

Nutrition Facts per serving: 181 cal., 8 g total fat (5 g sat. fat), 64 mg chol., 157 mg sodium, 20 g carbo., 9 g sugar, 0 g fiber, 6 g pro.
Daily Values: 8% vit. A, 1% vit. C, 8% calcium, 3% iron
Exchanges: ½ Starch, 1 Other Carbo., ½ Lean Meat, 1½ Fat

Cherry Clafouti

Clafouti is a traditional French, custardlike dessert, but its summer-ripe flavor and rich texture make it pleasing for breakfast. The most popular sweet cherries are the large, dark colored Bing or Lambert varieties.

1 Generously coat a 2-quart square baking dish with cooking spray; set aside.

2 In a medium mixing bowl beat together egg whites, whole eggs, granulated sugar, milk, orange peel, and almond extract with a wire whisk until combined. Blend in yogurt just until smooth. Gradually add flour, beating with whisk until smooth. Pour batter into the prepared baking dish. Sprinkle with cherries.

3 Bake in a 350° oven for 25 to 30 minutes or until a knife inserted near the center comes out clean. If desired, sprinkle with sifted powdered sugar.

Prep: 15 minutes
Bake: 25 minutes
Oven: 350°F
Makes: 8 servings

Nonstick cooking spray
3   egg whites
2   eggs
⅓   cup granulated sugar
¼   cup fat-free milk
½   teaspoon finely shredded orange peel
    Few drops almond extract
1   8-ounce carton plain fat-free yogurt
½   cup all-purpose flour
2   cups pitted dark sweet cherries
    Sifted powdered sugar (optional)

Nutrition Facts per serving: 129 cal., 2 g total fat (1 g sat. fat), 54 mg chol., 62 mg sodium, 23 g carbo., 15 g sugar, 1 g fiber, 6 g pro.
Daily Values: 4% vit. A, 5% vit. C, 8% calcium, 4% iron
Exchanges: 1 Fruit, ½ Starch, ½ Lean Meat

Pour-and-Bake Pear Pudding

If you don't have a quiche dish on hand, a deep-dish 10-inch pie plate works just as well. Avoid pans with removable bottoms such as springform pans or quiche pans; they may leak.

1 Drain pear halves, reserving ¾ cup syrup. Score the round side of each pear half by making shallow crosswise cuts across the top. Set pears and syrup aside.

2 In a blender container or food processor bowl combine flour and granulated sugar. Cover and blend or process until combined. Add yogurt, eggs, vanilla, and the reserved pear syrup. Cover and blend or process until smooth.

3 Grease a 9½×1½- or 10×1½-inch quiche dish. Arrange pear halves, flat sides down, in bottom of the prepared dish. Pour the batter over pears. Sprinkle with brown sugar.

4 Bake in a 375° oven for 25 to 30 minutes or just until center is set when gently shaken. Cool on a wire rack about 30 minutes. Spoon into dessert dishes. Serve warm.

Prep: 15 minutes
Bake: 25 minutes
Oven: 375°F
Makes: 6 servings

2   15-ounce cans pear halves in light syrup
⅓   cup all-purpose flour
¼   cup granulated sugar
½   cup plain low-fat or fat-free yogurt
2   eggs
1   teaspoon vanilla
3   tablespoons brown sugar

Nutrition Facts per serving: 177 cal., 2 g total fat (1 g sat. fat), 72 mg chol., 40 mg sodium, 36 g carbo., 30 g sugar, 3 g fiber, 4 g pro.
Daily Values: 2% vit. A, 5% vit. C, 6% calcium, 5% iron
Exchanges: 1 Fruit, 1½ Other Carbo., ½ Fat

Apricot Bread Pudding

Bread pudding—the ultimate comfort food—gets updated and slimmed down in this delectable dessert. To dry the bread, let it stand, loosely covered, at room temperature for 8 to 12 hours.

1 Grease a 10½-inch quiche dish; set aside. In a large bowl combine bread pieces, apricots, and currants. Place the bread mixture in the prepared quiche dish. In a medium bowl combine milk, egg product, sugar, vanilla, and cardamom. Pour evenly over bread mixture.

2 Bake in a 325° oven for 35 to 40 minutes or until a knife inserted near the center comes out clean.

Nutrition Facts per serving: 213 cal., 1 g total fat (0 g sat. fat), 2 mg chol., 269 mg sodium, 41 g carbo., 23 g sugar, 2 g fiber, 10 g pro.
Daily Values: 22% vit. A, 2% vit. C, 17% calcium, 12% iron
Exchanges: ½ Fruit, 1 Starch, 1 Other Carbo., ½ Very Lean Meat

Prep: 15 minutes
Bake: 35 minutes
Oven: 325°F
Makes: 6 to 8 servings

5	cups torn dry bread pieces (7 to 8 slices)
8	dried apricots, quartered
3	tablespoons dried currants or raisins
2¼	cups fat-free milk
1	8-ounce carton refrigerated or frozen egg product, thawed
⅓	cup granulated sugar
1	teaspoon vanilla
¼	teaspoon ground cardamom

23 g
carb

Lemon-Mango Pudding Cake

Remember Mom's pudding cake? Perhaps she called it sponge pudding, cake-top pudding, or upside-down pudding. No matter what the moniker, this simple dessert is delicious served warm from the oven.

1 Coat a 2-quart square baking dish with cooking spray. Arrange mango in bottom of the prepared baking dish. Set aside.

2 In a large mixing bowl stir together sugar, flour, and salt. Stir in lemon juice and melted margarine. In a small bowl combine egg yolks, yogurt, and milk. Add to lemon mixture; stir just until combined.

3 In a medium mixing bowl beat egg whites with an electric mixer on high speed until stiff peaks form (tips stand straight). Gently fold the beaten egg whites into the lemon mixture. Carefully spoon batter on top of chopped mango in baking dish. Place the baking dish in a larger baking pan. Set the baking pan on the oven rack. Pour boiling water into the larger baking pan around the baking dish to a depth of 1 inch.

4 Bake in a 350° oven about 40 minutes or until set. Remove from larger baking pan; cool on a wire rack for 30 minutes. Serve warm. If desired, garnish each serving with a mango wedge and/or raspberries.

Prep: 30 minutes
Bake: 40 minutes
Oven: 350°F
Makes: 9 servings

Nonstick cooking spray
1 large mango, seeded, peeled, and chopped (about 1¾ cups)
½ cup sugar
¼ cup all-purpose flour
Dash salt
2 tablespoons lemon juice
1 tablespoon margarine or butter, melted
3 egg yolks
1 8-ounce carton lemon low-fat yogurt
½ cup fat-free milk
3 egg whites
Mango wedges and/or raspberries (optional)

Nutrition Facts per serving: 136 cal., 3 g total fat (1 g sat. fat), 73 mg chol., 76 mg sodium, 23 g carbo., 19 g sugar, 1 g fiber, 4 g pro.
Daily Values: 26% vit. A, 16% vit. C, 7% calcium, 2% iron
Exchanges: 1½ Other Carbo., ½ Fat

17 g
carb

Mini Cheesecakes

Just a couple of bites each, these tiny cheesecakes burst with flavor and satisfy any sweet tooth. To create a colorful platter, top the petite desserts with an assortment of fresh fruits.

1 Coat ten 2½-inch muffin cups with cooking spray. Sprinkle the bottom and sides of each cup with 1 rounded teaspoon of the crushed vanilla wafers. Set aside.

2 In a medium mixing bowl beat the cream cheese with an electric mixer on medium speed until smooth. Add the sugar, flour, and vanilla; beat until smooth. Add egg product; beat on low speed just until combined. Divide evenly among the prepared muffin cups.

3 Bake in a 325° oven for 18 to 20 minutes or until set. Cool in muffin pan on a wire rack for 5 minutes. Cover and chill for 4 to 24 hours.

4 Remove the cheesecakes from muffin cups. Just before serving, top the cheesecakes with fresh fruit.

Nutrition Facts per cheesecake: 98 cal., 1 g total fat (0 g sat. fat), 5 mg chol., 22 mg sodium, 17 g carbo., 12 g sugar, 0 g fiber, 6 g pro.
Daily Values: 1% vit. A, 2% vit. C, 12% calcium, 1% iron
Exchanges: 1 Other Carbo., ½ Very Lean Meat

Prep: 20 minutes
Bake: 18 minutes
Chill: 4 to 24 hours
Oven: 325°F
Makes: 10 cheesecakes

Nonstick cooking spray
⅓ cup crushed vanilla wafers (about 8 wafers)
1½ 8-ounce tubs fat-free cream cheese, softened
½ cup sugar
1 tablespoon all-purpose flour
1 teaspoon vanilla
¼ cup refrigerated or frozen egg product, thawed
¾ cup assorted fruit (such as halved seedless grapes; cut-up peeled pineapple, kiwifruit, or papaya; red raspberries; blueberries; sliced strawberries or plums; and/or orange or grapefruit sections)

Crème Caramel

Thanks to aromatic and intensely flavored vanilla bean, no one will know that this cousin of flan doesn't have the whole milk, cream, and egg yolks of the traditional recipe.

1 Coat six 6-ounce custard cups with oil or cooking spray; set aside.

2 In a small saucepan heat milk, rosemary, vanilla bean, orange peel, and lime peel just until bubbly. Remove from heat. Pour milk mixture through a sieve lined with a double thickness of 100-percent-cotton cheesecloth to remove vanilla bean and peels. Discard vanilla bean and peels. Set aside milk mixture.

3 Meanwhile, in a medium mixing bowl combine egg product and sugar. Slowly whisk hot milk mixture into egg mixture.

4 Place the custard cups in a 3-quart rectangular baking dish. Set baking dish on an oven rack. Pour custard mixture evenly into cups. Pour enough boiling water into the baking dish to reach halfway up sides of cups.

5 Cover baking dish loosely with foil. Bake in a 325° oven for 35 to 40 minutes or until a knife inserted near the centers comes out clean. Remove custards from baking dish. Cool on a wire rack for 1 hour. Cover and chill until serving time.

6 To unmold custards, loosen edges with a knife. Invert a dessert plate over each custard; turn custard cup and plate over together. Pour maple syrup over custards and garnish with fresh berries.

Prep: 25 minutes
Bake: 35 minutes
Cool: 1 hour
Oven: 325°F
Makes: 6 servings

Cooking oil or nonstick cooking spray
2 cups reduced-fat milk
1 small sprig fresh rosemary
½ of a vanilla bean, cut in half lengthwise (about 3 inches)
1½ teaspoons finely shredded orange peel
¾ teaspoon finely shredded lime peel
1 cup refrigerated or frozen egg product, thawed, or 4 eggs
3 tablespoons sugar
2 tablespoons pure maple syrup
Fresh berries

Make-Ahead Tip: Prepare, bake, and cool the custards as directed. Cover unmolded custards and chill for 4 to 24 hours.

Nutrition Facts per serving: 115 cal., 2 g total fat (1 g sat. fat), 6 mg chol., 108 mg sodium, 17 g carbo., 16 g sugar, 1 g fiber, 7 g pro.
Daily Values: 6% vit. A, 24% vit. C, 12% calcium, 5% iron
Exchanges: 1 Other Carbo., 1 Very Lean Meat, ½ Fat

36 g
carb

Strudel Triangles with Brandied Apples

Call it an elegant take on apple pie—layer warm apple-and-raisin filling with cinnamon-sugar phyllo crisps and caramel topping.

1 Combine the graham cracker crumbs and granulated sugar; set aside. Coat a large baking sheet with cooking spray; set aside.

2 Cut phyllo sheets in half crosswise. Coat the phyllo halves with cooking spray. Sprinkle one-fourth of the crumb mixture on a phyllo half. Top with another phyllo half and another one-fourth of the crumb mixture; repeat with remaining phyllo halves and crumb mixture for a four-layer stack. Cut the stack into nine 4¾×3-inch rectangles. Cut each rectangle diagonally in half to form two triangles (18 total).

3 Carefully place triangles on the prepared baking sheet. Bake in a 375° oven for 6 to 8 minutes or until golden brown.

4 In a large skillet melt margarine. Stir in brown sugar until combined. Stir in apple slices, 3 tablespoons of the ice cream topping, the raisins, apple brandy, cinnamon, and nutmeg. Cook, uncovered, about 5 minutes or until apples are tender, stirring occasionally.

5 To serve, place a strudel triangle on each of 6 dessert plates. Spoon one-third of the apple mixture on strudel triangles. Place a second strudel triangle over apple mixture on each plate, with the points going in different directions than the first triangle. Top triangles with one-third of the apple mixture. Repeat with the remaining strudel triangles and the remaining apple mixture.

Prep: 35 minutes
Bake: 6 minutes
Oven: 375°F
Makes: 6 servings

¼ cup low-fat cinnamon graham cracker crumbs
1 tablespoon granulated sugar
   Nonstick cooking spray
2 sheets (18x14 inches) frozen phyllo dough, thawed
1 tablespoon margarine or butter
1 tablespoon brown sugar
3 medium apples, peeled, cored, and thinly sliced (about 1 pound)
⅓ cup caramel ice cream topping
¼ cup raisins, dried cranberries, or dried cherries
1 tablespoon apple brandy, apple cider, or apple juice
¼ teaspoon ground cinnamon
⅛ teaspoon ground nutmeg

6 Drizzle the remaining ice cream topping over apple mixture. Serve immediately.

Nutrition Facts per serving: 169 cal., 3 g total fat (1 g sat. fat), 0 mg chol., 133 mg sodium, 36 g carbo., 29 g sugar, 3 g fiber, 1 g pro.
Daily Values: 3% vit. A, 6% vit. C, 2% calcium, 4% iron
Exchanges: 1 Fruit, 1½ Other Carbo., ½ Fat

Lemon-Meringue Shells

The secret to successful meringue is adding sugar gradually so it dissolves into the egg whites. Rub a small amount of meringue between your index finger and thumb to see if the sugar is dissolved.

1 In a large mixing bowl let egg whites stand at room temperature for 30 minutes. Meanwhile, line a baking sheet with parchment paper or foil. Using a pencil, draw eight 3-inch circles on parchment paper or foil. Turn paper upside down on baking sheet; set aside.

2 For meringue, add lemon juice and cream of tartar to egg whites. Beat with an electric mixer on medium speed until soft peaks form (tips curl). Add sugar, 1 tablespoon at a time, beating on high speed about 7 minutes or until very stiff peaks form (tips stand straight) and sugar is nearly dissolved.

3 For shells, use the back of a large spoon to spread the meringue over circles on parchment paper, building up sides to form shells.

4 Bake in a 300° oven for 30 minutes. Turn off oven. Let meringues dry in oven, with door closed, for at least 1 hour. Remove from paper. If desired, store in an airtight container in a cool, dry place for up to 1 week.

5 Just before serving, spoon 1 tablespoon of the lemon curd into each meringue shell. Place a few berries on lemon curd.

Prep: 35 minutes
Bake: 30 minutes
Stand: 1 hour
Oven: 300°F
Makes: 8 servings

2 egg whites
1 teaspoon lemon juice
¼ teaspoon cream of tartar
⅔ cup sugar
½ cup lemon curd
1 cup blackberries, raspberries, or
     other berries

Nutrition Facts per serving: 141 cal., 1 g total fat (1 g sat. fat), 15 mg chol., 29 mg sodium, 34 g carbo., 30 g sugar, 3 g fiber, 1 g pro.
Daily Values: 1% vit. A, 7% vit. C, 1% calcium, 1% iron
Exchanges: 2 Other Carbo.

Nectarine Tart

The filling in this low-fat dessert tastes deceivingly rich. Fat-free cream cheese is the key. For a pretty finish, arrange the fruit in a pinwheel design before glazing with the apricot spread.

1 For pastry, in a medium bowl combine flour and salt. Using a pastry blender, cut in butter until pieces are pea-size. Sprinkle 1 tablespoon of the cold water over a portion of the mixture. Toss with a fork. Push to the side of the bowl. Repeat until mixture is moistened. Form into a ball.

2 On a lightly floured surface, flatten pastry. Roll pastry into a 12-inch circle. Ease pastry into a 10-inch tart pan with a removable bottom, being careful not to stretch pastry. Press pastry about ½ inch up the sides of pan. Prick the bottom well with the tines of a fork. Bake in a 450° oven for 12 to 15 minutes or until golden. Cool on a wire rack. Remove sides of tart pan.

3 Meanwhile, in a medium bowl combine the cream cheese, sugar, and vanilla. Beat with an electric mixer until smooth; spread over the cooled pastry. Arrange nectarines over cream cheese layer. Sprinkle with blueberries.

4 In a small saucepan heat apricot spread until melted; cut up any large pieces. Spoon melted spread over fruit. Chill for at least 2 hours or up to 3 hours.

Prep: 35 minutes
Bake: 12 minutes
Chill: 2 hours
Oven: 450°F
Makes: 12 servings

- 1 cup all-purpose flour
- ¼ teaspoon salt
- ¼ cup butter or margarine
- 4 to 5 tablespoons cold water
- 1 8-ounce package fat-free cream cheese, softened
- ¼ cup sugar
- 1 teaspoon vanilla
- 4 or 5 nectarines or peeled peaches, pitted and sliced, or one 16-ounce package frozen unsweetened peach slices, thawed and drained
- ½ cup blueberries
- ½ cup low-calorie apricot spread

Nutrition Facts per serving: 145 cal., 4 g total fat (1 g sat. fat), 2 mg chol., 196 mg sodium, 23 g carbo., 12 g sugar, 1 g fiber, 4 g pro.
Daily Values: 14% vit. A, 5% vit. C, 4% calcium, 3% iron
Exchanges: ½ Fruit, 1 Starch, ½ Fat

Tropical Tart

A little coconut, a little pineapple and a few kiwifruit on top of a gingersnap crust—it's a classic Caribbean flavor combination. You can almost feel the island breezes.

1 Generously coat a 10-inch tart pan with a removable bottom with cooking spray. In a small bowl combine gingersnaps, coconut, and melted margarine. Press the mixture onto the bottom and up the sides of the prepared tart pan.

2 Bake in a 350° oven about 8 minutes or until light brown. Cool on a wire rack.

3 For filling, in a medium saucepan combine the sugar and cornstarch. Stir in undrained pineapple. Cook and stir until thickened and bubbly. Cook and stir for 2 minutes more. Remove from heat. Stir in vanilla; transfer filling to a bowl. Cover surface with plastic wrap and cool to room temperature.

4 Spread the filling into the crust. Arrange kiwifruit and/or strawberries on filling. Cover and chill for 2 to 3 hours. To serve, remove sides of tart pan. If desired, spoon whipped topping on top of tart.

Prep: 20 minutes
Bake: 8 minutes
Chill: 2 hours
Oven: 350°F
Makes: 10 servings

Nonstick cooking spray
1 cup finely crushed gingersnaps (about 18 cookies)
½ cup shredded coconut
3 tablespoons margarine or butter, melted
⅓ cup sugar
3 tablespoons cornstarch
1 15¼-ounce can crushed pineapple (juice pack)
½ teaspoon vanilla
2 cups sliced peeled kiwifruit and/or sliced strawberries
Frozen light whipped dessert topping, thawed (optional)

Nutrition Facts per serving: 173 cal., 6 g total fat (2 g sat. fat), 0 mg chol., 124 mg sodium, 29 g carbo., 19 g sugar, 2 g fiber, 1 g pro.
Daily Values: 4% vit. A, 44% vit. C, 3% calcium, 6% iron
Exchanges: ½ Fruit, 1½ Other Carbo., 1 Fat

No-Sugar Apple Pie

Compared with a double-crust apple pie, this version has 130 fewer calories and 7 grams less fat per serving. The best part? It still has that comforting, home-baked flavor.

1 Prepare Baked Pastry Shell. For filling, in a small bowl combine apple juice and tapioca. Cover; let stand for 15 minutes. In a large saucepan combine apples, butter, cinnamon, nutmeg, and tapioca mixture. Cook, covered, over medium-low heat for 20 to 25 minutes or until apples are tender, stirring occasionally.

2 Spoon the filling into baked pie shell. Cool for 1 hour. Serve warm or cover and chill before serving. If desired, top with whipped topping.

Baked Pastry Shell: In a medium bowl stir together 1¼ cups all-purpose flour and ¼ teaspoon salt. Using a pastry blender, cut in ⅓ cup shortening until pieces are pea-size. Using 4 to 5 tablespoons cold water, sprinkle water, 1 tablespoon at a time, over flour mixture and toss with a fork until all of the dough is moistened. Shape into a ball. On a lightly floured surface, roll dough from center to edges into a 12-inch circle. Transfer to a 9-inch pie plate. Trim pastry to ½ inch beyond edge. Fold under extra pastry; crimp edge. Line pastry with a double thickness of foil. Bake in a 450° oven for 8 minutes. Remove foil. Bake for 5 to 6 minutes more or until golden brown. Cool on a wire rack.

Prep: 45 minutes
Bake: 13 minutes
Cool: 1 hour
Oven: 450°F
Makes: 8 servings

1 recipe Baked Pastry Shell
½ cup apple juice or water
2 tablespoons quick-cooking tapioca
8 cups peeled and thinly sliced Golden Delicious apples (about 3 pounds)
1 tablespoon butter or margarine
1 teaspoon ground cinnamon
½ teaspoon ground nutmeg
    Frozen whipped dessert topping, thawed, or frozen vanilla yogurt (optional)

Nutrition Facts per serving: 246 cal., 11 g total fat (3 g sat. fat), 4 mg chol., 83 mg sodium, 37 g carbo., 18 g sugar, 3 g fiber, 2 g pro.
Daily Values: 2% vit. A, 7% vit. C, 1% calcium, 6% iron
Exchanges: 1½ Fruit, 1 Starch, 2 Fat

Strawberry Bavarian Pie

Naturally low-fat ladyfinger sponge cakes form the crust for this light, strawberry-flavored pie. Shop for soft ladyfingers; the crispy ones will not work as well.

1 Place strawberries in a blender container or food processor bowl. Cover and blend or process until smooth. Measure the blended strawberries (you should have about 1¾ cups).

2 In a medium saucepan combine the sugar and gelatin. Stir in the blended berries. Cook and stir over medium heat until the mixture is bubbly and the gelatin is dissolved.

3 Gradually stir about half of the gelatin mixture into egg whites. Return all of the egg white mixture to gelatin mixture in the saucepan. Cook and stir over low heat for 2 to 3 minutes or until slightly thickened. Do not boil. Transfer to a bowl. Cover and chill just until the mixture mounds when dropped from a spoon, stirring occasionally.

4 Meanwhile, cut about half of the ladyfingers in half crosswise; stand on end around the outside edge of a 9- or 9½-inch tart pan with a removable bottom or a 9-inch springform pan. Arrange the remaining ladyfingers in bottom of pan. Slowly drizzle orange juice over ladyfingers.

5 Fold whipped topping into strawberry mixture; spoon into the ladyfinger-lined pan. Cover and chill for at least 2 hours or until set. If desired, garnish with additional whipped topping and strawberries.

Prep: 20 minutes
Chill: 2½ hours
Makes: 10 servings

- **3 cups strawberries**
- **¼ cup sugar**
- **1 envelope unflavored gelatin**
- **3 slightly beaten egg whites**
- **1 3-ounce package ladyfingers, split**
- **2 tablespoons orange juice**
- **½ of an 8-ounce container frozen light whipped dessert topping, thawed**

Nutrition Facts per serving: 97 cal., 2 g total fat (2 g sat. fat), 31 mg chol., 31 mg sodium, 16 g carbo., 9 g sugar, 1 g fiber, 3 g pro. **Daily Values:** 1% vit. A, 44% vit. C, 1% calcium, 3% iron
Exchanges: 1 Other Carbo., ½ Fat

8 g
carb

Date Bars

Lessen the temptation to eat more than you should from this batch. After they're baked, wrap and freeze half of them in freezer wrap or an airtight freezer container. If stored properly, they will keep in your freezer for up to 8 months.

1 In a small bowl pour boiling water over dates. Cover and let stand for 10 minutes. Drain liquid.

2 Coat an 8×8×2-inch baking pan with cooking spray; set aside. Combine flour, baking powder, cinnamon, and baking soda; set aside.

3 In a medium mixing bowl beat egg with an electric mixer on high speed until frothy. Add brown sugar; beat until combined. Stir in evaporated milk and drained dates.

4 Add flour mixture to egg mixture, stirring with a wooden spoon just until combined. Stir in nuts. Pour batter into the prepared baking pan.

5 Bake in a 350° oven about 15 minutes or until a wooden toothpick inserted near the center comes out clean. Cool in pan on a wire rack. Sprinkle with powdered sugar. Cut into bars.

Nutrition Facts per bar: 40 cal., 1 g total fat (0 g sat. fat), 9 mg chol., 21 mg sodium, 8 g carbo., 5 g sugar, 0 g fiber, 1 g pro.
Daily Values: 2% calcium, 1% iron
Exchanges: ½ Other Carbo.

Prep: 25 minutes
Bake: 15 minutes
Oven: 350°F
Makes: about 24 bars

½ cup boiling water
⅓ cup snipped pitted whole dates
  Nonstick cooking spray
½ cup all-purpose flour
½ teaspoon baking powder
¼ teaspoon ground cinnamon
⅛ teaspoon baking soda
1 egg
⅓ cup packed brown sugar
⅓ cup evaporated fat-free milk
2 tablespoons finely chopped walnuts, toasted
1 teaspoon sifted powdered sugar

Vanilla Bean Biscotti

Using vanilla bean is worth the extra expense in these twice-baked tender cookies. Easier to make than you think, they're a great accompaniment to a dish of fresh fruit or a cup of coffee.

1 Grease a very large cookie sheet; set aside. Scrape seeds from the vanilla bean, if using; set aside.

2 In a medium bowl combine flour, baking powder, and salt; set aside. In a large mixing bowl beat eggs with an electric mixer on high speed for 1 minute. Gradually beat in sugar, beating on high speed for 1 minute. Beat in butter and vanilla seeds or vanilla extract, if using, on low speed until combined. Beat in as much of the flour mixture as you can with the mixer. Stir in any remaining flour mixture with a wooden spoon.

3 Divide dough into thirds. On a lightly floured surface, roll each portion into a 14×1½-inch log. Place logs 2½ inches apart on prepared cookie sheet.

4 Bake in a 325° oven for 25 minutes or until firm and light brown. Cool on cookie sheet on a wire rack for 15 minutes.

5 Transfer each log to a large cutting board. With a serrated knife, gently slice each log diagonally into ½-inch slices. Arrange slices, cut side down, on the cookie sheet.

6 Bake slices for 10 minutes. Turn slices and bake 10 minutes more or until crisp and lightly browned. Remove and cool on the cookie sheet on a wire rack.

Prep: 30 minutes
Bake: 45 minutes
Cool: 1 hour
Oven: 325°F
Makes: 48 cookies

- 1 vanilla bean, split, or 2 teaspoons vanilla
- 3 cups all-purpose flour
- 1 tablespoon baking powder
- ¼ teaspoon salt
- 3 eggs
- ¾ cup sugar
- ½ cup butter, melted and cooled

Nutrition Facts per biscotti: 63 cal., 2 g total fat (1 g sat. fat), 19 mg chol., 62 mg sodium, 9 g carbo., 3 g sugar, 0 g fiber, 1 g pro.
Daily Values: 2% vit. A, 2% calcium, 2% iron
Exchanges: ½ Other Carbo., ½ Fat

Devil's Food Cookies

When you need a little something to satisfy a sweet tooth, try to fit one of these powdered sugar-dusted, chocolaty morsels into your carb allowance for the day.

1 Coat a cookie sheet with cooking spray; set aside. In a small bowl stir together flour, cocoa powder, baking soda, and salt; set aside.

2 In a medium mixing bowl beat butter with an electric mixer on medium to high speed for 30 seconds. Add the brown sugar. Beat until combined, scraping sides of bowl occasionally. Beat in buttermilk, egg product, and vanilla until combined. Beat in as much of the flour mixture as you can with the mixer. Using a wooden spoon, stir in remaining flour mixture.

3 Drop dough by rounded tablespoons onto prepared cookie sheet. Bake in a 350° oven for 7 to 9 minutes or until nearly firm. Cool on cookie sheet for 1 minute. Transfer to a wire rack; cool. Sprinkle cookies with powdered sugar.

Nutrition Facts per cookie: 73 cal., 2 g total fat (1 g sat. fat), 5 mg chol., 99 mg sodium, 12 g carbo., 6 g sugar, 1 g fiber, 1 g pro.
Daily Values: 2% vit. A, 2% calcium, 4% iron
Exchanges: 1 Other Carbo., ½ Fat

Prep: 15 minutes
Bake: 7 minutes per batch
Oven: 350°F
Makes: about 24 cookies

Nonstick cooking spray
1½ cups all-purpose flour
⅓ cup unsweetened cocoa powder
1 teaspoon baking soda
⅛ teaspoon salt
¼ cup butter, softened
⅔ cup packed brown sugar
½ cup buttermilk
¼ cup refrigerated or frozen egg product, thawed, or 2 egg whites
1 teaspoon vanilla
1 tablespoon sifted powdered sugar

Honey-Peach Frozen Yogurt

You can't go wrong with this combination. The tartness of the frozen yogurt accents the sweetness of the peaches. Add a little honey for good measure and you have a healthful version of peaches and cream.

1 Place 1½ cups of the chopped peaches in a food processor bowl or blender container with the yogurt and honey. Cover and process or blend until smooth. (If using a blender, blend a small amount at a time and do not overblend.) Stir in remaining chopped peaches. Pour into a 2-quart pan. Cover and freeze for 4 hours or until firm.

2 Break the frozen mixture into small pieces and place in a chilled mixing bowl; beat with an electric mixer on medium speed until fluffy, starting slowly and gradually increasing the speed. Return mixture to pan and freeze, covered, for 6 hours or until firm. Let frozen yogurt stand at room temperature for 10 to 20 minutes before serving.

Prep: 40 minutes
Stand: 10 minutes
Freeze: 10 hours
Makes: 12 (½-cup) servings

3 cups peeled, pitted, and finely chopped peaches or nectarines (about 4 medium)
2 16-ounce cartons low-fat vanilla yogurt
¼ cup honey

Nutrition Facts per serving: 109 cal., 1 g total fat (1 g sat. fat), 5 mg chol., 54 mg sodium, 23 g carbo., 22 g sugar, 1 g fiber, 4 g pro.
Daily Values: 6% vit. A, 6% vit. C, 14% calcium
Exchanges: ½ Milk, 1 Other Carbo.

Watermelon Sherbet

To save some work, look for packages of cut-up watermelon in the produce section of your grocery store. You'll still have to remove the seeds, unless you're fortunate enough to find cut-up seedless melon.

1 Place watermelon in a blender container or food processor bowl. Cover and blend or process until smooth. (You should have 3 cups of the watermelon mixture.) Stir in sugar.

2 In a small saucepan combine the gelatin and cranberry juice. Let mixture stand for 5 minutes. Stir mixture over low heat until gelatin is dissolved.

3 Stir the gelatin mixture into the melon mixture. Pour into an 8×8×2-inch baking pan. Cover and freeze about 2 hours or until firm.

4 Break up frozen mixture and place in a chilled mixer bowl. Beat with an electric mixer on medium to high speed until mixture is fluffy. Return to pan. Cover and freeze about 6 hours or until firm.

Prep: 25 minutes
Freeze: 8 hours
Makes: 8 (½-cup) servings

4   cups cubed, seeded watermelon
½   cup sugar
1   envelope unflavored gelatin
⅓   cup cranberry juice

Nutrition Facts per serving: 80 cal., 0 g total fat (0 g sat. fat), 0 mg chol., 4 mg sodium, 19 g carbo., 20 g sugar, 0 g fiber, 1 g pro.
Daily Values: 6% vit. A, 18% vit. C, 1% calcium, 1% iron
Exchanges: 1 Fruit, ½ Other Carbo.

Espresso Granita

The distinctive flavor of coffee—slightly bitter, slightly rich—oozes from this cool icy dessert. If needed, combine 3 cups of cold water and 3 tablespoons instant espresso powder to substitute for the strong brewed espresso in the recipe.

1 In a medium saucepan combine the water and sugar. Cook and stir over medium heat until sugar is dissolved. Remove from heat; cool about 30 minutes. Stir in espresso and, if desired, anisette liqueur. Pour into a 13×9×2-inch pan.

2 Cover and freeze about 1½ hours or until mixture is slushy on the edges. Stir, scraping the frozen mixture off bottom and sides of pan. Cover and freeze for 3 to 3½ hours or until all of the mixture is slushy, stirring every 30 minutes. Cover and freeze for at least 6 hours or until firm.

3 Before serving, let granita stand at room temperature for 5 to 10 minutes. Scrape the surface of the granita and spoon into chilled dessert dishes.

Prep: 15 minutes
Cool: 30 minutes
Freeze: 10½ hours
Stand: 5 minutes
Makes: 8 servings

1	cup water
½	cup sugar
3	cups very strong brewed espresso, cooled
1	teaspoon anisette liqueur (optional)

Nutrition Facts per serving: 48 cal., 0 g total fat (0 g sat. fat), 0 mg chol., 3 mg sodium, 12 g carbo., 12 g sugar, 0 g fiber, 0 g pro.
Exchanges: 1 Other Carbo.

Index

Metric Information

The charts on this page provide a guide for converting measurements from the U.S. customary system, which is used throughout this book, to the metric system.

Product Differences

Most of the ingredients called for in the recipes in this book are available in most countries. However, some are known by different names. Here are some common American ingredients and their possible counterparts:

- Sugar (white) is granulated, fine granulated, or castor sugar.
- Powdered sugar is icing sugar.
- All-purpose flour is enriched, bleached or unbleached white household flour. When self-rising flour is used in place of all-purpose flour in a recipe that calls for leavening, omit the leavening agent (baking soda or baking powder) and salt.
- Light-colored corn syrup is golden syrup.
- Cornstarch is cornflour.
- Baking soda is bicarbonate of soda.
- Vanilla or vanilla extract is vanilla essence.
- Green, red, or yellow sweet peppers are capsicums or bell peppers.
- Golden raisins are sultanas.

Volume and Weight

The United States traditionally uses cup measures for liquid and solid ingredients. The chart below shows the approximate imperial and metric equivalents. If you are accustomed to weighing solid ingredients, the following approximate equivalents will be helpful.

- 1 cup butter, castor sugar, or rice = 8 ounces = ½ pound = 250 grams
- 1 cup flour = 4 ounces = ¼ pound = 125 grams
- 1 cup icing sugar = 5 ounces = 150 grams

Canadian and U.S. volume for a cup measure is 8 fluid ounces (237 ml), but the standard metric equivalent is 250 ml. 1 British imperial cup is 10 fluid ounces.
In Australia, 1 tablespoon equals 20 ml, and there are 4 teaspoons in the Australian tablespoon.
Spoon measures are used for smaller amounts of ingredients. Although the size of the tablespoon varies slightly in different countries, for practical purposes and for recipes in this book, a straight substitution is all that's necessary. Measurements made using cups or spoons always should be level unless stated otherwise.

Common Weight Range Replacements

Imperial / U.S.	Metric
½ ounce	15 g
1 ounce	25 g or 30 g
4 ounces (¼ pound)	115 g or 125 g
8 ounces (½ pound)	225 g or 250 g
16 ounces (1 pound)	450 g or 500 g
1¼ pounds	625 g
1½ pounds	750 g
2 pounds or 2¼ pounds	1,000 g or 1 Kg

Oven Temperature Equivalents

Fahrenheit Setting	Celsius Setting*	Gas Setting
300°F	150°C	Gas Mark 2 (very low)
325°F	160°C	Gas Mark 3 (low)
350°F	180°C	Gas Mark 4 (moderate)
375°F	190°C	Gas Mark 5 (moderate)
400°F	200°C	Gas Mark 6 (hot)
425°F	220°C	Gas Mark 7 (hot)
450°F	230°C	Gas Mark 8 (very hot)
475°F	240°C	Gas Mark 9 (very hot)
500°F	260°C	Gas Mark 10 (extremely hot)
Broil	Broil	Grill

*Electric and gas ovens may be calibrated using celsius. However, for an electric oven, increase celsius setting 10 to 20 degrees when cooking above 160°C. For convection or forced air ovens (gas or electric) lower the temperature setting 25°F/10°C when cooking at all heat levels.

Baking Pan Sizes

Imperial / U.S.	Metric
9×1½-inch round cake pan	22- or 23×4-cm (1.5 L)
9×1½-inch pie plate	22- or 23×4-cm (1 L)
8×8×2-inch square cake pan	20×5-cm (2 L)
9×9×2-inch square cake pan	22- or 23×4.5-cm (2.5 L)
11×7×1½-inch baking pan	28×17×4-cm (2 L)
2-quart rectangular baking pan	30×19×4.5-cm (3 L)
13×9×2-inch baking pan	34×22×4.5-cm (3.5 L)
15×10×1-inch jelly roll pan	40×25×2-cm
9×5×3-inch loaf pan	23×13×8-cm (2 L)
2-quart casserole	2 L

U.S. / Standard Metric Equivalents

⅛ teaspoon	= 0.5 ml
¼ teaspoon	= 1 ml
½ teaspoon	= 2 ml
1 teaspoon	= 5 ml
1 tablespoon	= 15 ml
2 tablespoons	= 25 ml
¼ cup = 2 fluid ounces	= 50 ml
⅓ cup = 3 fluid ounces	= 75 ml
½ cup = 4 fluid ounces	= 125 ml
⅔ cup = 5 fluid ounces	= 150 ml
¾ cup = 6 fluid ounces	= 175 ml
1 cup = 8 fluid ounces	= 250 ml
2 cups = 1 pint	= 500 ml
1 quart	= 1 litre

THE AMERICAN GIRLS

1764 KAYA, an adventurous Nez Perce girl whose deep love for horses and respect for nature nourish her spirit

1774 FELICITY, a spunky, spritely colonial girl, full of energy and independence

1824 JOSEFINA, a Hispanic girl whose heart and hopes are as big as the New Mexico sky

1854 KIRSTEN, a pioneer girl of strength and spirit who settles on the frontier

1864 ADDY, a courageous girl determined to be free in the midst of the Civil War

1904 SAMANTHA, a bright Victorian beauty, an orphan raised by her wealthy grandmother

1934 KIT, a clever, resourceful girl facing the Great Depression with spirit and determination

1944 MOLLY, who schemes and dreams on the home front during World War Two